EDUCATION IN ZAMBIA

CATHOLIC PERSPECTIVES

BRENDAN CARMODY

Bookworld Publishers

Bookworld Publishers
PO Box 32581, Lusaka, Zambia.

Copyright © Brendan Carmody 1999

All rights reserved. No part of this publication may be reproduced, stored in a retrieval system, or transmitted, in any form or by any means electronic, mechanical, photocopying, recording or otherwise, without the prior permission of the publisher.

ISBN 9982-24-013-7

Typesetting and Graphics by Fergan Limited, Lusaka, Zambia.

Printed by Inter Africa Media Services, Cape Town, South Africa.

Dedicated to the memory of Margaret O'Shea-Priscott

TABLE OF CONTENTS

Acknowledgements	vi
List of Abbreviations	vii
Preface	ix
Introduction	xi

Chapter 1	Conversion and School 1891-1924	1
	Catholic Perspectives on Conversion and Schooling	4
	BSAC Perspectives on Schooling	6
	Catholic Schools in Zambia 1891-1924	8
	African Response to Catholic Schools	15
	Nature of Early Conversions	20
Chapter II	Conversion and School 1924-1964	38
	Catholic Perspectives on Schooling	39
	Colonial Government and Schooling	40
	Catholic Schools in Zambia 1924-1964	43
	Control of Catholic Primary Schools	50
	Catholic Teacher Training	58
	Catholic Secondary Schools	63
	Response to Catholic Schooling	70
	The School and Conversion	77
Chapter III	Conversion and School 1964-1996	93
	Catholic Perspectives on Schooling	94
	Zambian Government and Schools	99
	Catholic Responses to Post-Independence Educational Needs	106
	Control of Primary Schools	107
	Church Struggle for School Curriculum	115
	Teacher Training Colleges	120
	Secondary Schools	126
Chapter IV	Conversion and Schools Today	131
	New Context for Church State Co-operation: The Primary Schools	132
	Catholic Teachers' Colleges	138
	Catholic Secondary Schools	141

Conclusion	152
Selected Bibliography	158
Index	187

Maps
Catholic North-Eastern Zambia, 1895 onwards	2
Zambezi Mission	3
Bangweolo and Nyassa Vicariates; 1913-33	38
Bangweolo, Lwangwa, Zambezi and Nyassa Vicariates; 1933-37	38
Bangweolo, Lwangwa, Fort Jameson and Nyassa Vicariates; 1937-47	39
Bangweolo, Abercorn and Fort Jameson Vicariates; 1947-52	39
Catholic Parishes and Dioceses in Zambia	94
Aided Catholic Institutions	95

ACKNOWLEDGEMENTS

It is indeed a pleasure at the end of a work such as this to thank those who have helped me. As always, however, it would be impractical to mention everybody by name. There are some nonetheless to whom I feel specially indebted. These included administration, staff, and last but not least the students of the University of Zambia, Lusaka, between 1989 and 1998. Friends and relatives, many miles from the University campus, who supported me tirelessly. Research assistants, particularly K. Mwamba, D. Kangwa, and M. Chisulo need to be mentioned. Also "thank you" to those many people who completed surveys and agreed to be interviewed. I cannot fail to express appreciation to Missio and Propaganda Fidei who assisted both the research and the publication financially. A special word of gratitude to Fr. Vincent Cichecki S.J. who not only assisted me in finding materials but also by encouraging and advising me from the first day to the last. Also thanks to Fr. John Doyle S.J. who helped me to put the material on computer. Thanks finally to Ms. Fay Gadsden who did the final editing and who saw the manuscript to print. At this point I would also like to thank the Missionaries of Africa for permission to use their photographs and maps. In addition I wish to acknowledge permission received to reproduce a large section of Chapter IV from the editor of African Christian Studies, Nairobi.

Brendan P. Carmody
Religious Studies,
P.O. Box 32379,
University of Zambia
Lusaka.

ABBREVIATIONS

A.A.L.	Archbishop's Archives Lusaka
A.M.E.C.E.A.	Association of Member Episcopal Conferences in East Africa
A.N.C.	African National Congress
B.S.A.C.	British South Africa Company
C.A.R.E.	Catholic Association for Religious Education
C.C.D.	Confraternity of Christian Doctrine
C.F.C.	Christian Brothers
C.S.A.	Catholic Secretariat Archives
D.O.R.	Daughters of the Redeemer
E.R.I.P.	Educational Reform Implementation Project
F.M.S.	Marist Brothers
G.A.E.	Grant Aided Educationist
H.B.V.M.	Handmaids of the Blessed Virgin Mary
H.C.	Holy Cross Sisters
I.C.L.	Institute of Christian Leadership
J.A.C.	Jesuit Archives Chelston
J.A.D.	Jesuit Archives Dublin
J.A.L.	Jesuit Archives Lusaka
J.A.R.	Jesuit Archives Rome
J.C.T.R.	Jesuit Centre for Theological Reflection
K.A.A.	Kasama Archdiocesan Archives
L.E.A.	Local Education Authority
L.S.M.I.	Little Servants of Mary Immaculate
M.Afr.	Missionaries of Africa
M.I.C.	Missionaries of the Immaculate Conception
M.M.D.	Movement for Multiparty Democracy
M.S.O.L.A.	Missionary Sisters of Our Lady of Africa
N.A.S.	Native Authority School
N.A.Z.	National Archives of Zambia
O.F.M. Cap.	Order of Friars Minor Capuchin
O.F.M. Conv.	Order of Friars Minor Conventual
O.P.	Order of Preachers (Dominicans)
P.E.	Petit Echo
P.E.O.	Provincial Education Officer
P.N.	Petites Nouvelles
P.R.L.	Public Records London
R.A.	Rapports Annuels

R.C.I.A.	Rite of Christian Initiation of Adults
R.S.C.	Religious Sisters of Charity
R.S.H.M.	Sisters of the Sacred Heart of Mercy
S.A.P.	Structural Adjustment Programme
S.C.J.	Child Jesus Sisters
S.C.C.	Small Christian Community
S.C.O.	Sisters of Charity Ottawa
S.H.	Sacred Heart Brothers
S.M.	Marianist Brothers
S.J.	Society of Jesus
S.M.A.	Society of African Missions
S.N.D.	Sisters of Notre Dame
S.S.F.	Sisters of St. Francis
S.V.D.	Divine Word Missionaries
U.A.T.S.	United African Teaching Service
U.M.C.B.	United Missions in the Copperbelt
U.N.I.P.	United National Independence Party
U.N.Z.A.	University of Zambia, Lusaka.
W.F.R.	White Fathers Rome
W.F.L.	White Fathers Lusaka
Z.A.N.C.	Zambia African National Congress
Z.E.C.	Zambia Episcopal Conference
Z.M.R.	Zambezi Mission Record

PREFACE

In the context where government once again invites more close co-operation with the Churches, *Education in Zambia: Catholic Perspectives* is welcome. This book traces the history of the Catholic Church's contribution to the development of education in Zambia for more than a century. In so doing, the author provides much precious data not only on the Catholic endeavour but also on the overall educational history of Zambia.

Education in Zambia presents both the Catholic missionaries' perspectives and those of catechists, teachers, administrators and students. In this it has employed numerous interviews. While the Catholic Church authorities clearly articulated their purposes in setting up and maintaining schools, the author argues that it was not a one-way street. There often were conflicting viewpoints in terms of what government, students, and parents wanted from the Catholic schools. This on-going interaction is treated with care. During the colonial period, for instance, the Church's relationship with the state differed significantly from that which existed in post Independence times. Similarly, relationships between staff and students in the Catholic institutions altered considerably as evidenced by the gradual reduction in the number of student strikes after Independence.

After a somewhat slow start, Catholic schools responded to the demands of their students for academic schooling. As years went on, they excelled and today hold a high reputation for their achievements in this area. Although the author acknowledges this, he endeavours to place it in its religious perspective. Preparation of competent citizens is undoubtedly valuable, but do they carry with them the kind of religious vision that enables them to act responsibly?

Education in Zambia argues that Catholic schools have been instruments of liberation to both the Zambian men and women whom they educated. In the discussion, the author recognises the ambiguities of modernisation and the need to respect and acknowledge the riches of Zambia's traditions. It is not enough for Catholic schools to propel their students into a modern economy that is debt-ridden and swamped by poverty. Catholic graduates need to walk with both a sense of justice and of self-respect that yearns for greater autonomy.

Among other things, *Education in Zambia* reflects the on-going search of the Catholic schools for a greater sense of identity. Many factors eroded this not least of which was the emergence of a non-confessional Religious Educational programme. Various stages of this search are described and analysed. A new concept of Catholic school with a predominantly non-Catholic student population is one of the outcomes. Is this the type of school that will mould the character and outlook of a nation that is progressively more pluralistic and ecumenical?

On the rather controversial and once again topical issue of the hand-over of the Catholic primary schools to government in 1973, *Education in Zambia* is clear. Although Catholic authorities handed over the schools somewhat reluctantly, the hand-over brought much needed relief in terms of finance and administration. It is hardly any wonder that the Catholic Church remains cautious about accepting back these schools in any but piecemeal fashion.

This is a highly readable and informative book which should be of great assistance not only to students of education in Zambia but also to the Church and political history of the country. The theoretical issues raised should be of interest to specialists in international and comparative education, history, missiology, sociology, psychology and related disciplines.

Geoffrey Lungwangwa
Director,
Directorate of Research and Graduate Studies,
University of Zambia,
Lusaka.

INTRODUCTION

The subject of this work developed over a decade during which time I served as a senior lecturer in the Religious Studies section of the School of Education at the University of Zambia. These years, 1989-1998, coincided with significant political events for Zambia. In December 1990, President Kaunda, having seen the liberalisation taking place in Europe with the removal of the Berlin Wall and subject to much pressure from within and without the country, reopened the way for multipartyism in Zambia. Less than a year later, as a result of multiparty elections in October 1991, Mr. Frederick Chiluba, the leader of a newly formed party called the Movement for Multiparty Democracy (M.M.D.), replaced Dr. Kenneth Kaunda as President of the Republic of Zambia, after his twenty seven years in office.

By 1991, the Catholic Church in Zambia had grown to include roughly 26% of the country's population. That year, all its bishops were Zambian together with approximately 25% of the priests and 54% of the sisters. As the President of the day noted:

> Travelling throughout Zambia, whether in urban areas or in the remotest regions of the country, one is struck by the presence everywhere of Roman Catholic churches. The most striking thing is how widespread is the network of Catholic Churches that covers Zambia today.[1]

Since the establishment of the Church one hundred years earlier, many Zambians had become Catholics and a contention of this study is that the schools held a pivotal role in their conversion process.

Until 1991, the Catholic Church had co-existed in relative harmony with the one-party state headed by Kenneth Kaunda. Criticism of government always remained guarded, but as the era came to a close, it became somewhat more outspoken, much to the dismay of the then President. One of the areas of close Church-state co-operation over the years had been the provision of schooling. However, in 1973, the Church decided to hand over all of its primary schools to the government because of the increasing difficulty of retaining them. Moreover, over the years, at the Teacher Training and secondary school levels, government had greatly limited the autonomy of the Church-sponsored schools which proved unsatisfactory from the Church's viewpoint. Thus, when the new M.M.D. Government assumed office in 1991, one of its first gestures included an offer to revise the partnership

---

[1] Address of Kenneth Kaunda on the occasion of the centenary celebration. (August 1991). Jesuit Archives, Chelston. Henceforth, J.A.C.

that existed particularly in the area of education. This greatly interested the Catholic authorities for they continued to contribute in a major way to the provision of secondary schooling and teacher training. By so doing, however, they had progressively come to view themselves as instruments of the state with only minimal potential for promoting their religious message.[2]

What follows is an historical description and analysis of this complex issue of the co-operation between the Catholic Church and the state in the provision of schooling from 1891 to 1996. The study will focus primarily on the provision of academic education at the aided primary, secondary and teacher training levels, even though the Church has been and continues to be involved in many other forms of education, such as pre-schools, trades training, schooling of the handicapped and seminary education, to mention but a few.[3] Our concern will be grant-aided institutions under Catholic agency that provide academic schooling.

The study is primarily historical in approach. Its main sources of data include documents held at diverse locations in Zambia, namely, the National Archives, Lusaka, and diocesan archives at Lusaka, Kasama, Mansa, Monze and Livingstone as well as Jesuit and Missionary of Africa archives in Lusaka. Outside Zambia, research included the consultation of materials at the Westminster Archdiocesan archives, the Public Records Office, and the Jesuit Farm St. archives in London, as well as Jesuit archives in Harare, Dublin and Rome and those of the Missionaries of Africa in Rome. To complement the documentary data, I conducted over 200 interviews with past teachers, administrators, students and missionaries in conjunction with two major surveys involving about 3,000 people—684 of whom were graduates of Catholic institutions. Five further mini-surveys were carried out by research assistants between 1993 and 1996 in order to verify certain issues which appeared unclear. Despite efforts to obtain statistics, the overall study is

---

[2] Edward Berman, *African Reactions to Mission Education* (New York: Teachers' College Press, 1975), p. xi.

[3] For a discussion of grant aided schools in Africa, see: Berman, *African Reactions*, p. 17; P.D. Snelson, *Educational Development in Northern Rhodesia 1883-1945* (Lusaka: Kenneth Kaunda Foundation, 1974), pp. 143, 152; *The Provision of Education for All: Towards the Implementation of Zambia's Educational Reform under demographic and economic restraints: 1986-2000* (University of Zambia, 1986), pp. 145-148. In future, I will refer to this report as E.R.I.P. For details on other educational work by the Catholic Church in Zambia, see: *Impact* no. 139 (May, 1994), p. 5. Since 1970, Choma's Trades Training Institute together with Kasiya Secretarial College made significant contributions to Zambia's non-academic labour needs.

preponderantly qualitative. It will be divided into three chronological periods, corresponding with BSAC rule 1891-1924; the colonial era, 1924-1964; and the post Independence period, 1964-1996.

The major issues that I shall consider include: how did the institutions in question contribute at different periods to the growth of the Church in Zambia? Were the children in the institutions free agents or were they somewhat unwittingly socialised into the new religion? If so, what kind of Catholics did they become? Were they merely "school" Catholics who swiftly shed their Catholicism after they left school or did the schools help many of these young men and women carry the Word of God into their adult and professional lives? Thus, the study will focus on whether and how the schools promoted conversion. Conversion will assume different meanings over the periods in question. During the first and second time spans, we will take conversion primarily to mean a shift from an indigenous religious way of life or from another Christian denomination to Catholicism. In post Independence times, conversion in the above sense will remain but, in the educational settings, it will frequently mean a deepening of the initial commitment to Catholicism. Clearly, such a change of religious orientation will admit of a variety of understandings and commitments. In attempting to analyse this complex human phenomenon, we will mainly use the paradigm provided by the Roman Catholic theologian, Bernard Lonergan, where he speaks of conversion as a fundamental change which can be effected on a number of levels of the personality.[4] There is religious conversion which is our main area of interest. This is a change in the area of one's ultimate concern. There is intellectual conversion which is concerned with a fundamental change in the way we understand, and a moral conversion which has to do with a change in the values by which we live. There can be added further conversions which deal with change in our emotional and social orientations.[5]

Bernard Lonergan's theological paradigm will provide some of the elements of conversion which will be applied to the African context with the assistance of Robin Horton's sociological framework, elucidated by Humphrey Fisher's critique, which outlines three main phases in

---

[4] See: Bernard Lonergan, *Method in Theology* (New York: Herder & Herder, 1972), pp. 237-41.

[5] On the extension of Lonergan's concept of conversion to the emotional level, see: Robert M. Doran, *Subject and Psyche: Ricoeur, Jung, and the Search for Foundations* (Washington D.C.: University of America Press, 1977). Donald L. Gelpi, "The Converting Jesuit," *Studies in the Spirituality of Jesuits* 18 (January 1986), pp. 1-38; Lewis R. Rambo, *Understanding Religious Conversion* (New Haven & Yale University Press, 1993), pp. 146-8.

African conversion, namely, the quarantine, mixing, and reform stages.[6] In the interests of clarity, I shall briefly outline the Horton-Fisher discussion of African conversion. Horton's theory proposed that traditional African cosmology included two tiers, what he called the microcosm and the macrocosm. The microcosm included cults, rituals, and beliefs endemic to the local village. It focused on the spirits who were understood to control the local environment. The macrocosm, on the other hand, included the wider society where a supreme being as opposed to local spirits had overarching power. Horton contended that initial response to Christianity or Islam depended on the group's cosmological orientation at the point of contact with the new religion. Groups focused primarily on the microcosm tended to be unresponsive to the new religions whereas those with a more macrocosmic outlook responded more positively. The reason for this, according to Horton, was that Christianity or Islam provided more universal beliefs and values which presented a more adequate explanation of life in situations of major social change. In this way, both Christianity and Islam could be viewed more as catalysts than as causing the new worldview.

Humphrey Fisher criticised Horton's thesis mainly because he felt that Horton failed to account for the religious element of both Islam and Christianity. For him, Christianity or Islam were not mere catalysts. Instead, they shaped the new mentality. Thus, Fisher details the emergence of conversion in terms of three stages—quarantine, mixing, and reform. The quarantine exists when Christian or Muslim missionaries move into an area and have few if any converts. Mixing occurs when conversions begin. Fisher speaks of adhesion where converts tend to hold a foot in traditional religion as well as in the new religion. Thus the convert can be in Church or mosque in the morning and seeking the traditional healer in the afternoon. The reform stage often appeared in Islam in the form of a jihad where greater purity of faith was sought. Literacy could be a major factor at this point. As Muslims began to read and study the Koran, they discovered

---

[6] Robin Horton, "African Conversion," *Africa* XII, 2 (1971), pp. 85-108; "On the Rationality of Conversion, I", *Africa* 45, 3 (1975), pp. 219-35; "On the Rationality of Conversion, II", *Africa* 45, 4 (1975), pp. 373-99; Humphrey Fisher, "Conversion Reconsidered: Some Historical Aspects of Religious Change in Black Africa," *Africa* XLIII (1973), pp. 27-40; "The Juggernaut's Apologia: Conversion to Islam in Black Africa," *Africa* 55, 2 (1985), pp. 153-73. See also: N. Etherington, "Recent Trends in the Historiography of Christianity in Southern Africa," *Journal of South African Studies* 22, 2 (1996), pp. 215-6; T. Ranger, "The Local and the Global in Southern African Religious History," in R.W. Hefner, ed. *Conversion to Christianity* (Cambridge: Cambridge University Press, 1993).

discrepancies between what they believed and practised and what the book spoke about. Something similar happened within Christianity resulting in numerous independent churches.

In the context of this study, we will utilise the Horton-Fisher discussion to identify and clarify elements of the conversion process of Zambians to Catholicism over a hundred year period. In doing so, we will also attempt to focus on the deeper psychological underpinnings of conversion including the degree to which Zambian Catholics today are energised primarily by the Catholic message or traditional cosmology.

In our description of the activity of the Catholic Church in Zambia between 1891 and 1924, we will outline the beginnings of the Church's commitment to schooling. This roughly coincides with the British South Africa Company's (B.S.A.C.) rule. It was a period when two major Catholic religious societies, the White Fathers (today known as the Missionaries of Africa) and the Jesuits, operated in the country. Schools were generally catechetical centres, providing basic literacy in the three Rs and leading towards Baptism within what was considered to be the true (Catholic) Church. What motivated early conversions is difficult to say. The attraction of the new message certainly operated in some instances, but the prospect of material gain perhaps remained a motivating factor.[7] In terms of Lonergan's scheme, this period represents a strong emphasis on the intellectual and moral aspects of conversion through the catechism approach of the Jesuits and White Fathers. It is true that elements of religious conversion were promoted through the Roman Catholic Mass and Sacraments as well as through devotional practices like the Rosary and Stations of the Cross. Nonetheless, all came packaged in a foreign mode and permitted minimal integration of Catholicism with indigenous beliefs and practices.

The second period described is that of the colonial government which assumed control of the territory in 1924 and yielded power on October 24th 1964, when Zambia, until then Northern Rhodesia, became an independent republic. In many respects, this was the period when the Catholic Church contributed very substantially to the educational development of the country. The colonial government assumed some responsibility for the provision of education and as copper mining developed, migration which was already an established way of life increased, opening the way to urbanisation and its demands for wage labour. While Catholic missionaries initially seemed somewhat lukewarm if not hostile to such development, their Roman superiors

---

[7] Brendan Carmody, "Conversion and School at Chikuni, 1905-39," *Africa* 58, 2 (1988), pp. 193-209.

realised that the Church would need to be part of the modernising process. Thus, the arrival in Northern Rhodesia of Monsignor Hinsley in 1928 marked a definite turning point in the Catholic missionaries' attitude to modernisation especially in so far as it affected provision of schooling with a largely secular curriculum.

In the years that followed the Catholic Church in Northern Rhodesia built up a network of government-supported primary schools as portals to the Church. School children became the main source of new membership. It is difficult to say how free or how deep such conversions were. Undoubtedly, many remained rather superficial, but good numbers also became highly committed to the beliefs and practices of their adopted Church. Conscious of the need to train leaders for the future, Catholic authorities opened seminaries in the 1920s and secondary schools from 1949. The attempt to provide Catholic secondary schools proved difficult in that the Protestants seemed threatened by such a prospect and urged government to resist. For various reasons, not least of which was financial, government permitted Church aided secondary schools. Thus, in 1949, the Catholic Church opened what became a very influential institution, Canisius College. Such an initiative enabled the Catholic authorities to become a more integral part of he country's modernisation process. It was moreover a profoundly political act in that it provided much needed secondary education at a time when government tended to drag its feet. It is unclear how much the Catholic leaders were conscious of the political impact of opening secondary schools in the late colonial period. Some awareness certainly existed as the take-over by a Communist party and expulsion of the Church in China often featured in discussions. People frequently repeated that the same should not happen in Northern Rhodesia and, if it did, the Church should have well-trained Catholic leaders.[8]

On a political level, the Catholic Church of the 1950s presented itself as apolitical. On the one hand, the Church authorities did not wish to alienate themselves from the colonial government. At the same time they were aware that the country was headed for new nationalist leadership, despite the imposition of the Federation with Nyasaland and Southern Rhodesia in 1953. It could be said that in Northern Rhodesia the Catholic Church remained relatively independent of European secular power.[9] The Church's links with the new leaders, Harry

---

[8] On this see: Brendan Carmody, "Jesuit Mission School: Ally of Zambian Nationalism?" *Zambia Journal of History* no. 5 (1992), pp. 37-56.

[9] J. Haynes, *Religion and Politics in Africa* (Nairobi: East African Educational Publishers Ltd., 1996), p. 43.

Nkumbula and Kenneth Kaunda, were forged largely through the influence of Fr. Patrick Walsh who did much not only to eliminate the colour-bar but to create trans-racial alliances. This he managed to do especially through his membership of what was known as the Kabulonga Club in Lusaka which provided the only forum where black and white could meet and discuss their problems.[10] Walsh helped to keep the Catholic Church from being seen as an enemy of nationalism. Thus, not only in terms of provision of schooling but in terms of some support for the nationalist cause, the Catholic Church emerged from this difficult period as a friend of the new leadership. From the perspective of Catholic conversion, much of the characteristics of the earlier period survived in that the approach remained largely unchanged until after the Second Vatican Council in the 1960s. The Catholic Church's support for the nationalist aspirations gave the conversion process a somewhat political tone, though this did not yet lead to any significant integration of Catholicism with tradition. It was the Church's experience with the Lenshina movement in Northern Province in the mid 1950s, where many left the Catholic Church at least for a period, that led to the adoption of a more truly vernacular missionary approach. Conversion, however, remained a rather foreign and perhaps alien experience for many Zambians.

As in many newly independent African countries, the Zambian state indicated its intent to take over the primary schools in the immediate aftermath of Independence. Already, many Protestant Churches had handed over their schools to government in the 1950s, when it became more difficult to maintain sufficient autonomy for evangelistic purposes. Most of the other Protestant groups surrendered their schools soon after Independence. The Catholic Church, however, clearly declared that it wished to continue administering its primary schools even though various concerned groups within the Church were less than enthusiastic. While the government accepted the Catholic partnership, it made clear that it was in charge and progressively made the administration of Catholic primary schools so difficult that in 1973 the Catholics handed over all their primary schools. Meanwhile, the Church continued to maintain its secondary schools and two teachers' colleges. However, even here, all was not so well. By the 1970s, much of its autonomy was eroded particularly in the area of admission of students, choice of staff, curriculum, discipline, and finances. For many proprietors, the Catholic nature and value of such schools became

---

[10] "Profile of a Priest," *The Northern Star* (June 4, 1964). Confirmed by Dr. K.D. Kaunda during an interview in Lusaka, 19 February 1999.

questionable especially in the mid 1970s.

In this period the alliance between the Catholic Church and the Zambian state was rather tenuous. The State clearly wished to direct the educational endeavour. Its commitment to education for all entailed policies that were somewhat non-denominational. Such an ideal of non-denominational schooling was by no means new. It stretched back into the early days of grant-in-aid in the 1930s. Finally, however, the new government was in a position to pursue this policy and, to a large extent, it succeeded. The result was that many denominational schools, like it or not, became religiously mixed. Such religious pluralism formed part of a trans-ethnic outlook which was very much part of the ideology behind the slogan: "One Zambia one nation."[11] For the most part the desire to have non-denominational schools did not necessarily mean that the government wanted purely secular schooling. On the contrary, it supported an interdenominational religious education programme from the early 1970s in the educational institutions.

It is true that in the late 1970s and early 1980s the one party state adopted a socialist orientation.[12] In itself, this did not lead to an open attack on the provision of religious education. In the 1976 Educational Reform Programme, religious education was not mentioned, but when questioned the government denied that this omission was intentional and so it was quickly restored. In the early 1980s, government made many attempts to introduce political education in the primary and secondary schools as well as in the teachers' colleges. Much of this was atheistic, but when the matter was brought into the open during a meeting of parents and administrators with the President in 1982, he denied that it was designed to be atheistic.

This briefly then is the context in which the M.M.D. government invited discussion on the way ahead in late 1991.[13] Though the Catholic Church had been forced to relinquish its primary schools twenty years earlier, it was prepared to reconsider some form of renewed commitment in the 1990s. While the administration and operation of its two teacher colleges and roughly twenty six secondary schools entailed much investment in an enterprise that had become dominated by the state, it

---

[11] Elizabeth Colson, "The Bantu Botatwe: Changing Political Definitions in Southern Zambia," in *The Politics of Cultural Performance*. Edited by David Parkin, Lionel Caplan, & Humphrey Fisher. (Oxford: Berghadn Books, 1996), pp. 61-80.

[12] See: Clive Dillon-Malone, *Zambian Humanism, Religion and Social Morality* (Ndola: Mission Press, 1989).

[13] Letter from Chief Education Inspector of Schools for Permanent Secretary, Ministry of Education, to Vicar General, Diocese of Mansa, December 1991 (Mansa Diocesan Archives); "FJT Assures Church," *Sunday Times* (16 March 1997).

was happy to look at ways in which these institutions could be reclaimed. Nonetheless, over the years, the Catholic Church's own outlook too had changed so that in the discussions of the early 1990s there was no question of wanting an all-out Catholic institution of the type that existed in the 1950s. The Church, too, had come to appreciate more fully the value of religious pluralism in contemporary Zambia.

Academically, the Church's schools remain exemplary. Although they provided only about 6% of the schooling at the final Grade XII level, they formed 23% of the 1996-7 intake to the University of Zambia. In this respect they have earned a reputable place in the country's educational history. However, from the Church's own perspective of justice and liberation of the poor, this contribution has some ambiguity. By becoming more integrated into the national system of schooling, somewhat ironically, the Catholic Church has also become more closely allied to the process of class formation and thus tends disproportionately to favour the rich. It has not, for instance, been able to address in a major way the issue of the many boys and girls who have to drop out of the system annually. Does this mean that the Church schools are being progressively distanced from the poor?

It is true that many Catholics and non-Catholics of slender means pass through the doors of the Catholic schools. Apart from a solidly academic formation, what do they carry into the world? Religiously, they have generally learned to live with and respect other denominations even if this has not been always explicitly and intentionally promoted. From a Christian perspective, their formation in the Religious Education programmes seems positive and many gain some sense of justice. From a Catholic perspective, bonds with priests, brothers, and sisters have been forged. A minority have profited from some form of catechetical formation. From a moral and religious perspective it is not clear that they perform significantly better than the students leaving other secondary schools or colleges. In some instances, it may even be that they are less well prepared for the rigors of responsible adult life. As Chilufya states, "they jump from large scale control in the convent setting to much freedom."[14] Thus the overprotection in Catholic girls' schools may need to be reviewed.

From the perspective of conversion, there is often some evidence of

---

[14] Rosemary Chilufya, "The Impact of Catholic Secondary Schools on University of Zambia Students' Academic and Religious life," (Project for RS 400, University of Zambia, 1996). It was found that past convent school students tend to do poorly academically at University while in general their religious and moral lives do not appear greatly different from others.

a deepening, especially where the atmosphere is free and where there is no great need to pretend. It is not so clear that much has been done, however, to promote on-going dialogue with traditional religion. Although as adolescents, there would normally be much search for meaning and integration, it is far from evident that sufficient is being done either in the classroom or out of it to enable young Zambian boys and girls to indigenize their faith or to enable them to find the Christian message relevant to their needs. In some respects, it is possible that the Catholic Church tends to be too 'liberal', when many youths desperately need the kind of clear-cut answers which sects frequently provide.[15]

To what degree the Zambian Catholic schools have served as instruments of liberation or domestication in the sense in which the highly influential contemporary educator Paulo Freire uses these terms is difficult to say.[16] In order tentatively to answer this question, let me outline some of the salient features of Freire's work. For him, pedagogy of liberation pivots on dialogue whereby the teacher no longer simply teaches but is herself/himself taught. Such dialogue exists where there is a profound love of others. To promote this liberation, Freire designed "problem posing" learning. This method entails critical reflection on present reality where people are empowered to act as a result of reflection on their historical experience.

In his discussion of pedagogy, Freire speaks of levels of human consciousness. The lowest is intransitive consciousness. At this level, people are preoccupied with meeting elementary needs. They are immersed in time which is expressed as a one-dimensional oppressive present. Semi-intransivity constitutes the second level of consciousness and is found most often in so-called Third World situations. It is the dominant consciousness of so-called closed societies. People take the facts of their sociological situation as given. It often means the presence of a fatalistic mentality where all is explained in terms of destiny or forces beyond one's control. Naïve consciousness forms Freire's third level. Here people seriously question their situation but in a naïve way. Cultural situations are seen to be determined by others and so one tends

---

[15] Ibid. Many young boys and girls leave the Catholic Church at least for a while mainly because they do not appear to find the Church's message as vital as those of some of the sects. See: Paul Gifford, "Some Recent Developments in African Christianity," *African Affairs*, 93 (1994), pp. 513-534; Lewis R. Rambo, *Understanding Religious Conversion*, p. 31.

[16] For clarification of these terms see: B. Carmody, "Conversion to Roman Catholicism in Zambia: Shifting Pedagogies," *African Christian Studies* Vol. 4, no. 2 (June 1988), pp. 5-24; R. Mackie, ed. *Literacy and Revolution: The Pedagogy of Paulo Freire* (New York: Continuum, 1981).

not to assume responsibility for one's life. Freire's fourth and final level of consciousness is achieved through a process of conscienticization and is marked by critical interpretation of social reality.

Learning, in Freire's framework, entails the process by which one moves from one level of consciousness to another. It includes becoming aware of the contingency of social reality. It presumes that there is an essential difference between the givenness of the natural world and the contingency of the social. The contingent world can be changed while learning is the process of challenging and being challenged by the givenness of one's situation. Such learning results from a "problem posing" as opposed to what Freire calls a banking approach where learners are viewed as storers of knowledge deposits. Problem posing pedagogy is liberating whereas that of banking is domesticating.

From the perspective of this study, we will attempt to specify the degree to which the Catholic schooling process in Zambia liberated and empowered its students to create their social reality. During the colonial era, it appears that Catholic secondary schooling embodied a kind of hegemony akin to what McLaren found in some contemporary minority schools of Toronto.[17] Adapting McLaren's terminology in the Zambian pre-Independence context, one might say that the instructional rites entailed a rather hegemonic character reinforcing colonial dominance with the teacher as hegemonic overlord. Clearly, however, there was periodic resistance, as we shall see, when teachers became entertainers and liminal servants, teachers who encouraged a more open style of teaching. After Independence, while the hegemony of the colonial state disappeared, that of the one-party Independent state could be no less oppressive. During this time, Catholic aided schools became more closely integrated into the national educational system and, despite Vatican II's emphasis on justice, it remained difficult to review the "friendly fascism" of the post-colonial, democratic socialist Zambian state.

In many respects the Catholic schools did not have sufficient autonomy either in the colonial or the post Independence periods to provide schooling that truly liberated individuals. Yet, even in the colonial situation, the school was not entirely class reproductive as it provided allies and leaders for the nationalist movements.[18] It had an

---

[17] Peter McLaren, *Schooling as a Ritual Performance* (London: Routledge & Kegan Paul, 1986), pp. 82, 112-3.

[18] M. Carnoy, *Education as Cultural Imperialism* (New York: David McKay, 1974); Michael W. Apple, *Education and Power* (London: Routledge & Kegan Paul, 1982), p. 17; Carmody, "Jesuit Mission School: Ally of Zambian Nationalism," *Zambia Journal of*

element of anti-structure. Despite decreasing autonomy in the post-Independence era, the possibility of anti-structure remains, even if in general it appears that the Catholic school system became too closely identified with support for the status-quo rather than with reform.[19] As the Catholic institutions gain more autonomy, they may have more opportunity not only to deliver education in a cost-effective way but to promote greater personal and social transformation.[20] Nonetheless, in a society where a tiny minority are growing more affluent at the expense of the majority of the population who are faced with greater and greater poverty, the Church needs to become more concerned with the educational needs of the poor. Moreover, in a context where participatory democracy has become part of the so-called new culture, Catholic educational institutions may need to provide models of democratic governance and leadership which will involve:

> making room for the 'way of Jesus', the way of non-dominating power, in the political arrangements under which members of society and nation will relate to one another.[21]

Thus, the task ahead should include a clearer articulation of what this "way of Jesus" means for personal and social transformation. As far as this study is concerned, the challenge for Catholic schools remains the need to develop the total person or, in other words, to promote conversion at the various levels of the personality.

History, no. 5; M. Carnoy & H. Levin, *Schooling and Work in the Democratic State* (Stanford: Stanford University Press, 1985), p. 22.

[19] Brendan Carmody, "Denominational Secondary Schooling in post-Independence Zambia: a case study," *African Affairs* Vol. 89, 355 (April 1990), pp. 261-63; "Roman Catholics and African Politics," Pro Mundi Vita Dossiers 7/8 (March 1979), p. 37.

[20] There is evidence that schools which are more autonomous are more cost-effective. See: Emmanuel Jimenez and Marlaine E. Lockheed, *Public and Private Secondary Education in Developing Countries* (Washington, D.C.: The World Bank, 1995), p. 121; See also: E.R.I.P., p. 147; Here I concur with Samoff's concern for vision: See: Joel Samoff, "African Education and Development: Crisis, Triumphalism, Research, Loss of Vision," *Alberta Journal of Educational Research* Vol. XLII, 2 (June 1996), pp. 121-47.

[21] Kwame Bediako, *Christianity in Africa* (Edinburgh: Edinburgh University Press, 1995), p. 247.

CHAPTER ONE

CONVERSION AND SCHOOL: 1891-1924

Before discussing the Catholic Church's contribution to schooling in Northern Rhodesia during the B.S.A.C. period, in the interest of clarity we shall give a brief outline of the development of the Church.

In 1891, the White Fathers, a Catholic missionary Congregation, founded by Cardinal Lavigerie, entered Zambia from the north.[1] Mambwe became their first mission in Zambia, though it did not prosper.[2] Despite severe criticism from Chitimukulu, Paramount Chief of the Bemba, the Fathers opened another mission at Kayambi in 1895. This was the first European settlement in Bembaland. It was directed by Fr. Joseph Dupont (later Bishop), more popularly known as Moto-Moto (Fire-Fire). In Holmes' words:

> Dupont was a man of considerable presence, some would say flamboyance, a good hunter and excellent marksman apart from being a competent physician and a good preacher. He understood the protocol required when dealing with chiefs, and often behaved more like a chief himself than as a missionary shepherd of a flock[3]

Dupont made further efforts to penetrate Bemba territory, but chief Mwamba would not entertain any such idea until 1898, when he became ill and sent for Dupont whose healing skills had become well known. As a result of what he did for Mwamba, Dupont was appointed successor to the chieftainship. He swiftly informed the Governor of the situation and, after consultation with thirty-three local chiefs, he urged the Governor to take control in order to prevent the customary human sacrifices on the death of a chief and possible civil war. In his letter to the Governor at

---

[1] Brian Garvey, *Bembaland Church; Religious and Social Change in South Central Africa, 1891-1964* (Leiden: E.J. Brill, 1994), pp. 28-39; John Weller & Jane Linden, *Mainstream Christianity to 1980 in Malawi, Zambia and Zimbabwe* (Gweru: Mambo Press, 1984), pp. 49-57: J.M. Ogez, *Where it all began* (Lusaka: Missionaries of Africa, 1991), p. 69.

[2] The White Fathers abandoned Mambwe mission in 1895 and sold it to the B.S.A.C. The present Mambwe mission is about twenty miles west of the old one and opened in 1938, see: Michael O'Shea, *Missionaries and Miners* (Ndola: Mission Press, 1986), p. 44; Ogez, *Where it all began*, pp. 123-31.

[3] Timothy Holmes, "French Missionaries and British Treaties in Southern Africa 1830-1900," *Zambia Journal of History* 6/7 (1993-4): p. 17.

Blantyre on the occasion of Mwamba's death, Dupont wrote:

> Il (Mwamba) m'a dit qu'il me faisait venir pour me donner son pays après sa mort. Il m'a redit la même chose chaque jour.[4]

On November 3rd, the British administrators sent two men, MacKinnon and Young, to take possession of the territory. However, to the astonishment of Dupont, they told him that he had no permission to remain. They informed him that this was the order of the new Governor, Sir R.T. Codrington. Dupont was not a person to accept a decision of this nature easily, especially since, as he emphasised, he had opened Bembaland to British control. As might be expected, Dupont remained, and, as a gesture of reconciliation on the part of the administration, he was invited to sit beside Codrington at the installation of Mwamba's successor in June 1899.[5]

A government post was meanwhile set up in the country.[6] Moreover, Dupont lost no time in starting a mission at Chilubula in 1898, Chilonga in 1899, Chilubi in 1903, Ngumbo in 1905, and Chibote in 1909. The rather rapid spread of the missions was achieved by the increasing number of priests and nuns. The arrival of White Sisters in 1902 signalled the beginning of Sisters' apostolates among the Bemba. Another pivotal element in the mission's expansion was the establishment in 1897 of a boarding primary school at Kayambi, which had as one of its purposes the recruitment and training of catechists. Catechists formed a central part of the White Fathers' outreach strategy which had been well established elsewhere. These first Roman Catholic missions in Bembaland were administered as part of the vicariate of Nyasa, which Bishop Dupont managed from Chilubula. After Dupont's retirement the territory was divided into two new jurisdictions: the vicariate of Nyasa and the vicariate of Bangweulu, where Bishop Etienne Larue became the administrator in 1913. The first White Father mission

---

[4] He (Mwamba) told me that he wanted me to come in order to give me his territory after his death. He told me the same thing each day. J. Dupont, Lettre à Son Excellence, Monsieur Le Gouverneur de la British Central Africa à Blantyre, 26 October 1898. (Doss 106: 2, White Fathers' Archives, Rome. Henceforth, I shall refer to these archives as WFR.) J. Flies, *The Missionaries of Africa: 100 Years in Zambia* (Ndola: Mission Press, 1991), p. 10; Hugo Hinfelaar, *Bemba-Speaking Women of Zambia in a century of Religious Change* (Leiden: E.J. Brill, 1994), p. 40; O'Shea, *Missionaries and Miners*, pp. 40-41.

[5] J. Perraudin, "Mons. Dupont, l'apotre des Babemba Notice Biographique" (B2. Divers 5. WFR.)

[6] KDH 1/1 Kasama Notebook compiled by P.C. Cookson (1902), p. 404 (National Archives of Zambia: henceforth, I shall refer to these archives as N.A.Z.); At Ipenburg, *All Good Men: The Development of Lubwa Mission, Chinsali, Zambia 1905-1967* (Frankfurt am Main: Peter Lang, 1992), p. 67; O'Shea, *Missionaries and Miners*, pp. 41-43.

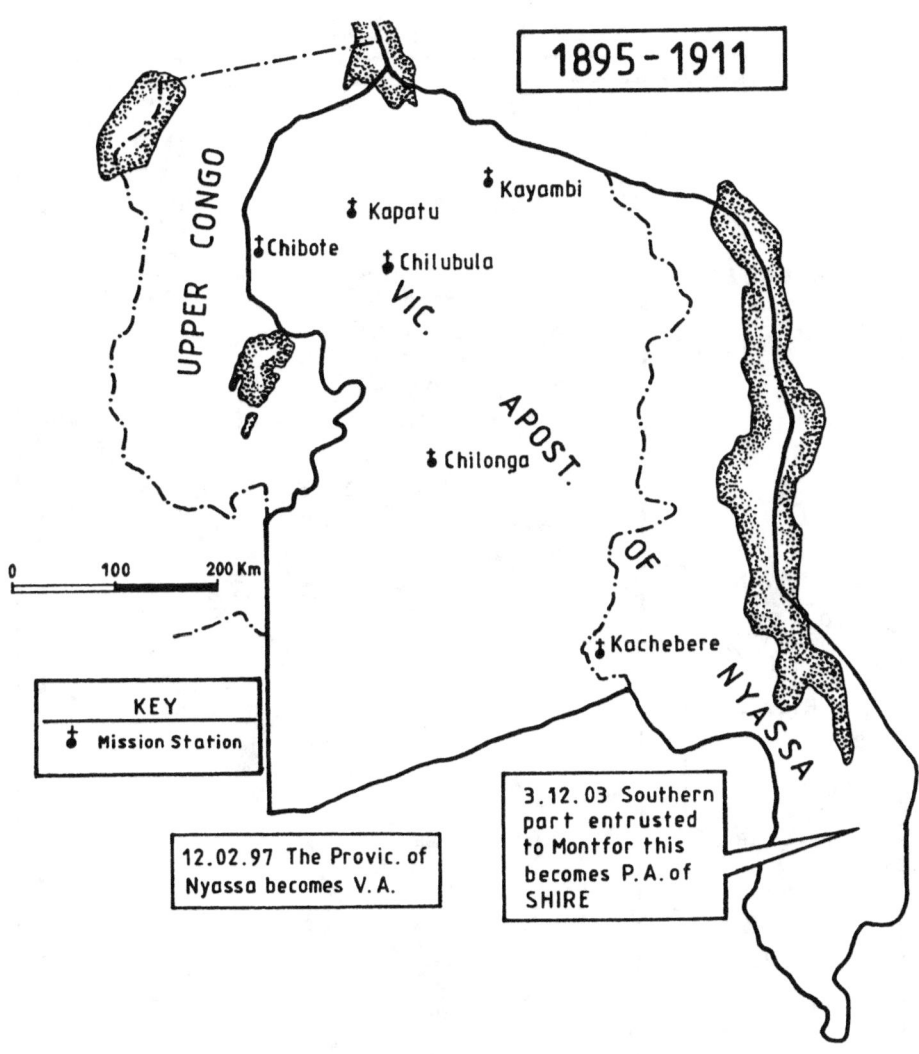

ZAMBEZI MISSION

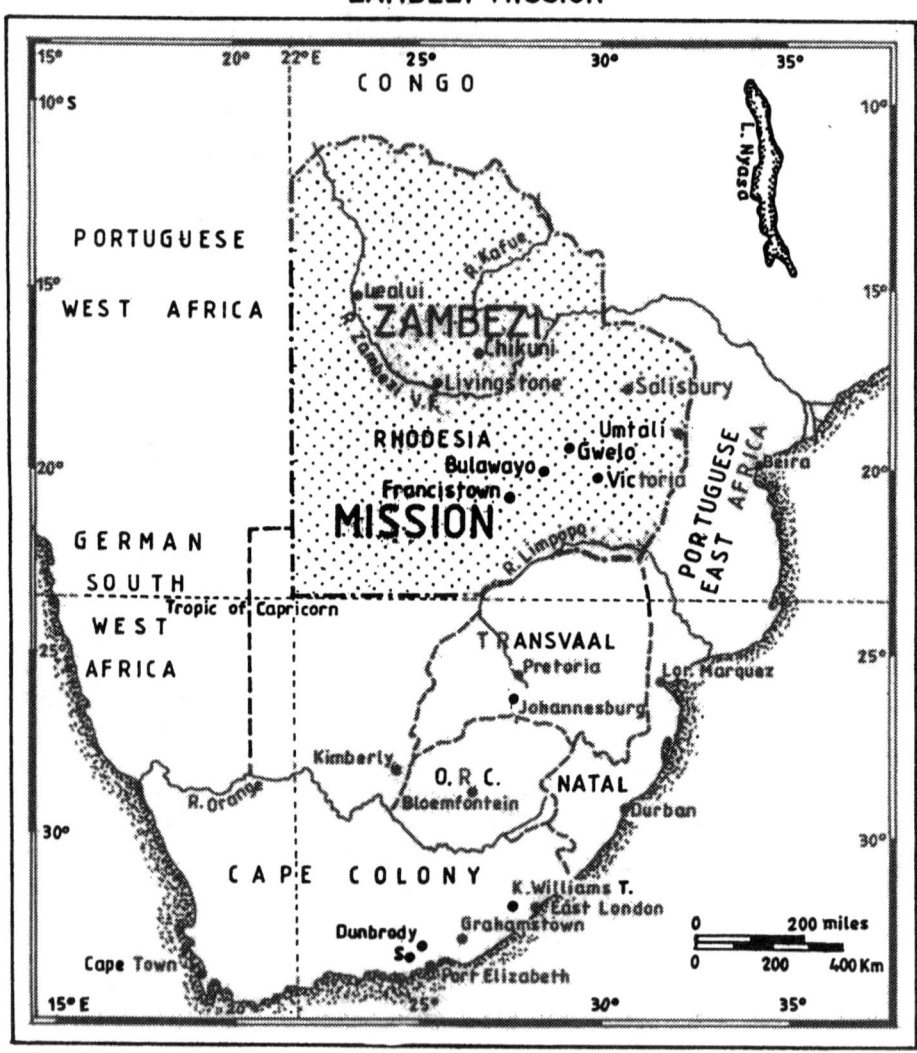

SOURCE Zambezi Mission Record III (January 1919)

in Eastern province opened in 1903 as part of Nyasa at Kachebere on what is today the border between Zambia and Malawi. Subsequently, in 1924, despite much opposition from the Dutch Reformed Church, a further mission was started at Minga.

Already by 1905, 1,000 people had been baptised. The new Catholics were mainly adults. What motivated many of these early converts is difficult to say. Some priests felt that they were often moved by the fear of Divine Justice and Hell which was a central part of the White Fathers' message in these early days:

> Mais vienne le moment de mourir! Oh! Alors, bien vite, ils envooient chercher le Bwana pour qu'il les baptise, car ils ne veulent pas mourir en paiens et craignent d'être jetés dans le feu de l'enfer. [7]

In 1905, two French Jesuits, Frs. Joseph Moreau and Jules Torrend, arrived at Chikuni in the southern part of Zambia. Some years before, in 1879, the Jesuits had been entrusted with responsibility for what was known as the Zambezi Mission which stretched from the Limpopo river northwards to Congo, present-day Democratic Republic of the Congo.[8]

As soon as Fr. Moreau arrived in Chikuni, he introduced the first plough to the area and so attracted many of the locals. Within a short time, Fr. Moreau's companion, Fr. Torrend, left the Chikuni mission and settled in what is presently Kasisi, some miles north east of Lusaka.

In 1910, because of anti-clerical leadership in Portugal, Jesuits working in Mozambique, most of whom were Polish, were forced to leave. As a result they migrated into Northern Rhodesia and started missions at Kapoche in 1910, Katondwe in 1911, and Chingombe in the Luangwa valley in 1914. In typical Jesuit tradition of founding schools, Chingombe, Kasisi and Katondwe soon began catechists training centres. In 1921, Kasisi, through the influence of Fr. Torrend, became the centre of the Jesuit missionary endeavour in the area. By 1924, there were about 7,000 Catholics within the Jesuit missionary orbit which stretched from Livingstone to the borders of present-day Republic of Congo.

---

[7] But when the time of death approaches! Oh, then, they quickly send for the priest so that he can baptise them, for they don't want to die as pagans fearing to be cast into eternal fire. *Rapports Annuels* 1909-10, p. 448. These are newsletters from the White Father's missions and one set is available at the White Fathers' Archives in Rome. I will in future refer to these as R.A.

[8] In 1879, the Zambezi Mission was entrusted to the Jesuits. For details: see: Brendan Carmody, *Conversion and Jesuit Schooling in Zambia* (Leiden: E.J. Brill, 1992), p. 8; For more detail on the Jesuits, see: Joseph de Guibert, *The Jesuits, Their Spirituality, Doctrine and Practice* (Chicago: Loyola University Press, 1964).

By that same year, White Father and Jesuit missionary endeavours had resulted in a Catholic population in Northern Rhodesia of approximately 47,000.

CATHOLIC PERSPECTIVES ON CONVERSION AND SCHOOLING

The Catholic missionary revival of the nineteenth century had begun as a response to the Protestant investment in missions. In 1816, the Roman Propaganda Fidei was re-established and endowed by Pope Pius VII as the chief authority of the missions. Another major contributing factor to the expansion of the Catholic missionary endeavour was the establishment of the Society for the Propagation of the Faith by Pauline Jaricot in 1822. Perhaps, as Schmidlin suggested, it was no accident that France, where the Church had been persecuted during the revolution became the most fruitful soil for the support of the missionary movement.[9]

The missionary outreach of the nineteenth century stressed the role of the Christian village where, in its Catholic version, much emphasis was placed not so much on the individual but upon the social and structural aspect of conversion.[10] However, by the early part of the twentieth century, this mission strategy was gradually superseded by the school as a means of evangelisation. In Eastern Nigeria, for example, it was the school rather than the Christian village approach that proved to be more effective in the evangelisation of the area. In 1905, the Roman Catholic Vicar in Calabar, Father Joseph Shanahan (later Bishop) claimed that he would use the newly established schools to strike the last blow at the Presbyterians. Shanahan, following the lead given by his predecessor, Fr. Lejeune, concentrated on creating and maintaining a vast network of state-subsidised schools and, in doing so, acquired a

---

[9] J. Schmidlin, *Catholic Mission History* (Techny, Illinois: Mission Press, 1933), p. 558; see also Elizabeth Isichei, *A History of Christianity in Africa* (London: S.P.C.K., 1995), pp. 84 ff; John Baur, *2000 Years of Christianity in Africa* (Nairobi: Paulines Publications, 1994), pp. 106-9; Richard Gray, *Black Christians and White Missionaries* (New Haven: Yale University Press, 1990), pp. 89-91; Adrian Hastings, *The Church in Africa* (Oxford: Clarendon Press, 1994), pp. 295-305.

[10] T.J.M. Burke, ed. *Catholic Missions: Four Great Missionary Encyclicals* (New York: Fordham University Press, 1957), p. 291; Adrian Hastings, *Church and Mission in Modern Africa* (London: Burns and Oates, 1967), p. 81; Isichei, *A History of Christianity in Africa*, p. 135; Nicholas I. Omenka, *The School in the service of Evangelisation* (Leiden: Brill, 1989), pp. 34-5; T.O. Beidelman, *Colonial Evangelism: A Sociohistorical study of an East African mission at the grassroots* (Bloomington: Indiana University Press, 1982), p. 21.

dominant position among the Igbo.[11] On this Donovan commented:

> Just after the turn of the century, about the year 1906, Joseph Shanahan, Bishop of Southern Nigeria, took money which was coming from the Propaganda in Rome, money sent specifically to ransom slaves, and used it to begin the building of an extensive school system in Southern Nigeria. He not only affected the destiny of a tribe, the Ibos; he helped to change the missionary history of all Africa. A new era began in the African missions with Bishop Shanahan.[12]

In 1919, Pope Benedict XV's encyclical, *Maximum Illud*, provided further direction for the Catholic missionary endeavour. This encyclical reiterated the long-perceived need to carry light to those in the shadow of death. Echoing the theology of the day, the Pope underlined the belief that it was either impossible or next to impossible to be saved without baptism and explicit membership of the Catholic Church. Thus, he highlighted the need for local clergy. Such clergy should, according to the encyclical, be well prepared and equal to European clergy in terms of formation. The Pope emphasised:

> He (the mission superior) must make it his special concern to secure and train local candidates for sacred ministry. In this policy lies the greatest hope of the new churches....If the indigenous clergy is to achieve the results we hope for, it is absolutely necessary that he be well trained and well prepared. We do not mean a rudimentary and slip-shod preparation, the bare minimum for ordination. No, their education should be complete and finished`, excellent in all its phases, the same kind of education for priesthood that a European should receive.[13]

Omenka speaks of *Maximum Illud* as a milestone in the Church's attitude to the planting of a local church.[14]

Thus, in the late nineteenth century, the Church renewed its

---

[11] Isichei, *A History of Christianity*, pp. 196, 271; P.B. Clarke, "The Methods and Ideology of the Holy Ghost Fathers in Eastern Nigeria 1885-1905," *Journal of Religion in Africa* VI, 2 (1974), pp. 81-108; Omenka, *The School in the Service of Evangelisation*, p. 47; E.K. Ekechi, "Colonialism and Christianity in West Africa: The Igbo case, 1900-1915," *Journal of African History* XII, 1 (1971), pp. 103-115; Baur, *2000 Years of Christianity*, pp. 149-52; Hastings, *Church and Mission*, p.81; Weller & Linden, *Mainstream Christianity*, p. 125; E.H. Berman, "African Responses to Mission Education," *African Studies Review* XVII, 3 (December 1974), p. 527; Adrian Hastings, "Patterns of African Mission Work," *Afer*, VIII, 4 (October 1966), p. 291.

[12] Vincent J. Donovan, *Christianity Rediscovered* (New York: Orbis, 1978), p. 6.

[13] "Maximum Illud," in Burke, *Catholic Missions*, p. 13; See also Ian and Jane Linden, *Catholics Peasants and Chewa Resistance in Nyasaland* (London: Heinemann, 1974), p. 178.

[14] Omenka, *The School in the Service of Evangelisation*, p. 4; Hastings, *Church and Mission*, p. 23.

emphasis on Christian mission outreach, focusing on the ideal of the Christian village. However this was, to some extent, superseded by the school in the twentieth century.

BSAC PERSPECTIVES ON SCHOOLING

In 1890, the British South Africa Company gained control of the territory of Northern Rhodesia through the Lochner Concession. However, the history of schooling during the subsequent thirty-four years was one of consistent neglect. It established one school during its period of administration. This was the Barotse National School. Except for this school in the Barotse district, education was in the hands of missionaries.[15]

The British South Africa Company assumed no financial responsibility for schooling. However, it did try to exercise some control over mission appointed teachers. A Jesuit from Katondwe wrote in 1915:

> Government is doing its best to make schools impossible in order to keep people in the darkness of paganism and ignorance. "Native teacher" is the person we call "catechist." The government offers no pecuniary aid either for catechists or for the erection of their houses; it nevertheless arrogates to itself the right to judge whether or not a catechist is a worthy and fit person to teach.[16]

In 1918, government introduced a Proclamation thereby demanding the registration of all schools which it defined in such a way as to encompass any setting where people received instruction. Moreover, anybody found subverting the tribal authority of the chief or headman, or spreading teaching of a seditious tendency was subject to a large fine. In addition, the Proclamation empowered magistrates and native commissioners to inspect schools. These regulations and attempts to control education by the B.S.A.C. were prompted by the Chilembwe revolt in Nyasaland where it was felt that the teachers and those educated by the missions had played a leading role.[17]

Although the Company showed little interest in promoting native

---

[15] Snelson, *Educational Development in Northern Rhodesia*, pp. 121, 123-127; Franklin Parker, "Early Church-State Relations in African Education in Rhodesia and Zambia," *The World Year Book of Education* (London: Evans Bros., 1966). pp. 200-216.

[16] John Coyne, *History of the Jesuits in Zambia* (Lusaka, n.d.), p. 74.

[17] N.A.Z.BS3/197 vol. 1; Snelson, *Educational Development in Northern Rhodesia*, p. 131; J. P. Ragsdale, *Protestant Mission Education in Zambia, 1880-1954* (London: Associated University Press, 1986), pp. 56-60.

schooling, many mission groups who directed schools considered that the Company ought to share some financial responsibility for schooling in the territory. Missionaries, in some cases, viewed the 1918 Proclamation as government interference without corresponding financial commitment. Ragsdale notes:

> The Administration was attempting to control an activity to which they contributed nothing. The regulations were not designed to improve the quality of education; they merely added an administrative burden of reports and applications. The missions objected strongly, and a period of negotiations began the process towards a government – mission educational system.[18]

Because of fairly widespread criticism of the Proclamation, the High Commissioner instructed the administrator to solicit amendments from missionary representatives. Subsequently, the 1919 Missionary Conference discussed the Proclamation at length. In response, the Company replaced the Proclamation of 1918 with the Native Schools Proclamation of 1921. At the 1921 Conference, members repeated their demand for government aid to missionary education work. These developments in Northern Rhodesia coincided with the appointment of an Advisory Committee to the Colonial Office on Education in British Tropical Africa by the Secretary of State in November, 1923. This Committee invited the Phelps-Stokes Commission to undertake a survey of whatever schooling was being done in the African colonies. In 1924 the Commission visited Northern Rhodesia and met the General Missionary Conference in Kafue.[19]

The rather exclusive mission of the Catholic Church of that time meant that even Protestants were regarded as being in the shadow of death.[20] Because of this general Catholic attitude to Protestants at this time, Catholics did not wish to be an integral part of these conferences. Nonetheless, there were Jesuit representatives at the earlier conferences. In a rather unusual ecumenical spirit for that time, Catholics sat with Protestants as full members. Catholic participants were elected on to various committees though their apparent detachment was regretted by the Protestants and even by people like the Jesuit Father Moreau: "I am afraid that we are rather left behind. Our policy of aloofness is not very

---

[18] Ragsdale, *Protestant Mission Education*, pp. 59-60.

[19] Snelson, *Educational Development*, pp. 140-141.

[20] Louis Oger, *Where a Scattered Flock Gathered: Ilondola* (Ndola: Mission Press, 1991), p. 64: Isichei, A *History of Christianity*, p. 81.

wise and will work against us in the end."[21]

The British South Africa Company government did little to provide schooling in Northern Rhodesia. By 1924, approximately 50,000 of the 200,000 school age children were receiving basic schooling almost exclusively in mission schools.[22]

CATHOLIC SCHOOLS IN ZAMBIA: 1891-1924

The early mission history of the White Fathers and Jesuits in Zambia needs to be set in the context that I have briefly outlined. It may be worth noting that, while individual White Fathers and Jesuits had some autonomy in the decisions they made, they were limited by the directives of the Roman Church and by directives from their higher superiors. In most cases, the White Fathers' mission superiors reported back to their headquarters in Algiers. In the case of the Jesuits, they generally related directly with the provincials of the particular provinces of which they were offshoots. Special issues were referred to the General in Rome.

From the early days, though not from the outset, the White Fathers attempted to establish Christian villages. In such villages, a potential convert had to live monogamously and attend catechism class. Similarly, the Jesuits concentrated on setting up Christian villages within their area. The Jesuits were very much aware that this notion of the Christian village constituted part of their long heritage:

> When mention has been made of these native missions in previous numbers of the Record, it is not unlikely that our readers may have been reminded of the once famous Jesuit Reductions of Paraguay. And not without reason, Our present missions in South Africa are very much upon the same lines.[23]

Though the method of forming Christian villages was widespread, there were different perspectives on its efficacy. At the 1920 Jesuit Conference in Bulawayo, some members felt that, though it was an ideal, it was not appropriate in a context where there was a great shortage of priests:

---

[21] Coyne, *History of the Jesuits in Zambia*, p. 14; see also N.A.Z. RC 365 "Resolutions adopted at the General Missionary Conference of Northern Rhodesia," p. 2; W. Lane, "Jesuit Religious Education, Zambezi to Zambia: 1875-1975." (University of Dublin, M. Ed. thesis, 1976). pp. 57-9, 125-8; O'Shea, *Missionaries and Miners*, pp. 268-9; Garvey, *Bembaland Church*, pp. 41, 43, 101; Carmody, *Conversion and Jesuit Schooling*, p. 36; 65-78; Harold Peters, "Education and Development among the Tonga. (Ph.D. thesis: Urbana-Champaign, 1976), pp. 108, 127.

[22] *Education in East and Central Africa* (London: Edinburgh House Press, n.d.), pp. 259-60; Ragsdale, *Protestant Mission Education*, pp. 73-74.

[23] Z.M.R. III, 37 (July 1907), p. 277.

> To have Christian kraals is, of course, the ideal thing: but the time for this has not come yet; for the existence of Christian kraals means too much centralisation, whereas our great need is to widen our spheres of influence, and we have, as it is, far too few missionaries for this.[24]

Nonetheless, the Christian village approach continued. In his memorial of 1924, the visitor to the Jesuit mission remarked:

> On each station, as far as it is possible, native Christians should be gathered into Christian villages in the neighbourhood of the Mission Church.[25]

Though he advocated some segregation between Christians and pagans, the visitor warned against anything like what he called Pharisaical aloofness. The Christian village approach of both the White Fathers and the Jesuits entailed basic schooling, though many of these so-called schools remained rather crude:

> Teaching was in the hands of young men who had been given a grounding in the three Rs and a little hygiene and, having acquired the elements of the Catholic faith, were appointed as teacher evangelists. The schools operated a few weeks at a time until the teacher exhausted his material or until the interest of the class evaporated to vanishing point.[26]

It was nonetheless these "schools" that became the missionaries' mode of access to the local population. As a result, it became important for a mission to have a "school" in as many areas as possible. Competition with other denominations proved to be an important motivating factor in opening schools.[27] When a "school" had been set up, one could begin to claim a rather exclusive right to the population of the area under what became known as the "spheres of influence" policy.[28] This policy was adopted by the government to settle the claims of conflicting societies, particularly:

---

[24] Minutes of Missionary Conference held at St. George's, Bulawayo, June 22-27 1920. Jesuit Archives, Rome. Future reference will be to JAR.

[25] *Memoriale of the Visitation of the Zambezi Mission 1924-1925*, p. 40. (Zimbabwe Jesuit Archives, Harare, Box 48A).

[26] Snelson, *Educational Development*, p. 88.

[27] Garvey, *Bembaland Church*, p. 101. Clearly, the term school is ambiguous for while the earliest White Fathers in the area used schools as a means of creating Christian villages, the system was abandoned in 1904 in favour of itinerant catechists.

[28] N.A.Z. RC 711; *Proceedings of the General Missionary Conference of Northern Rhodesia 1924* (Lovedale Press, 1929), pp. 27-8; Carmody, *Conversion and Jesuit Schooling*, pp. 30, 35; Reinhard Henkel, *Christian Missions in Africa: A social geographical study of the impact of their activities in Zambia* (Berlin: Dietrich Reimer Verlag, 1989), pp. 103-112; O'Shea, *Missionaries and Miners*, pp. 45-8; Lane, "Jesuit Religious Education," pp. 51-3.

> ...to limit the operations of the French Fathers whose avowed intention is to establish missions throughout the whole country and to upset the influence of the Protestant Societies.[29]

Thus we find that in 1922, the White Father Bishop of Bangweulu, Etienne Larue directed: "Do not speak of schools, but only of houses of prayer."[30] For him, the two were quite distinct. In this way, he gained a foothold in the Chinsali district. If he had tried to open a more secular type of school, government would not have permitted him to do so. In general the Catholics, especially the White Fathers, refused to accept the "spheres of influence" policy. The White Father Bishop Guilleme disclaimed concurrence with the spirit of the Missionary Conference where the issue was discussed and stated openly that he could not admit the principle involved by agreeing to reservations of spheres for different missions.[31] Hardly surprisingly, government officials viewed such non-compliance negatively:

> I regret having to appear unsympathetic towards the White Fathers for whose devoted labours on behalf of the natives I have the highest regard and with some of whom I had most cordial relations in the past...From an administrative point of view I am of the opinion that it is not desirable under the present conditions of the territory to have missions teaching widely different doctrines side by side for native converts and pupils.[32]

As Holmes implies, the White Fathers may not have considered this sort of religious apartheid an appropriate tribute for the assistance they had rendered the B.S.A.C. in gaining a foothold in Bembaland. As a result, they did not feel obliged to conform to such, at least in their eyes, arbitrary legislation.[33]

The Jesuits appear to have accepted the policy in principle, yet they tended to ignore it when it did not fit their interests especially in the Katowdwe region. Referring to the Jesuits, the Acting Secretary for Native Affairs wrote:

> There is now I am afraid a tendency on the part of several missionaries to aim at enlarging their range of influence regardless of their means for

---

[29] N.A.Z. A3/10/2-4; "Report on Native Affairs, 31 March 1925 (Public Records Office, Kew, London: CO 799), p. 430. Future reference P.R.L.

[30] Oger, *Where a Scattered flock*, p. 46; Hinfelaar, *Bemba-Speaking Women*, p. 59.

[31] N.A.Z. RC/365.

[32] N.A.Z. RC/711; Acting Administrator, Richard Goode, to His Excellency, Acting High Commissioner for South Africa, Cape Town, Sir Rudolf Bentinck, 17 December 1923.

[33] N.A.Z. RC/711; Holmes, "French Missionaries," *Zambia Journal of History* 6/7, p. 21; Henkel, *Christian Missions in Africa*, p. 109.

providing effective European supervision over the native teachers and preachers. I feel more good would be done with less chance of friction and with less risk of upsetting the native mind or of disturbing the regular channels of community control if their efforts were devoted to consolidation and sound organisation rather than occupying new fields.³⁴

However, the Catholics were not the only offenders. In 1910, the White Father superior of Kayambi complained to the District Commissioner about London Missionary Society (L.M.S.) trespassing and concluded by warning:

> But the Kawimbe Mission may rest assured that we will not withdraw, and retire before them. If they enter our territory, we shall advance into theirs.³⁵

Schools in the more secular, academic, sense of providing more than religious instruction at this stage were probably few. In any case, it would appear that in general the White Fathers were not enthusiastic about them. As Garvey noted:

> Schoolmastering was not popular among White Father missionaries who greatly preferred the physical discomforts of their bush stations to the strict regime and petty restrictions of the seminary.³⁶

Moreover, according to Garvey, lack of interest in secular learning characterised all White Fathers' missions in Central Africa and reflected their founder's principle that communities should be Christianised with as little as possible disruption of traditional culture.³⁷ In addition to this lack of desire to tie themselves to a classroom on the part of the White Fathers, there may have been a more serious reason in that the French Fathers wanted to maintain a distance from the B.S.A.C. and the system of schooling associated with the British.³⁸

These early schools were rather primitive. As a student of the 1920s, Fr. Lyamibaba, recalled: "At the beginning we used rags for writing and

---

³⁴ Letter from Acting Administrator, Richard Goode, to His Excellency, Acting High Commissioner, Sir Rudolf Bentinck, 17 December 1923. (N.A.Z. RC/711). Lane, "Jesuit Religious Education," pp. 38-39; Peters, "Educational Development among the Tonga," p. 104. In general however, the Jesuits were considered to be more co-operative than the White Fathers. See: *Education in East and Central Africa*, pp. 163-4.
³⁵ N.A.Z. A3/10/9; E. Puett, Superior to Mr. Leyer, 18 July 1910.
³⁶ Garvey, *Bembaland Church*, p. 136; Oger, *Where a scattered flock*, p. 46; Brian Garvey, "Colonial Schooling and Missionary Evangelism," *History of Education* Vol. 23, 2 (1994), p. 197.
³⁷ Garvey, *Bembaland Church*, p. 136; Garvey, "Colonial Schooling and Missionary Evangelism," p. 106.
³⁸ Flies, *The Missionaries of Africa*, p. 10.

we came together in a cow shed. Some time later we were given slates."³⁹ In many cases, there were no copybooks, and children wrote with charcoal on white stones. Reading was said to come without much difficulty, but writing was poor and arithmetic abysmal.⁴⁰ In fact, Ipenburg states that the Catholic catechists were frequently illiterate. However, Oger's comment on this statement was: "If he (Ipenburg) means not able to read and write, he is definitely wrong.... If he means ignorant in a particular field, then he is right".⁴¹ Thus the teachers were catechists, and minimally literate, people who knew some religious doctrine but had little real training.

> Nos catéchistes ne sont pas des puits de science, mais pour faire bien il n'est pas besoin d'être grand intellectuel.⁴²

When asked by his superior about the catechists, one White Father replied:

> Are they masters of their mission? ... Yes in that they catechise the people. What they lack is secular knowledge. They are not capable of being good primary teachers, and the British want genuine schools.⁴³

Dupont wanted well-established men of good living as catechists rather than youths of academic ability.⁴⁴

Despite the rather basic, perhaps crude, nature of the White Father's schools, they were not the subject of major criticism by government. After the Proclamation of 1918, it was noted that the White Fathers had little to complain about since the government asked for nothing which they did not already practice regarding the careful recruitment of evangelist-teachers. The Magistrate at Kasama simply requested the Bishop to furnish him with a list of villages receiving catechetical instruction.⁴⁵

Conscious of the need to provide schools for girls as well as boys, the White Fathers invited the White Sisters in 1902 to Chilubula. Gadsden

---

³⁹ Fr. John Lyamibaba, Interview, Chilubula, 16 July 1996.

⁴⁰ Garvey, *Bembaland Church*, p. 140.

⁴¹ At Ipenburg, *All Good Men*, p. 47. L. Oger, Personal letter to author, 24 November 1995.

⁴² Our catechists are not fountains of knowledge but in order to do good they do not need to be great intellectuals. R.A. 1920-21, p. 281.

⁴³ WFA F108; Welfare to Livinhac, 23 May 1908, as quoted in Garvey, *Bembaland Church*, p. 35.

⁴⁴ Ibid.

⁴⁵ Garvey, *Bembaland Church*, p. 140.

noted that, before the advent of Sisters, Roman Catholic societies only educated girls to puberty. Even after the arrival of Sisters, however, girls did not remain in school for long. There was little desire for girls' schooling for a variety of reasons but especially because of early marriage, very limited opportunity to get paid employment and men's fear that educated girls would become too independent.[46]

Unlike the White Fathers, it would seem that the Jesuits did not attempt to create a crew of catechist-teachers. They opened schools piecemeal and held regular meetings for the teachers:

> The Fathers did a good deal in these early years to help the teachers to reach a proper standard of efficiency. Regular meetings were held at which usually eight to ten teachers from schools in the area were brought together for a few days even for a whole week on occasion.[47]

Their teachers had a very basic education. Fr. Torrend of Kasisi demanded that a teacher should be proficient in reading and writing one of the local languages and should know the elements of arithmetic.[48] Much of the instruction was done by the Jesuits themselves. At their 1920 Missionary Conference in Bulawayo, it was reported that older priests were unequal to the drudgery of teaching day after day in elementary schools. In this regard, one of the recommendations of the mission's visitor in 1924 included:

> I have just mentioned the part which the trustworthy catechists can play in the extension of your apostolic work. At no time are such catechists indispensable allies more than at present, when they alone can in some measure make up for the dearth of priests.[49]

As mentioned already, government suspected that Jesuits were more intent on occupying the field than on real schooling. However, in 1915, the Jesuits invited the Sisters of Notre Dame de Namur to Chikuni, though they did not arrive until 1920. From the earliest times at Chikuni, Fr. Moreau desired to have a convent where girls could learn. In 1909, he wrote:

> The native girls and young women are coming to the mission with the

---

[46] Fay Gadsden, "Patriarchal Attitudes: Male control over and policies towards female education in Northern Rhodesia: 1924-1963," *Zambia Journal of History* 1993/4 Nos. 6/7 (1993-4), pp. 33, 39.

[47] Coyne, *A History of the Jesuits in Zambia*, p. 140.

[48] Ibid.

[49] Minutes of the Missionary Conference held at St. George's, Bulawayo, 22-27 June 1920, p. 10. J.A.R; Memoriale of the Jesuit Visitor to the Province 1924-5, p. 31. J.A.C.

greatest good will, and are anxious to learn. Had we a convent here their wish could be complied with, and the work would develop much more rapidly.[50]

A group of Dominican Sisters arrived in Kasisi in 1924, initiating a commitment that was to have a profound impact on the history of education in the country.[51] Both White Fathers and Jesuits recognised that having all male missionaries was far from satisfactory. They knew the importance of including women and girls in their schooling programmes. It is true of course that the White Fathers employed women as evangelists and baptisers from very early on.[52] Reflecting on the Katondwe diarist's notes of 1915, Coyne commented:

> He (the diarist) touches an important side of missionary work in Africa, the education of women, which has been neglected with the result that children when they leave the neighbourhood forget even that they were baptised....we have often heard that the woman is the slave of the man, here it is quite the contrary, the man is slave of the wife's mother. She is consulted in everything, from travel to baptism, to attendance at school. The grandmother is more powerful than the head of the family. Woman has great influence, and as she, so are the children. If she was educated, religion would send deep roots among the Africans, and in case the Missions were abolished traces of Christianity would not vanish so quickly. But for this, Sisters are needed.[53]

Like the White Fathers, the White Sisters did not specialise in teaching and tended to be more directly pastoral in orientation. Even by 1927, none of the White Sisters had received any formal teacher training.[54] Similarly, at Chikuni, though the Sisters of Notre Dame attracted large numbers to their school initially, they placed little emphasis on academic training.[55] As late as 1933, there were only 18 girl boarders, because the Sisters did not yet want to alienate girls from their tribal life.[56] Instead, they encouraged the girls to attend the day school and thus remain close to their roots. At Chikuni as in the northern parts of the territory, it

---

[50] Z.M.R. III, 45 (July 1909), p. 615.

[51] O'Shea, *Missionaries and Miners*, p. 103; *In God's White-robed Army* (Cape Town: Maskew Miller Ltd n.d.), pp. 216-222.

[52] Fay Gadsden, "Education and Society in Colonial Zambia," in Samuel N. Chipungu, ed. *Guardians in their Time* (London: MacMillan, 1992), p. 107.

[53] Coyne, *A History of the Jesuits in Zambia*, p. 8.

[54] Garvey, "Colonial Schooling and Missionary Evangelism," p. 204.

[55] Carmody, *Conversion and Schooling*, p. 41; Lane, "Jesuit Religious Education," pp. 46-7.

[56] P. Robertson, "History of Chikuni Mission." P.G.C.E. Report, 1967. (Special Collections, University of Zambia) p.13

needs to be stressed however that in general there was significant resistance on the part of parents and guardians to sending girls to school:

> The old folks say among themselves: we want to dispose of our daughters as we like, and school girls cannot be disposed of, therefore, no school for them.[57]

By 1925, the Jesuits were running 83 schools for 4,300 children. In the White Fathers' 500 schools there were 25,000 pupils. Overall the Catholic Church operated approximately 35% of the primary schools in Northern Rhodesia in 1925.[58] Though both the Jesuits and the White Fathers had been more than two decades at work in the territory, the White Fathers' endeavours were much larger. This may be attributable not only to larger numbers of personnel, but to the strategy of effectively using catechists to evangelise.[59]

AFRICAN RESPONSE TO CATHOLIC SCHOOLS

Throughout the period 1901-1924, the missionaries complained about the difficulty either of attracting students to their schools or of sustaining their interest.[60] The first White Father school opened at Kayambi in 1896. The first students included fourteen boys who had been ransomed from Arab slave traders. But soon Dupont began recruiting children, sons of chiefs in particular, from the surrounding villages, within a radius of 100 kilometres, who became boarders.[61] In order to encourage regular attendance, pupils were paid a penny a day. The prospect of casual employment may also have been an incentive.[62] However, even when children came to school their attendance records were poor. It was reported that at Chilubula in 1902:

> there were rarely more than sixty pupils at a time in attendance. It was accepted that village life militated against strict regularity, but it was

---

[57] Z.M.R., VI, 79 (January 1918): 102.

[58] Reinhard Henkel, *Christian Missions in Africa*, p. 128.

[59] In 1924, the Jesuits had 5 stations, 20 Europeans and 70 outschools whereas the White Fathers had 12 stations, 32 Europeans, 570 outschools and 218 native teachers. (*Education in East Africa*, pp. 263-4). One needs to keep in mind the rather vague distinction between school and catechetical centre. We are mainly dealing with catechetical centres at this time.

[60] R.I. Rotberg, *Christian Missionaries and the creation of Northern Rhodesia 1880-1924* (Princeton: Princeton University Press, 1965), p. 107.

[61] L. Oger, letter to author. 24 November 1995; Oger, *Where it all began*, pp. 46, 169

[62] Snelson, *Educational Development*, p. 67; Garvey, *Bembaland Church*, p. 67.

regretted that for this reason standards would have to be low.[63]

Nevertheless, the number of schools increased dramatically over the next twenty five years leading to more regular attendance and more consistent and efficient standards.[64] For this they trained itinerant catechists, prayer leaders, and baptisers. Catechists resided at central villages from which they would tour the surrounding area. Part of their task included the setting up of chapel schools (*chapelles-ecoles*), which they used both for religious services and classes in the basics of the Catholic faith. Occasionally, the priest came to provide Mass and to oversee development.

It would appear that people often came to the White Fathers' schools in those days because of their interest in the new religion and their desire for baptism. Elderly men and women came with the youth, though young men were predominant:

> C'est la jeunesse et surtout la jeunesse masculine qui compose cette partie de notre troupeau. Nous disons, la jeunesse, car les vieux, pour la plupart, n'ont pas encore dit adieu à leurs fétiches et á leurs superstitions...Nous avons ajouté: la jeunesse masculine. Si nous avons des femmes parmi nos catéchumens, elles son t loin d'être légion.[65]

People desired baptism and the new religion frequently because of the teaching of the evangelists. Fear of Hell and the prospect of Heaven featured as part of the motivation. Personal salvation and forgiveness for sin formed part of the message. According to Hinfelaar, the common people regarded the missionaries as liberators, who, because of their medical and social work appeared to have preferential regard for the poor and those who suffered. Catholic emphasis on purity and monogamy initially restored the central role of the women in the family and thus resembled earlier Bemba practise.[66]

Much of the instruction centred on the catechism which was learned by rote. On Sundays after prayers a catechist would:

> make the congregation repeat one or two chapters of the official catechism, which had been taught by an itinerant catchiest and which had been

---

[63] Garvey, *Bembaland Church*, p. 70.

[64] Oger, *Where a Scattered flock*, p. 55.

[65] It is the youth especially the young men who form this part of our flock. We are saying the youth because the old, for the most part, have not bid "Goodbye" to their fetishes and superstitions. We emphasise: young men. If we have any women among our catechumens, they certainly are not many. R.A. 1914-15, p. 351.

[66] Hinfelaar, *Bemba-Speaking Women of Zambia*, p. 30.

learned by heart.⁶⁷

What seems to have featured less clearly here than elsewhere was the desire for secular learning.

> Si tous en général ont compris l'importance de l'instruction religieuse, less enfants n'ont point encore admis l'utilité de l'instruction profane...savoir lire et écrire est le dernier de leurs soucis, et leurs parents ne s'en soucient guère pour eux.⁶⁸

If people wanted secular learning, they were more likely to go to the Protestant missions which were nearby. The Lubwa mission for instance viewed schools, in the more secular sense, as the most potent barrier against the inroads of Roman Catholicism. In fact, school and Protestantism became synonymous.⁶⁹

Inevitably, those students in the White Fathers' schools who wanted to learn English so as to enable them to secure paid employment experienced some frustration.⁷⁰ Migration of young men seeking employment remained a constant feature during this time:

> Ce que nous avons eu à regretter, ce fut le départ des jeunes gens officiellement recrutés pour les mines du Sud. Ils sont partis nombreux, revant d'étoffes et de livres sterling.⁷¹

In 1922, Bishop Larue, who had succeeded Dupont as bishop, regretted the fact that nearly 40% of the Christian male population had migrated.⁷²

In the South and East, where the Jesuits operated, the local response to schools proved slow. In Chikuni, Fr. Moreau found that the Tonga were less enthusiastic about schooling than he had expected. He wrote:

---

[67] Oger, *Where a scattered flock*, p. 55; Garvey, *Bembaland Church*, p. 90; Brendan Carmody, "Conversion to Roman Catholicism in Zambia: Shifting Pedagogies," *African Christian Studies*, 4, 2 (1988), p. 10.

[68] If all have understood the importance of religious instruction, the children have not yet appreciated the use of secular instruction....knowing how to read and write is the least of their worries, and their parents do not care about them. R.A. 1912-13. pp. 634-5.

[69] Ipenburg, *All Good Men*, p. 50; Oger, *Where a scattered flock*, p. 53; Hinfelaar, *Bemba-Speaking Women*, p. 47.

[70] Flies, *The Missionaries of Africa*, p. 10.

[71] What we regret is the departure of the youth who were recruited officially for the mines of the South. Many have gone dreaming of clothes and pounds sterling. R.A. 1908-9, 329; "Report on Native Affairs," 31 March 1925. P.R.L.

[72] Henkel, *Christian Missions in Africa*, p. 113.

> ...a school has proved a great difficulty; it has been started half a dozen times and had to be given up; children find all sorts of excuses for absenting themselves and parents connive at it.[73]

Moreau felt that the only way in which he could maintain regular attendance was through employing youths during the day and teaching them in the evenings. He was to write later:

> People were not anxious for schools or religious instruction at first but what they wanted keenly was cash to pay their tax which was still then a novelty.[74]

In 1911, a day school had to be abandoned because of "the apathy of the natives."[75] The response to the girls' school in 1920 appeared better but regular attendance continued to be a problem. Because of the slow development of schooling in the Chikuni region, Moreau was perceived to lack interest in schools by his Jesuit superiors. He strongly denied this and was greatly pained by such criticism. What is clear is that by this time schooling had come to assume a major role in Jesuit evangelisation.

Moreover, it would appear that what the early schools offered frequently did not coincide with what the local population wished to receive. This became particularly evident when in Chikuni the students demanded to be taught English. In these years, English was perceived by Africans to be the gateway to wage employment. As one student of the time related:

> I wanted to learn English very much as I wanted to be filled with the knowledge of the white man. I insisted on asking Fr. Moreau to teach me but he refused. I wanted to know English because I thought if I went to town I could use English for seeking employment.[76]

Undoubtedly, the prospect of wage employment featured greatly in those early days. In 1912, it was reported:

> There has, of late, been an exodus of our Christian boys, more than half of whom have gone in search of work. Tonga boys are extremely fond of dressing in a showy way, and the sight of a boy returned from work and brilliantly clad from head to foot gives them all "Bulawayo fever."[77]

---

[73] N.A.Z. ZA/7/1/1/3.

[74] N.A.Z. RC 1691; Moreau to D.C. Mazabuka, 11 December 1935.

[75] N.A.Z. KDB 6/6/1 as quoted in Carmody, *Conversion and Jesuit Schooling*, p. 52.

[76] Ibid, p. 54; Berman, "African Reactions", p. 211; Omenka, *The School in the service of Evangelisation*, p. 99.

[77] Z.M.R. IV, 58 (October 1912): 450; Kenneth Vickery, *Black and White in Southern Zambia* (New York: Greenwood Press, 1986), p. 95.

Dixon-Fyle notes that labour migrancy was under way in the 1890s.[78] However, this was exacerbated further by the introduction of the hut-tax in 1904 which, in Gann's words, meant that;

> the need to earn cash became a steady and predictable feature of life, not an occasional adventure which a man might undertake once or twice in the course of his career, in order to get a pot, a knife, or a gun.[79]

Unfortunately, Fr. Moreau, like many missionaries of the time, was initially unsympathetic to the students' demands for English as a means to wage employment. The reasons behind such reluctance to teach English may have come from Moreau's perception of how schooling had effected his own country for the worse. According to one of Chikuni's earliest students:

> Moreau used to tell us the effect of education–it would change the world for the worse. He told us that in his own home (back in France) the country had died because of education...He hated education. It is only today that I look back and believe what Fr. Moreau said about education.[80]

Moreau's unwillingness to teach English may have thus resulted not so much, as Rotberg suggests, from the fact that it would divert Africans from the paths of religion or because it would ultimately produce "half-educated" Africans with an unfortunate awareness of their own independence, but from a desire to preserve Tonga traditional community.[81]

The local population responded to the missionary schools in somewhat different ways. Whereas among the White Fathers the peoples' response to schools seemed to be primarily in terms of their desire for the new message, in Jesuit areas, the response appears to have been coloured much more by the perspective of wage employment.

---

[78] M. Dixon-Fyle, "Reflections on Economic and Social Change among the Plateau Tonga of Northern Rhodesia, 1890-1935," *International Journal of African Historical Studies* 16, 3 (1983), p. 426.

[79] L.H. Gann, *A History of Southern Rhodesia* (London: Chatto & Windus, 1965), p. 124.

[80] Wilson Beenzu, Interview, Chisekesi, 23 March 1984. Interpreter and translator, Cletus Mwila.

[81] Rotberg, *Christian Missionaries*, p. 109; For a somewhat similar dynamic in Karoland, see: M.M. Steedly, "The Importance of proper names: language and "national" identity in colonial Karoland," *American Ethnologist* 23, 3 (1996), pp. 447-75. This may have been partly the idea of "Christian villages." See: Jon Miller, "Missions, Social Change and resistance to authority: notes towards an understanding of the relative autonomy of Religion," *Journal for the Scientific Study of Religion* 32, 1 (1993), pp. 45-6.

NATURE OF EARLY CONVERSIONS

In 1924, as we noted, there were approximately 47,000 Catholics in Northern Rhodesia, the majority of whom came from the White Father Vicaraiate of Bangweulu and about fifteen percent from Jesuit missions. We now wish to attempt to identify more clearly to what were these people converted?

Our discussion will utilise Horton's thought-provoking theory of conversion which has been outlined earlier. As noted, Horton identified what he termed the microcosm and the macrocosm. For him, the microcosm was linked to the local spirits while the macrocosm included the more universal spirits among whom was the Supreme being.

Amidst the White Fathers' missionary endeavour, we thus find that the Bemba had already been introduced to the macrocosmic forces by the 1890s. Since the mid-nineteenth century, the Bemba had been part of the Arab-Swahili trade in ivory and slaves. They had become a formidable people often encroaching on their neighbours. To what degree they had come to give prominence to the concept of a supreme being is not clear. In 1902, a colonial administrator wrote:

> The Babemba recognise the existence of God under the name *Lesa*, translated, all powerful, but they address their prayers and sacrifices to the souls of their ancestors, to spirits they think can work ill or good.[82]

A Tonga convert of the period, when speaking of Chief Monze, recalled: 'he (the chief) was happy that Moreau was talking about God who he already knew.'[83] The Tonga also had become familiar with the larger world since the 1850s.[84] Most Tonga converts of the time felt that the traditional God and the Christian God were one and the same. An early Chikuni convert replied thus to the question: Was the Christian God the same as the traditional one?

> Of course, yes. Only that we Africans go to special places (shrines) where we pray to God through our ancestral spirits whereas the white people pray to God through the priests.[85]

The Jesuits adopted the traditional word *Leza* for supreme spirit to translate the Christian concept of God. As Colson, an anthropologist who spent many years among the Tonga, noted when speaking of this

---

[82] N.A.Z. KDH/1/1; Kasama Notebook, p. 402.

[83] Wilson Beenzu, Interview, Chisekesi, 23 March 1984.

[84] See Vickery, *Black and White in Southern Rhodesia*, pp. 35-67.

[85] Mr. Tilimboyi, Interview. Chikuni, 8 August 1986, by R.L. Sishawa.

period:

> I think there had been a revision in religious belief very generally, in that *Leza* had been reinterpreted as God, and as God concerned with human beings, while the spirits that were concerned with the small local communities had become of much less importance.[86]

On the other hand, among the Bemba, the White Fathers appeared more hesitant to use the traditional word, *Leza*, and preferred the word, *Mulungu*, which they imported. As Professor Kashoki noted:

> The word *Leza* (in many White Fathers' minds) was associated with paganism, the imported word *Mulungu* was preferred. *Leza* was not used when I was growing up.[87]

It appears that the notion of a high god was prevalent among both the Bemba and the Tonga at the time of the missionaries' arrival in their areas. This may have facilitated the conversion process. However, formal acceptance of Catholicism entailed more than acceptance of a new concept of God and may not have featured as a dominant element in motivating conversion. It would seem that among the Bemba new eschatological ideas like Hell and Heaven featured more decisively, confirming Gray's observation on Horton's thesis that the appeal of eschatological elements was often more decisive in the conversion process than the notion of a High God.[88] On the other hand, among the Jesuit converts, social structural factors seemed to be foremost in motivating

---

[86] Elizabeth Colson, letter to author, dated 2 July 1987 (J.A.C.). The traditional word *Leza* seems to have been accepted by the missionaries from the beginning. See: J. Torrend, *A Primer of Tonga Language* (Trappist Mission Press, Marianhill, 1906); *An English-vernacular dictionary of Bantu Botatwe dialects* (Marianhill Mission Press, 1931); C.R. Hopgood, "Conception of God amongst the Tonga of Northern Rhodesia (Zambia)", in E.W. Smith, ed. *African Ideas of God* (London: Edinburgh House Press, 1966), pp. 61-77. Fr. Norman MacDonald S.J. who did much work on an ecumenical translation of the Bible into Tonga and who has been a missionary since the early 1950s confirmed to the author that he never noted any hesitation about using the word *Leza* for the Christian God. (Personal communication, 20 March 1997).

[87] Professor Mubanga Kashoki was the son of a catechist and grew up in the Kasama area in the early 1940s. Interview, Lusaka, 13 March 1997; See: Mubanga Kashoki, "Migration and language change: the interaction of town and country," in David Parkin, ed. *Town and Country in Central and Eastern Africa* (London: Oxford University Press, 1975), pp. 237 ff.; See also Kevin Maxwell, *Bemba Myth and Ritual: The Impact of Literacy on an Oral Culture* (New York: Peter Lang, 1983), pp. 99 ff; Isichei, *A History of Christianity in Africa*, pp. 122, 262; Hastings, *The Church in Africa*, p. 333.

[88] Richard Gray, "Christianity and Religious Change in Africa," *African Affairs* 77, 306 (January 1978), pp. 96-8.

them to convert.[89] Writing about those early days, Fr. Moreau recalled:

> In those days the Christians and catechumens were few in number, and the first step towards conversion was to prove to the natives that missionaries had not come to teach them religion but to improve their material conditions.[90]

As we have already indicated, there was widespread desire for wage employment throughout the territory. Among the reasons for this was the need for money to pay the hut tax which had been introduced in 1904.

Horton's thesis thus helps explain why conversion may have been facilitated by the social changes that were operating at the time of the arrival of the White Fathers and Jesuits. However, there are a variety of factors, some of which we have mentioned, which led to the choice, as opposed to the automatic acceptance, of Catholicism. One such factor included the nature of the message presented, which could vary considerably with missionary groups within the same denomination.

While the White Fathers and the Jesuits shared much of the common Catholic worldview of the day, their approaches to evangelisation clearly differed. Both groups of missionaries were predominantly of French origin, but White Father and Jesuit formation differed considerably. The White Fathers tended to be prepared for more direct pastoral work while, as we earlier indicated, the Jesuit programme of studies was more school oriented. In any event, the White Fathers appear to have had a clearer approach to preparing candidates for Baptism. From the beginning they stressed a four-year long catechumenate with strict conditions for its successful completion. As Oger commented:

> The road to baptism was a long one. In those days the White Fathers followed strictly the four year catechumenate, which had been the express wish of the founder, Cardinal Lavigerie. Converts would become postulants and receive a medal. A cross would make the entry into the catechumenate proper. Once the catechumens had a satisfactory Christian conduct and a fair knowledge of the Faith, they became candidates for baptism and were called to the central mission for a full month of intensive immediate preparation for baptism and eventually confirmation.[91]

---

[89] Carmody, *Conversion and Jesuit Schooling*, p. 57; "Conversion and School at Chikuni, 1905-1939," *Africa* 58, 2 (1988), pp. 193-209.

[90] Z.M.R. IX, 130 (October 1930), p. 104.

[91] Oger, *Where a scattered flock*, p. 51; see also Garvey, *Bembaland Church*, pp. 71, 89; This systematic approach to the catechumenate may have been part of Lavigerie's special legacy. See: Hastings, *The Church in Africa*, p. 298.

The instruction was highly conceptual and moral in focus, but the emphasis was not so much on understanding as on memorisation:

> Assiduity at instructions and the knowledge by heart of prayers and catechism formulae were required before candidates were formally admitted to their grades.[92]

Among the Jesuits, at least initially, admission to baptism appears to have been easier and for a long time depended a good deal on the personality of the priest rather than on a definite policy. As a result, there were complaints that many were baptised without sufficient instruction. In a letter from Fr. Czarlinski, superior of the mission, to the Prefect Apostolic in April 1921, he commented on Fr. Torrend's approach to baptisms:

> I ask your advice: Fr. Torrend baptises crowds of people without a minimum preparation, both children and adults as one would baptise dying people only. They are taught occasionally by a Christian, not even a catechist, and know nothing beyond the prayers and some hymns and have not the slightest idea of Christian living and its demands.[93]

At the Conference in Bulawayo in June 1920, however, a clearer overall policy on admission to baptism was formulated, whereby a candidate for baptism should:

> show a serious and sincere will to observe the commandments...regular attendance at religious instructions, in coming to church on Sunday and the greater festivals.[94]

This conference further stressed that the catechumenate should last for at least two years. In 1924, the official Jesuit visitor to the mission cautioned:

> The policy of "slow but sure" is undoubtedly the better. Useful and cheering as figures and statistics may be, they are not the sole standard by which the gains made in the spiritual business of conversion of souls may be safely judged. They take no account of quality, and quality is worth a great deal

---

[92] Brian Garvey, "The Development of the White Fathers' Mission among the Bemba-speaking Peoples 1891-1964." (Ph.D. thesis, University of London, 1974), p. 178. Lane, "Jesuit Religious Education," pp. 112-117.

[93] Coyne, *History of the Jesuits*, pp. 23, 124. 133; See also Lane, "Jesuits in Zambia", p. 23; Similar complaints were made about Father Moreau's practice. "After six lessons in Christian doctrine Fr. Moreau baptised one of the girls...As I was instructing her, I saw that she knew nothing and I protested, but he said: I am the superior..." Letter from A. Casset to Superior, 22 December 1919 (J.A.C.).

[94] Z.M.R. VI, 91 (January 1921), p. 381.

more than quantity. The value of missionary results is to be estimated less from long entries in the baptismal record than from the list of those – sometimes, alas, a considerably shorter one – whose lives tally with their baptismal vows.[95]

Both White Father and Jesuit approaches however, in typical Roman Catholic fashion of the time, made extensive use of a catechism.[96] Among the White Fathers, Dupont insisted: "Imprint the text firmly in their memories. They will understand it when they need to."[97] As already mentioned, the emphasis was not so much on understanding as on memorisation to assist subsequent understanding. This approach lasted into the 1950s. As Kashoki recalled:

> There was a lot of stress on memory. When I went to Colgate (university), I realised that indoctrination had played a great part in my early years...in those days, questioning religion had been almost taboo. When you questioned it was as if something was wrong.[98]

It should be recognised however that the Catholic rituals played a significant role in the socialisation of converts into the Church. The Mass of course was recited in Latin and both its celebration and that of the sacraments were standardised. The socialisation approach of the Catholic church perhaps paralleled that of traditional ritual.[99] Oger notes that in addition to the liturgy the White Fathers made extensive use of the Roman ritual. According to him, the pioneer missionaries did not hesitate to replace "pagan" practices like the blessing of fire at the beginning of cultivation with a Catholic version. In fact, Dupont was accused of sorcery because of the superior power which some of the rituals he used appeared to have. The Jesuits similarly made extensive use of such things as house, well, and crop blessings in their ministry.[100]

The approach of the White Fathers in the early days appears to have been more in accord with an oral rather than a literate orientation. As noted, many of the early catechists were barely literate. Gann contended that the Catholic rituals probably appealed to the tribesman's love of ceremonial.[101] Maxwell's proposal that Christian missionaries substituted

---

[95] Memoriale of Visitation, p. 18.
[96] Garvey, *Bembaland Church*, p. 90; Lane, "Jesuits in Zambia", p. 44.
[97] Garvey, *Bembaland Church*, p. 90.
[98] Kashoki, Interview, 13 March 1997.
[99] Garvey, *Bembaland Church*, p. 90.
[100] Louis Oger, "La Sorcellerie lieu d'inculturation," *Petit Echo* 1994/5 (860), p. 183; Lane, *Jesuits in Zambia*, p. 45.
[101] Gann, *Birth of a Plural Society*, p. 41; See: David Heise, "Prepatory Findings in the

a literate currency in place of one that was oral is hardly accurate in these early days of the White Fathers' evangelisation of the Bemba.[102]

In terms of practical demands made upon the convert, there are similarities between Jesuits and White Fathers. Both viewed Baptism within the Roman Catholic Church, which was seen to be the only true church, as essential for salvation. In the words of one of the missionaries of the day:

> Christianity must be exclusive; if Christ is the Son of God, no heathen deity can be of God...Now compare such a concept of a Protestant missionary the Catholic missioner, who is sent to convert the heathen in foreign lands. He has no halting and hesitating beliefs. He is no Mr. Facing Both Ways. He holds with absolute conviction, with the certainty of Divine Faith, not only that Christ is God and that there can be no compromise between him and false deities but he also knows on like grounds that the Catholic's form of Christianity is the only true form of the only true religion. This is the real motive power behind the Catholic missioner.[103]

In this respect, the White Fathers abhorred the Protestant view that baptism was not absolutely necessary for salvation.[104]

In concord with their theology which viewed membership of the Roman Catholic Church as essential for eternal salvation, both groups of missionaries emphasised the practice of baptising those in danger of death. From Mambwe in 1894, we read:

> Our nyampara (caretaker), Mwene Hama, seeing that his young daughter is in danger of death, comes to call Father Superior during the night and wishes his child to be baptised.[105]

The fact that people had not learned to call a priest when a person was in danger of death was taken to be a clear indication of inadequate instruction:

> Neglect, too, to summon a priest to the dying was a great trial for the Fathers: a pagan girl of eight had been brought to Katondwe in a starving

---

Sociology of Missions," *Journal for the Scientific Study of Religion* VI,1 (Spring 1967), p. 57, who contends that groups tend to be more receptive of a religion whose church organisation bears structural resemblance to the native social organisations.

[102] Maxwell, *Bemba Myth and Ritual*, pp. xvi-xvii: See: Ranger, "The Local and the Global in Southern African Religious History," pp. 85-86.

[103] Z.M.R., III (April 1908), p. 376: See also Carmody, *Conversion and Jesuit Schooling*, pp. 25-6; Lane, "Jesuit Religious Education," p. 19; Gann, *Birth of a Plural Society*, p. 38.

[104] Ipenburg, *All Good Men*, p. 178; Hastings, *The Church in Africa*, p. 509.

[105] Mambwe Diary: 1 June 1894, taken from The Mponda-Mambwe Diary 1891-1895 (Kasama: Archives Missionaries of Africa, 1994), p. 59; R.A. 1912-13, p. 614.

condition. Being given food she died. Her relations failed to call the priest and she was secretly buried to the accompaniment of pagan rites.[106]

Both White Fathers and Jesuits demanded that new Church members be monogamous, attend Sunday Mass, where possible, and receive the Sacrament of Penance frequently. From the Catholic perspective of the time, Sunday Mass constituted one of the prime obligations for Catholics. It was a key criterion of conversion. In a report from Chikuni in January 1906, less than six months after the mission had been started, we read:

> No conversions have yet been made, but the work of instruction on Sunday has begun in earnest. The people know and already observe the Sunday.[107]

As already indicated, Mass was conducted in Latin and in accord with standard rubrics. It included hymns that had been selected for worship in Europe. Though it may have enhanced the sense of mystery surrounding the Eucharist, it was very foreign. As Garvey mentions, this rite was closely linked to prior purification through Confession of sin, and so weekly Confession was a normal practice.[108]

For various reasons, polygyny was accepted in traditional life, and divorce was permitted on occasion.[109] According to Roman Catholic practice, neither was allowed. Garvey contends that this led to trial unions among Christian couples who were unwilling in youth to risk an indissoluble church marriage.[110] Among the Bemba, Dupont introduced a rule that restricted adult baptism to those who were living monogamously. Oftentimes, when one became a polygamist, he was expelled from the Christian village or mission reserve. Strict adherence to the practice of monogamy was sometimes incorrectly perceived to be a sign that Catholics as opposed to Protestants were selective in terms of the quality of people they attracted:

> An old chief said: "Your religion is a true religion. The Protestants recruit all the undesirable characters and make them more insolent and thievish." One of our men was sent away from our village because of polygamy. He went to Kawimbe and after a few months he was baptised together with all his wives.

---

[106] Coyne, *History of the Jesuits*, p. 23.

[107] Z.M.R., III, 31 (January 1906), p. 62

[108] Garvey, *Bembaland Church*, p. 106.

[109] Elizabeth Colson, *Marriage and the Family among the Plateau Tonga of Northern Rhodesia* (Manchester: Manchester University Press, 1967), pp. 119-36. A.I. Richards, *Chisungu* (London: Faber and Faber, n.d.)

[110] Garvey, *Bembaland Church*, p. 106.

> They accept anyone and they pick up all the weeds we throw over the hedge.[111]

The B.S.A.C. administration recognised as legal, marriages according to both traditional custom and churches. However, at one point, the administration urged Fr. Torrend of Kasisi to refuse the religious ceremony to couples who had not complied with the native custom, which did not recognise marriage as binding until it was consummated. Clearly, this was unacceptable to Torrend and all Catholic missionaries.[112] Neither White Fathers nor Jesuits appear to have been very successful in making marriage within the Church something that was expected of all Catholics.[113] Despite constant efforts to make marriage within the church normative, by 1924, it was reported from the Jesuit mission that:

> slowly but surely our Christian idea of marriage being a sacramental contract, not a chase, is bearing fruit in our Christian girls.[114]

Both White Fathers and Jesuits were aware of the importance of promoting a local clergy.[115] The White Fathers started a seminary at Chilubula in 1919. Although the Jesuits did not set up a seminary in these early years, they accepted candidates for the priesthood from the 1930s and sent them for their studies to Salisbury (present day Harare). Many of the early priests in the country did their studies there. However, the White Fathers and the Jesuits could be said to have embodied a Eurocentric Catholic culture and psychological outlook, probably resembling that of Europeans generally at that time, described thus by Hastings:

> ...the whole psychology of Europe in the second half of the nineteenth century—the Victorian age—with its enormous self-confidence, belief in progress as incarnated in its own achievement, and consequent sense of superiority, was most inimical to a supple missionary approach or to the commencement of what today we describe as dialogue. Missionaries inevitably shared this general psychology just as they shared the ecclesiastical attitudes of their age and country.[116]

---

[111] Mponda-Mambwe diary, 21 March 1895.

[112] Coyne, *History of the Jesuits*, p. 116.

[113] Garvey, *Bembaland Church*, pp. 105-7.

[114] Z.M.R., VII, 103 (January 1924), p. 315; Z.M.R., VI, 91 (January 1921), p. 382.

[115] Garvey, *Bembaland Church*, p. 136; O'Shea, *Missionaries and Miners*, p. 58; Weller & Linden, *Mainstream Christianity*, p. 160.

[116] Adrian Hastings, *Church and Mission in Modern Africa* (London: Burns & Oates, 1967), p. 27.

The Catholic Church's official attitude to local customs and rites remained rather conservative in the preservation of its traditionally western way of operating.[117] However, individual White Fathers and Jesuits of the time were sensitive to aspects of local cultures which they did not consider to be outrightly against the Christian way of life. In Chikuni, for instance, Fr. Moreau, while unenthusiastic about the psychological and social effects of the custom of girls' initiation, remained for mary years undecided about the custom from the Christian perspective:

> How far is the rite opposed to Christianity I have not yet fully ascertained, but the sequestration (sic) of a young woman just entering womanhood in a dark evil smelling hut day and night for one, two, or three months or even more...cannot but have a debasing influence on the mind of the young woman. I think the female portion, or rather the coming generation of young women in these parts would owe a great debt of gratitude if the rite of initiation of girls were abolished.[118]

Moreover, at their Bulawayo Conference in 1920, the Jesuits including Fr. Moreau, carefully reflected on, and tried to be sensitive to, traditional customs, resolving that on the issues of marriage they should ask Africans what they themselves thought.[119]

It appears nonetheless that Africans were rarely consulted with the result that religiously and morally neutral customs were often condemned as pagan. For this reason, many Zambian Catholics perceive the early missionary approach to have been rather negative towards local culture. On being asked if the Church had helped him to cherish his Zambian heritage, one Catholic replied:

> No. Especially in the early days. To a large extent in the early days, the Catholic Church was "anti." From the point of view of African heritage, there were too many negatives. That unfortunately has remained with me up to now.[120]

Though, among the White Fathers and Jesuits, as we have mentioned, there was fairly universal insistence on monogamy, prohibition of widow-inheritance as well as divorce, Professor Elizabeth Colson recalls that Fr.

---

[117] J.A. Kieren, "Some Roman Catholic Missionary Attitudes in 19th century East Africa," *Race* (10), pp. 341-59; Z.M.R., IX, 29 (July 1930), p. 71.

[118] N.A.Z. KDB 6/6/1; "Report on Chikuni." 1916.

[119] Minutes of Missionary Conference held at St. George's, Bulawayo, 22-27 June 1920. J.A.R.

[120] Kashoki, Interview, 13 March 1997.

Moreau told her that he requested the Roman Curia to allow some latitude on polygamy. It appears that no such licence was granted.[121] He also attended rain shrine ceremonies among the Tonga. After one such occasion, he reported to his superior:

> Last Thursday there was a great gathering at Monze's grave, at least 1500 people. I went there myself and I preached to the crowd from a heap of stone. I told them that I thought my place was also to be with them, their joys as well as their sorrows. I told them about Monze whom I had known 30 years ago, who was then living on the very spot where they were gathered. I told them that if they his children gather now and then at his grave there was nothing wrong in that. If they gather to pay honour and show loyalty to the departed chiefs there was nothing wrong. In that the Batonga meet us, we all believe that our departed friends are still in communion with us. In this the Batonga think more rightly than some who pretend to have come to teach them the word of God...The dead who have died in the state of grace have gone to heaven, they can know us, hear us and intercede for those who have gone to Purgatory. But above all there is God to whom Supreme Honour is due.[122]

Jesuits and White Fathers respected the custom of bridewealth though with some modification. In considering the custom of bridewealth, the Jesuits strongly emphasised the freedom of the girl:

> Pagan girls have little to say on this point (accepting the man who pays the bridewealth), but Christian girls know their right, and they insist on it. One of our Christian girls was partly paid for by a leper. Her parents put great pressure on her to consent to the marriage, as they could not restore the money and other presents. The girl very sensibly refused.[123]

In general, however, there is scant evidence to suggest that the missionaries used traditional patterns of ritual or symbolism to express the Christian message, though clear parallels existed between such things, for instance, as rain shrine and Catholic Corpus Christi processions. It seems nonetheless too sweeping to say that the missionaries came purposefully to transform African society and especially its belief systems, whereby African religion was studied so that it could be refuted or absorbed.[124] Hastings contends that in general Catholics were less

---

[121] Personal communication with the author.
[122] Moreau to Superior, letter dated 27 August 1932. J.A.C.
[123] Z.M.R., IV, 51 (January 1911), p. 173; Garvey, *Bembaland Church*, p. 109.
[124] Garvey, *Bembaland Church*, p. 87; Maxwell, *Myth and Ritual*, p. xvi; For a contrary view, see: L. Sanneh, "The Yogi and the Commisar: Christian Missions and the New World Order in Africa,' in W.C. Roof, ed. *World Order and Religion* (Albany: State University Press of New York, 1991), pp. 173-92.

negative than Protestants towards African custom and certain ethnic groups of Catholic missionaries especially the French were more tolerant than others.[125] Moreover, as Mulaisho's novel, *The Tongue of the Dumb*, set in the Jesuit mission region of Katondwe, illustrates, even within the same mission with missionaries of similar ethnic background, attitudes to local customs and practices varied. In the novel, although Fr. Chiphwanya had little respect for local ways, this could not be said of the superior, Fr. Gonzago. On the occasion of Bro. Arrupe's death, Chiphwanya complained:

> You (Fr. Gonzago) and your natives, you both believe in witchcraft. How could you have approved the people's dramatic display of mourning, the kind of mourning that is only possible among people who do not share our belief in eternity...Yes, it is you who allowed his (Bro Arrupe) death to be mourned by pagans, as if our prayers were not enough.[126]

For Mulaisho, it is significant that it is the Jesuit superior who is open to traditional ways because he is more mature and has lived long among the people. In Mulaisho's view, this formed the more paradigmatic Catholic approach. Indeed, there were plenty of Chiphwanyas, newcomers and full of their own importance, but they did not represent the dominant Catholic approach. It appears correct, however, to say that there was little cultural adaptation even by the Fr. Gonzagos. The Catholic culture of the day, however, with its heavy emphasis on ritual, devotions of various kinds, statues, medals, rosaries and pious objects appealed to peoples whose traditions entailed much ritual. As Hogan pointed out, Catholicism provided an impressive array of techniques which might be used to enable people to cope with the daily problems of life.[127] In terms of Lonergan's paradigm of conversion, we could say that there was some emphasis on religious conversion as manifested in these pious objects and practices as well as in the liturgy of Mass and sacraments. Nonetheless, there was little attempt to integrate this into the overall intellectual and moral aspects of conversion which the catechisms presented.

On the other hand, both White Fathers and Jesuits did much to learn and become competent in the local languages. In fact, their

---

[125] Hastings, *The Church in Africa*, p. 590; See: Kaplan, *Indigenous Responses to Western Christianity*, pp. 9-28, who argues that missionaries were more tolerant than might be assumed.

[126] Dominic Mulaisho, *The Tongue of the Dumb* (London: Heinemann, 1971), p. 157.

[127] Edmund Hogan, "Conversion to Roman Catholicism," *Afer* Vol. 24, 2 (April 1982), p. 77; Gann, *Birth of a Plural Society*, p. 41.

contributions to the development of a vernacular literature remain significant.[128] As an internationally recognised scholar in language studies put it:

> On the matter of language alone there is no way that we ourselves as the owners could have done anything comparable to what we have been given by those people (early White Fathers). Take for example the Bemba dictionary, a most thorough work recognised in academic circles and Sambeek's grammar remains a classic.[129]

In communicating their versions of Catholicism, the White Fathers and Jesuit missionaries brought a new social vision. The early days of the White Fathers mission among the Bemba had an overtly political dimension even if the missionaries were to claim that they were different from colonialists. Garvey demonstrates how the authority of the Bemba chiefs was greatly undermined with the advent of the White Fathers. Unlike the Presbyterians, however, the White Fathers had not come to Bembaland in order to lead subsistence agriculturalists into a production for exchange society.[130] They assumed that their parishioners would

---

[128] For some of the Jesuit contribution, see: Carmody, *Conversion and Schooling*, p. 44; Some of the White Father contribution includes: *Essai de Grammaire* (Paris: St. Cloud, 1900); *Catechisme en langue Kibemba* (Paris: St. Cloud, 1900); Louis Schoeffer, *Bemba Grammar: A Grammar of the Bemba language as spoken in Northern Rhodesia* (Oxford, 1907); W. Lammond, *Lessons in Chibemba*; L. Guillerme, *Dictionnaire Francais-Chibemba* (Malines, 1920); *Bemba-English Dictionary* (Algiers, 1947, reprinted by Mission Press, Ndola, 1991); J. Van Sambeek, *A Bemba Grammar* (Longmans, 1955); *Milumbe yakwa Banana Isa* (1909); *Amafundishyo yakwa Banana Isa* (1910); *Fipeshya mano fyakwa Banana Isa* (1910); *Chitika ca bakristyani* (1910); *Chitabo ce sali* (1910); *Milandu yakwa Mulungu* (1920, 1929); *Milandu yakwa Banana Yesu* (1921, 1932, 1967); *Evangelio ifyo alembelwa kuli Mateo mutakatifu* (1929); *Evangelsio ifyo alembelwa kuli Joanni* (1932); *Evangelio ifyo alembelwa kuli Mariko* (1934). The whole Bible was not translated until 1971. See: Oger, *Where a scattered flock*, p. 74; Oger, "Language and early Catholic missionaries in Bembaland, Zambia." Paper sent to author 26 Nov 1995. J.A.C. On the general significance of such vernacular work, see: Lamin Sanneh, *Translating the Message: The Missionary Impact on Culture* (New York: Orbis, 1989); *Encountering the West: Christianity and the Global Cultural Process: The African Dimension* (London: Marshall Pickering, 1993); "Christian Mission in the Pluralist Milieu: The African Experience," *Missiology* Vol. XII, 4 (1984), pp. 421-432.

[129] Kashoki, Interview, 13 March 1997.

[130] Garvey, *Bembaland Church*, p. 105; For Nyasaland, see: Patrick A. Kalilombe, "From "Outstation" to "small Christian Communities,": A comparison between two Pastoral Methods in Lilongwe Diocese." (Berkeley, California: Graduate Theological Union, Ph.D. dissertation, 1983), pp. 82, 95, 355, 357; John McCracken, "Underdevelopment in Malawi: The Missionary Contribution," *African Affairs*, 76, 303 (April 1977); Garvey, "Bemba Chiefs and Catholic Missions, 1898-1935," *Journal of African History* 18 (1977): Holmes, "French Missionaries and British Treaties," *Zambia Journal of History* 6/7.

remain subsistence farmers while being introduced to new religious and moral beliefs and the requirements of the Catholic church. Yet, clearly this assumption proved false because even by 1922 it was estimated that forty percent of the male population below the age of fifty were absent from their homes because of labour migration to the Copperbelt:

> Quand nous arrivons dans les villages, nous éprouvons fréquemment la tristesse de les trouver presque vides. La plupart des jeunes gens de vingt à trente ans sur lesquels nous fondions des espérances et qui sont appelés à former dans chaque centre le noyau de Chrétiens sont partis aux mines de Bulawayo, Salisbury, la Katanga.[131]

At Chikuni, Fr. Moreau felt that what a people who had practically no money, almost annual famine, and scarcity of clothing most needed was:

> food and a bit of money to buy the most elementary of clothing and especially to pay the personal tax which had been recently imposed.[132]

Thus he set himself the task of improving the farming methods of the people, an activity which a number of his own confreres felt was not priestly work.[133] For Moreau, the promotion of new ways of cultivating embodied a larger vision of the development of Tonga society. It was Moreau's hope that the Tonga would become "a large class of intelligent, prosperous and contented peasants who would own the soil they tilled."[134] In order to achieve this ideal, Moreau envisioned that the Tonga would have to break with their traditional, tribal, land tenure system in favour of individual ownership. Thus each landowner could become prosperous and produce for the market. In 1926, he happily related that:

> ...from May to October, 1926, the traders at Pemba and Monze which lie on a stretch of only twenty miles of railway, brought from natives no less than 13,000 bags of mealies, besides other produce such as beans and monkey-nuts.[135]

---

[131] When we arrive in the villages we are often saddened to find them practically empty. Most of the youth from about twenty to thirty years of age on whom we set our hopes and who were called upon to form a nucleus of Christians have gone to the mines of Bulawayo, Salisbury, and Katanga. R.A. 1920-21, p. 630.

[132] Carmody, *Conversion and Jesuit Schooling*, p. 38.

[133] M. Dixon-Fyle, "Politics and Agrarian Change among the Plateau Tonga of Northern Rhodesia 1924-63." (Ph.D. University of London, 1976), p. 94.

[134] *Proceedings of the Missionary Conference of Northern Rhodesia* (1927) (Lovedale Illustration Press; 1928) p. 139 See also: Vickery, *Black and White in Southern Zambia*, pp. 159-77.

[135] Ibid.

It was this vision of a prosperous peasantry that partly explains why Moreau refused to teach his school pupils English for he considered that ability to speak and write English would lead to a major rural exodus of young men to the towns and industrial centres. Students at the mission in the early days recalled:

> Fr. Moreau never encouraged those who were educated to go to the towns for employment. Instead he encouraged them to work on the land and for the good of their families.[136]

He viewed the early schooling of girls somewhat similarly. In 1910, he wrote:

> For the present the girls are not taught any schooling. It is the custom among these people for girls to remain constantly with their mothers, and they are all the better for being left under the maternal charge. At present it does not appear wise to disturb this custom by trying to get girls to school.[137]

Long after the Sisters of Notre Dame had started a school, Moreau advised:

> The aim of the Sisters is not so much to impart to the girls academic knowledge as to fit them for later life, good housekeepers, good wives, and good mothers of family who will know how to keep their house clean and rear healthy children.[138]

A woman who had been a student at Chikuni mission in its earliest days noted in Chitonga: "We used to make baskets and some clay pots and some were sewing dresses."[139]

Thus the early Catholic missionaries in Northern Rhodesia exhibited a certain degree of ambivalence with regard to economic and social development. In some respects, the Jesuits under Moreau and the White Fathers wanted their school graduates to avail themselves of the material benefits which the emergence of capitalism was bringing. They wished their peoples to become prosperous peasants while their school graduates wanted white collar jobs in the towns. Option for rural and peasant community development at this stage in the history of the Church tended to be the missionaries' choice. It meant a certain neglect of the urban-oriented, more modernised, sectors of the populations. Among

---

[136] Gabriel Mainza and Jerome Mpile, Pre-1924 students at Chikuni. Interview, Chikuni, 3 March 1984.

[137] Carmody *Conversion and Jesuit Schooling*, p. 41.

[138] Report of Education work at Chikuni, 1933 J.A.C.

[139] Cynthia Mooya, Student at Chikuni in 1920s. Interview, Chikuni, March 1984.

missionaries of the late nineteenth and early twentieth century, this approach was widely shared. As Isichei commented:

> The missionaries who embarked on these social transformations were often, paradoxically, hostile to westernisation and education, believing these fostered worldliness.[140]

Missionaries tended to hold a romantic idea of rural life which led them to be anti-capitalist and to reject such aspects of modernity as urbanisation particularly when it involved male migration and the absence of men from village and family.[141]

As we have seen during the period under consideration, the White Fathers and the Jesuits introduced the Catholic Church to the peoples of Northern Rhodesia. It was a preponderantly institutional model of church, with special emphasis on obedience to laws and rubrics. The priest tended to be the key actor, though catechists had what was perceived to be a crucial, if subordinate, role.[142] During those early days, the school, in a rather primitive sense, progressively assumed a central role in the evangelisation process. The extent to which the school included secular learning depended on particular missionaries' viewpoints. Initially, among the White Fathers there was little. Schools became the vehicle for evangelisation rather than for political or social development. It is true that most schools of the era had a firm practical orientation, where artisans could be trained. In the case of the Jesuits at Chikuni, this practical, non-academic, vernacular orientation proved to be a source of friction in that local boys and young men were more interested in schooling from an academic perspective as a means of social mobility than of conversion.[143]

Given different motivations on the part of the missionaries and their students, it is not surprising that becoming a Catholic often entailed a certain measure of outward conformity to church and school rules in order to placate the missionary without corresponding interior conviction. Such pretence could be poorly addressed, if at all, where

---

[140] Isichei, *A History of Christianity*, pp. 94-5; Elizabeth Isichei, "Seven Varieties of Ambiguity: Patterns of Igbo Response to Christian Missions," *Journal of Religion in Africa* III, (1970), p. 216; Brendan Carmody, "Secular and Sacred at Chikuni 1905-1940," *Journal of Religion in Africa* XXI, 2 (1991), pp. 130-48.

[141] Ipenburg, *All Good Men*, p. 106; Beidelman, *Colonial Evangelism*, pp. 27, 133; Ranger, "The Local and the Global in Southern African Religious History," p. 36.

[142] A. Dulles, *Models of the Church* (New York: Image Books, 1978), pp. 39-50; Hastings, *Church and Mission*, p. 26; Hastings, "Patterns of African Mission Work," pp. 291-98.

[143] See also Berman, *African Reactions*, p. xii

there were large numbers forming the catechumenate, who were required to learn the catechism by heart and where there was no possibility of dialogue between a person's traditional, African, religious experience and his/her experience of the Christian message.[144]

A consequence of this was the promotion of conversion as adhesion in Fisher's sense, where people stood with one foot on either side of the fence. Strictly speaking, however, conversion of this kind entailed no mixing, at least from the Church's point of view.[145] Rather the converts held both their tradition and Catholicism side by side, operating out of both in different circumstances with or without a sense of their incompatibility. Even many years later, a long-time convert responded to the question: After conversion did you continue to believe in worship of ancestors?

> Yes, I did. In fact, the blackman today is suffering and dying in great numbers because he has abandoned the power of his ancestors.[146]

One might ask whether tradition or the new message had the preponderant influence on behaviour. This evidently depended on individuals, but persistence of traditional beliefs and practices would indicate that at least in the early days, converts selected Catholic beliefs and practices in terms of what Horton has termed the "basic" cosmology. This does not necessarily mean that the message of Catholicism embodied nothing new. The oldest Chikuni convert, when asked if he felt happy when he changed from worshipping many gods to worshipping one God, replied:

> Get this clear, young man. This is very important. When we were converted at first, people found it very difficult to change. Even now people still worship gods.[147]

As earlier indicated, the politico-social changes taking place in Northern Rhodesia at this time probably facilitated the emergence of a new religious system. As Van Binsbergen has argued, the relationship between Christian missionaries and the emergence of new modes of

---

[144] Berman, *African Reactions*, pp. 208-9.

[145] Humphrey Fisher, "Conversion Rediscovered: Some Historical aspects of Religious Change in Black Africa," *Africa* XLIII (1973), p. 31; "The Juggernaut's Apologia: Conversion to Islam in Black Africa," *Africa* 55, 2 (1985), p. 170; Carmody, "Conversion to Roman Catholicism in Zambia," pp. 12-3.

[146] Patrick Mweemba. Born 1912. Old convert. Interviewed, Chikuni. August 1986.

[147] George Chisenga, Born 1890s. Oldest convert at Chikuni. Interviewed by Kenneth Hamwaka at Chikuni, July 1986.

production entailed elements of correspondence and dialectic.[148] Missionaries paved the way for the entry of the B.S.A.C. among the Bemba. Elsewhere, they benefited by receiving substantial land grants. On occasion, Catholic missionaries lauded the imposition of the hut tax while they also defended Africans against cruel extraction methods:

> A white man was responsible for the tax collection. Willie Levin was his name. He had men who used to collect for him. They sometimes got money illegally by beating. Those who did not pay were beaten. When Fr. Moreau came, he used to protect people against tax collectors...What Fr. Moreau did not want was beating because they failed to pay.[149]

Because of his determination to protect local people's land rights, Fr. Torrend of Kasisi wanted to write directly to the local B.S.A.C. administrators. As he tended to be rather blunt, the administrators complained and Torrend's superior forbade him to communicate with the administrators without approval in future. This greatly pained Torrend in his desire to see justice done as the following extract from his reply to his superior illustrates:

> If you join the fight against Government, I hand you over command. Come and tell yourself the natives how they must behave in these trying circumstances when an unscrupulous lot of freemasons have made up their minds to reduce them to a tutelage akin to slavery. Then write yourself to the officials courteous letters that will change their minds as if by magic.[150]

Torrend felt that without direct access to administrators, much injustice could be done because of delays in communication and perhaps also, as the text illustrates, because of over civility in communicating.[151]

As employers of African wage earners and as harbingers of new technologies, both the White Fathers and the Jesuits helped to create both new structures of extraction and circulation and new attitudes towards economic subsistence.[152] In the Chikuni area, they were the main source of money:

---

[148] W.M.J. van Binsbergen, *Religious Change in Zambia* (London: Kegan Paul, 1981), pp. 63-4.

[149] Gabriel Mainza & Jerome Mpile. Old Chikuni converts. Interviewed, 11 March 1984; For Catholic missionaries support of the new tax system, see: NAZ A3/10/9 "Les Peres Blancs report by Father Guilleme (1902)."

[150] Letter from J. Torrend to R. Sykes. 4 January 1914. J.A.C.

[151] Letter from J. Torrend to R. Sykes, 4 January 1914. Letter from J. Torrend to Pater Generalis, 6 January 1914. J.A.C.

[152] Elmer S. Miller "The Christian Missionary: agent of Secularisation," *Missiology* vol. 1 (January 1973), p. 102.

> There was little money in those days. Apart from Fr. Moreau, there was none. We used to go to Monze to use any money we got.[153]

Possibly because of what both the Jesuits and the White Fathers perceived to be poverty in the lives of the people, they demanded little by way of voluntary contribution to the church. What resulted was that people began to see the missionaries as the source of finance, with rather unsatisfactory consequences for later.[154]

Although the White Fathers and the Jesuits inevitably helped the emergence of new economic and social relations, being predominantly non-British, they do not appear to have had interest in fostering British colonial interests. Moreover, as we have seen, neither group enthusiastically promoted full-scale integration into the capitalist economy. By 1924, many Northern Rhodesians had become Catholic converts through the Christian villages and schools, perhaps not so much because of individual religious choice but as a result of a much deeper structural dynamic beyond individual reflection, fostered by these Catholic institutions and the personal relationships that they embodied.

---

[153] Louis Chobana. Old convert. Chikuni. Interviewed 16 March 1984.
[154] Garvey, *Bembaland Church*; Weller & Linden, *Mainstream Christianity*, p. 159.

CHAPTER TWO

CONVERSION AND SCHOOL: 1924-1964

As the White Fathers extended their missionary outreach over much of the north-eastern part of Northern Rhodesia, they needed further assistance. Similarly, the Jesuit mission was greatly hampered by the lack of personnel. Administratively, the territories occupied by both the White Fathers and the Jesuits were large and needed to be divided. As we mentioned earlier, Nyasa vicariate was set up in 1897 under the White Father Bishop Joseph Dupont M. Afr. In 1913, this vicariate was divided into Nyasa and Bangweolo. Bishop Larue M. Afr. succeeded Dupont in the administration of Bangweolo.

Between 1913 and 1964, the territory was divided a number of times. By 1964, Zambia had the archdiocese of Lusaka and seven dioceses, Chipata, Kasama, Livingstone, Mansa, Mbala, Mongu and Monze.[1]

---

[1] In 1933, the present districts of Chama, Chinsali, Isoka, Mbala, Mpika, and Serenje were separated from Bangweolo to form what was known as the Vicariate of Lwangwa. Subsequently this Vicariate was renamed Abercorn and later Mbala, under the administration of Bishop Van Sambeek M. Afr. Between 1938 and 1946, Bishop Horst administered this area until Bishop van den Biesen succeeded him. Upon retirement in 1957, van den Bisen was replaced by Bishop Fustenburg who was administrator until 1987. In 1955, the Bishop's residence moved from Ilondola to Mbala.

In 1937, for administrative reasons, the current districts of Chama, Lundazi, and Chipata were separated from Lwangwa to form the Prefecture of Fort Jameson under Bishop Martin, M. Afr. As we noted earlier, stations had been started at Kachebere and Minga in 1903 and 1924 respectively. In 1947, Bishop Courtemarche M. Afr. succeeded Bishop Martin and continued until his retirement in 1970, by which time the territory was renamed Chipata.

The western part of the Bangweolo territory, the Luapula province, had become the Prefecture Apostolic of Fort Rosebery (Mansa) under Mgr. Rene Pailloux in 1952. In 1961, Mansa became a diocese with Bishop Pailloux as its first bishop. Two years later, Fr. Clement Chabukasansha became the first Zambian auxiliary Bishop of Fort Rosebery which in 1967 was renamed the diocese of Mansa. Meanwhile, the original territory of Bangweolo had been administered by Bishop Roy and later Bishop Daubechies until 1965, when it was renamed diocese of Kasama. In that year, Bishop Clement Chabukasansha moved to Kasama from Ft. Rosebery as the first Zambian Bishop.

In the southern part of the territory, the Prefecture of Broken Hill was constituted in 1927. This included the whole southern region of Zambia where Monsignor Bruno Wolnik S.J. became Prefect Apostolic. Since the area to be covered by the missionaries was large and the numbers of Jesuits remained rather limited, Monsignor Wolnik invited Irish Capuchins to open a mission in Livingstone in 1930, while the Franciscan

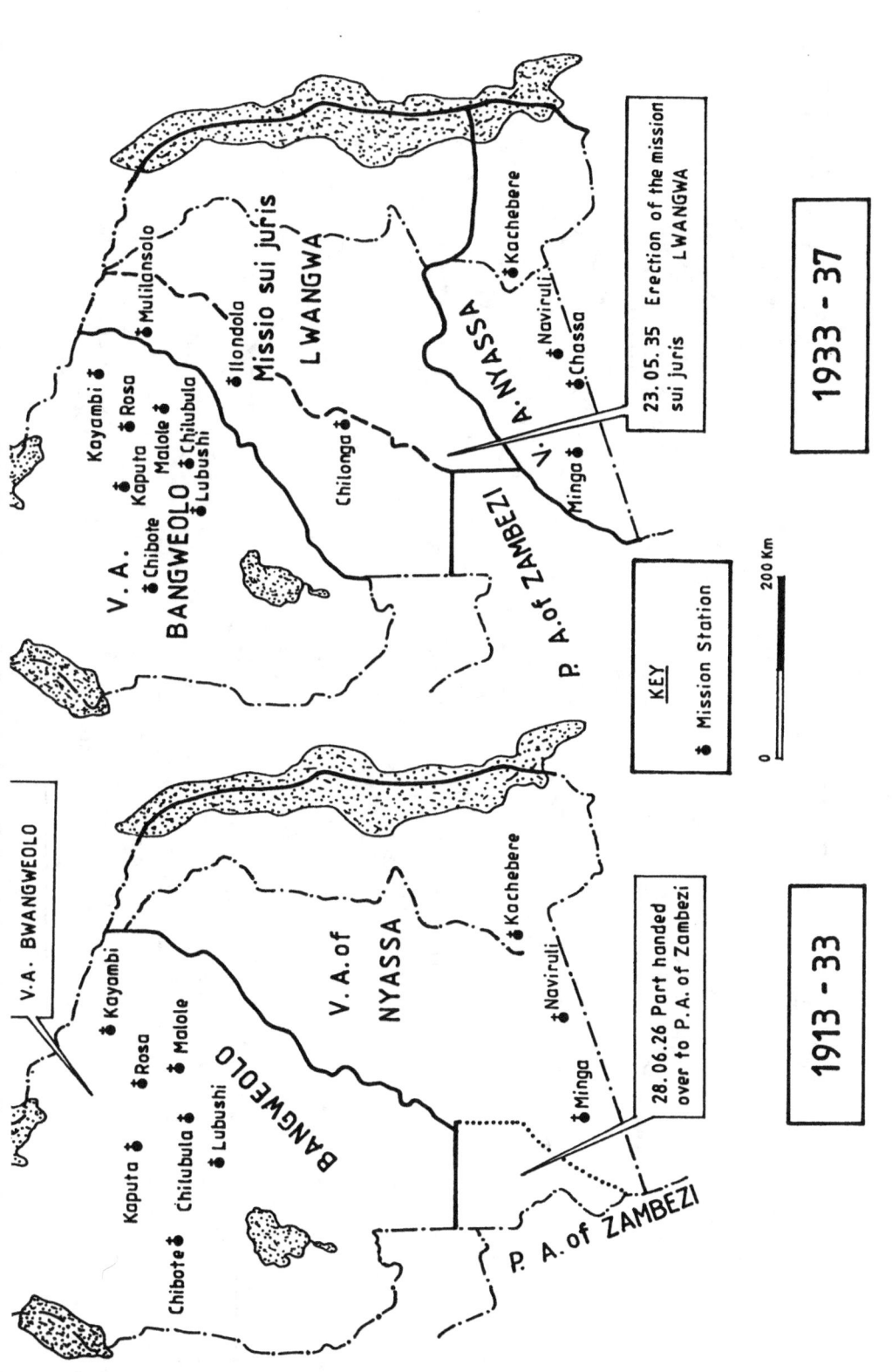

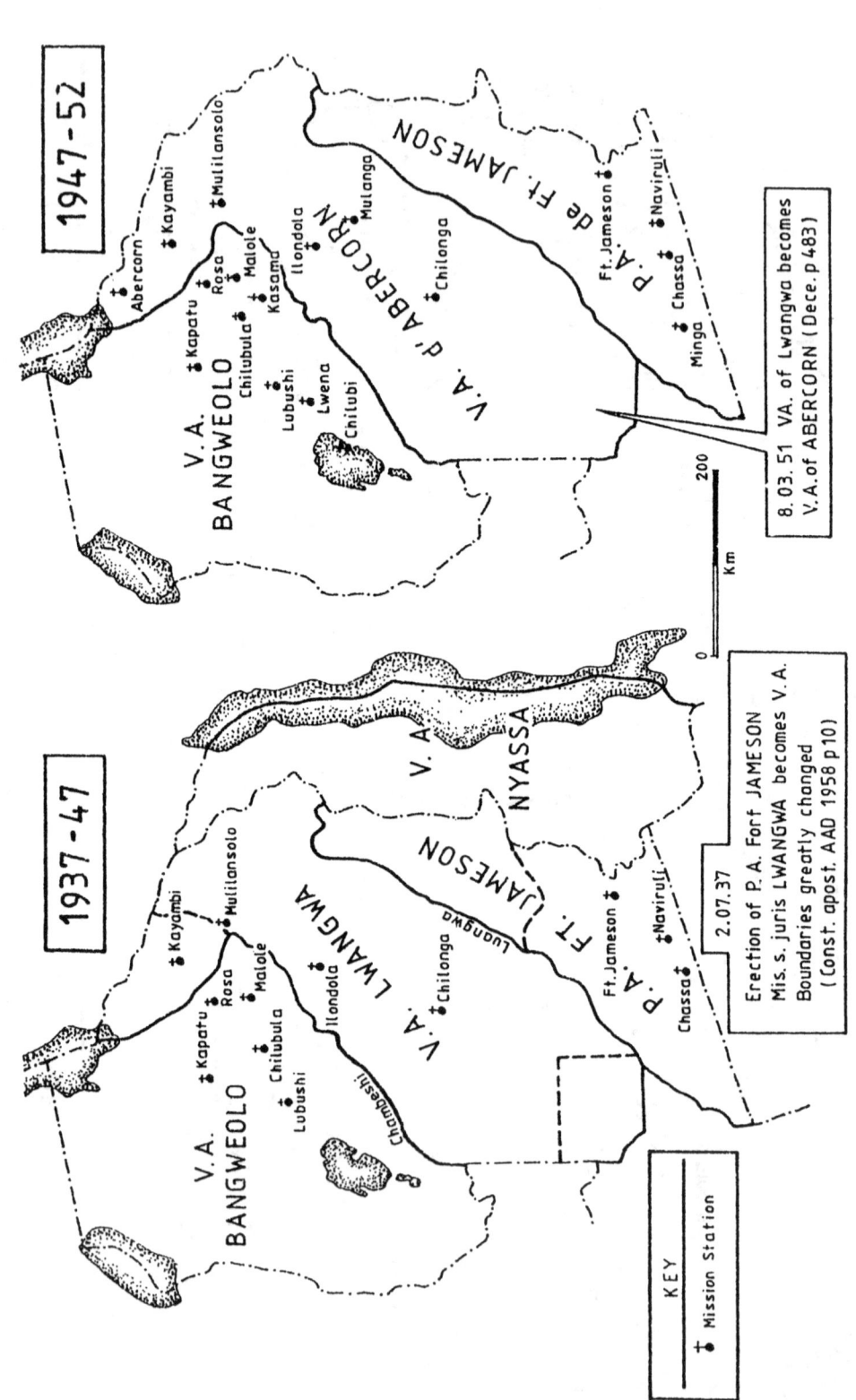

CATHOLIC PERSPECTIVES ON SCHOOLING

In the 1930s, the Catholic Church envisaged its outreach in the light of the papal encyclical, *Maximum Illud*, where the Pope urged missionaries to make education of the indigenes the primary purpose of the missionary enterprise.[2] From the standpoint of the Church of that era, membership of the Catholic Church remained essential for salvation. Pope Pius XII's encyclical of 1951, *Evangelii Praecones*, did not alter the Church's view on the need to convert the pagan to Catholicism.[3]

Alongside the emphasis on the need for conversion to Catholicism went an urgent appeal to form native clergy. In 1919, Pope Benedict XV had emphasised this. When speaking of a native clergy, the Church intended to produce a clergy who would be equally well educated as those in Europe or America. There should be no question of a second class clergy. The school came to be seen as a key means of both achieving a native clergy and of promoting the growth of the local Church. In 1922, Pope Pius XI petitioned missionaries to build schools and hospitals instead of churches and episcopal palaces.[4] The focus on the school as an instrument of Church growth came most unambiguously from Monsignor Hinsley when he visited East Africa, including Northern Rhodesia, in 1928. At a special meeting of Bishops in Dar-es-Salaam, Hinsley's instructions were:

> Collaborate with all your power: and where it is impossible for you to carry on both the immediate task of evangelisation and your educational work, neglect your Church to perfect your schools.[5]

Hinsely made a similar plea at Kachebere on the border between Northern Rhodesia and Nyasaland when he met the Northern

---

Conventuals started at Ndola in 1931. A few years after the arrival of the Capuchins, Livingstone became a Prefecture Apostolic in 1936 under Monsignor Killian Flynn O.F.M. Cap. This territory became a Vicariate Apostolic under Bishop O'Shea in 1950. Likewise, Ndola became an Apostolic Prefecture in 1939 and a Vicariate Apostolic in 1949 under Bishop Mazzieri O.F.M. Conv. In 1959, Solwezi, which formed part of Ndola, became a Prefecture under Monsignor Hillerich as Prefect Apostolic. After Monsignor Wolnik's retirement in 1955, Fr. Adam Kozlowiecki S.J. replaced him as administrator and in 1959, with the inauguration of a hierarchy, Mgr. Kozlowiecki S.J. was ordained Bishop, thereby becoming Vicar Apostolic of Lusaka. In 1962, Bishop James Corboy S.J., an Irish Jesuit, became Bishop of Monze, which previously had formed part of Lusaka.

[2] Nicholas I. Omenka, *The School in the Service of Evangelisation*, p. 4.

[3] Carmody, *Conversion and Jesuit Schooling*, p. 65.

[4] Omenka, *The School in the Service*, pp. 4-5.

[5] Ibid., pp. 133, 221-224.

Rhodesian Church representatives in 1934. He noted that the school would be the chief means of contacting the youth.[6]

During this period the Church had come to view the school as the most important means not only of spreading the gospel but of establishing itself structurally. By the 1930s, the Catholic Church in British Africa was clear-minded on this issue.[7] A decade later, the Church was not simply thinking in terms of primary schooling in Northern Rhodesia. It also had secondary schooling and higher education in mind. In his 1951 encyclical, *Evangelii Praecones*, the Pope wrote:

> The youth, especially those of them who have gone through the high schools, will control the destiny of their countries in the future. The importance of education at the elementary, secondary, and university levels is generally recognised as deserving the greatest care.[8]

The school had by then unquestionably assumed pivotal significance in the Catholic Church's outreach and development strategy.

COLONIAL GOVERNMENT AND EDUCATION

As noted in the last chapter, the B.S.A.C. government took little interest in education. It attempted to control the enterprise through various ordinances and regulations, but it provided no financial support to the mission societies' schools. It could be said that the Company government, particularly after the 1916 Chilembwe revolt in Nyasaland, regarded schools with suspicion.[9]

During the dying days of the Company rule, the missionary societies succeeded in drawing attention to the need for government investment in schools as well as its responsibility to do so. Because of missionary dissatisfaction in British African colonies the British Secretary of State appointed an Advisory Committee on Native Education in Tropical Africa. This group consulted the Phelps-Stokes Commission which subsequently undertook surveys of African education in West and East Africa. The Phelps-Stokes Commission visited Northern Rhodesia and met the General Missionary Conference in Kafue in 1924.[10] The Phelps-Stokes report stressed the need for "adaptation" to the conditions and

---

[6] Paper held at Archbishop's Archives, Lusaka. Henceforth, A.A.L.
[7] Omenka, *The School in the Service*, p. 223.
[8] Ibid., p. 5.
[9] Ragsdale, *Protestant Mission Education*, p. 56.
[10] Ibid., pp. 70-74.

needs of society. Whatever schooling would be given, it should help to raise the standard of life at the village level. Among other things, the Commission recommended the appointment of a Director of Native Education, the establishment of an Advisory Committee, and the availability of grants-in-aid to missionaries. It gave priority to teacher training to improve the overall educational standards in the territory. Subsequently, the Advisory Committee incorporated many of the Phelps-Stokes recommendations in its 1925 report, which became the main educational policy statement for much of the colonial period. The philosophy of "adaptation" underlined the Advisory Committee's memorandum. This idea of "adaptation" came from the American experience of negro schools, and was based on the questionable assumption that there was little difference between the native problem in Africa and the negro situation in the United States. It envisaged a dual educational system where there would be education for the masses and for a small elite. The system of negro education in the United States consisted of basic schooling that was utilitarian and agriculturally biased. It downplayed literacy. *Education Policy in British Tropical Africa*, in its promotion of the notion of "adaptation," stressed the need for the kind of education that would prepare people for life in the village or life within the tribal community. The envisaged educational system entailed a rather conservative perspective on political development. It essentially meant preserving the status-quo.[11]

Because of the newly formulated policy on education, the first Governor of Northern Rhodesia, Sir Herbert Stanley, created a sub-department of Native Education, with a man called G.C. Latham as its director. The government felt that the time had come to co-ordinate and supervise the education of the African, using the services of the missions. In the early years, the missions had strong representation on the newly formed Advisory Board, which first met in July 1925. On this first board three of the fifteen members were Catholics while nine represented Protestant mission societies. One of the first tasks of the Advisory Board was to produce a Native School Code. The purpose of this was to upgrade the schools that were in existence. In most cases, attendance at these schools was irregular, books and equipment were lacking, the teachers were untrained, while the schools opened for only a few weeks each year.[12] It was hoped that the new code would ensure

---

[11] Cmd. 2374., H.M.S.O: See also: E.H. Berman, "American Influence on African Education: The Role of the Phelps-Stokes Fund's Education Commissions," *Comparative Education Review* XV (June 1971); Carmody, *Conversion and Jesuit Schooling*, p. 49.

[12] Snelson, *Educational Development in Northern Rhodesia*, p. 151.

that schools in the future would be open for at least 150 days a year, with two hours secular learning daily and nine periods to be devoted each week to learning English.[13] Improving school standards, including the quality of teaching, became a priority in the new system. The new director, Mr. Latham, encouraged missions to set up teacher training centres or normal schools as they were called. To enhance this initiative, grants would be given towards the salaries of qualified missionary educators. Moreover, after 1928, there would also be certified African teacher grants. An additional means of improving the quality of the teaching included the establishment of a Jeanes training centre in Mazabuka in 1928. The overall aim of Latham and his sub-department remained:

> ...to curb the multiplication of village schools and to persuade Missionary Societies to concentrate more on the training of efficient teachers for the schools already in existence.[14]

After Latham's departure in 1931, the educational policy of the government continued to advocate mass education. Even in 1943 a highly placed administrator wrote: "The aim of Native development should not be to produce a small intelligentsia or aristocracy, but to raise the standard of all Africans."[15] This policy was designed to spread literacy and elementary education widely. It however had a further aim, to keep any higher-level schooling at a stage where it would not produce a large semi-educated class for whom there would be no employment and who would be so far ahead of the masses that they would be out of sympathy with them.[16] It was this conservative social vision that precluded significant expansion of secondary schooling in the territory until the late 1940s. When the question of secondary schooling was raised in 1936, the then Director of Native Education wrote:

> The policy of this government has always been to build a solid foundation of village education, to improve and develop the primary school and diffuse education as widely as possible among the people rather than concentrate attention (and expenditure) on the higher education of a select few.[17]

Coombe has argued that it was the De La Warr Commission, appointed

---

[13] Ibid., pp. 151, 161.
[14] Ibid., p. 158
[15] G. Beresford Stooke, "Memorandum on Native Education in Northern Rhodesia," (22 January 1943), as quoted in Carmody, *Conversion and Jesuit Schooling*, p. 79.
[16] J.M. Winterbottom, "Looking Back," *Rhodes Livingstone Journal* XIII (1953), pp. 30-34.
[17] Quoted by T. Coombe, "The Origins of Secondary Education in Zambia," *African Social Research* 3 (June 1967), p. 189.

by the Colonial Office to consider measures to develop Makerere College in Uganda into a university, and Colonial Office pressure, not the Northern Rhodesian government or its educational department, which stimulated a secondary education policy.[18] Even in the 1950s, the official policy of government remained "mass" oriented, emphasising higher education only for a few. The Binns Commission, however, part of the Cambridge Conference on African education stated:

> The minority which in Africa will move away from a purely agricultural environment to the growing centres of administration and commerce are a most important minority. [19]

This perception came late to Northern Rhodesia and it is little wonder that by 1964 the country had so few who had completed secondary school. With its 50 secondary schools most of which were junior and opened during the autumnal days of the colonial state, the country had only 1,000 secondary school graduates at Independence.

CATHOLIC SCHOOLS IN ZAMBIA: 1924-1964

Soon after the colonial government assumed power in Northern Rhodesia in 1924, it attempted, as we have indicated, to co-ordinate and upgrade the quality of educational provision in the territory. In 1926, grant-aided primary schools and normal schools were established.[20] When the Governor of the Protectorate visited the White Fathers' mission at Chilubula in 1925, he warned that if a Catholic normal school was not opened by January 1927, the responsibility for teacher training in the area would go to the Protestants. In response to such a threat, the White Fathers appointed a Dutch priest, Fr. Jan van Sambeek, as director of education for their schools. One of his first tasks was to open a normal school at Rosa, north of present-day Kasama, in 1926. Similarly, Mr. Latham, the Director of Native Education, requested Fr. Moreau of Chikuni, near Monze, to open a normal school. In doing so, Latham emphasised the need for agriculture in the new school system. As Fr. Moreau of Chikuni had done much to improve the agricultural methods of the area around Chikuni, he reacted

---

[18] See: Coombe, "The Origins of Secondary Education in Zambia: A study in Colonial Policy-making." Ph.D. diss., Harvard University, 1968. This was later substantially published in *African Social Research* 3, (June 1967), pp. 173-205; 4 (December 1967), pp. 283-315; and 5 (June 1968), pp. 365-405.

[19] *African Education: A Study of Educational Policy and Practice in British Tropical Africa* (Oxford: The Colonial Office, 1953), p. 65.

[20] For the origins of the grant aided system, see: Berman, *African Reactions*, p. 17.

enthusiastically to Latham's offer of a normal school that would provide training in agriculture. Thus, Catholic agencies started two normal schools—at Rosa near Kasama and at Chikuni near Monze.[21]

In the following year, 1927, the new Native Education Code[22] adversely affected the Jesuits' and White Fathers' schools. Many of the old schools failed to meet the requirements of the Code so that of the White Fathers 547 schools only 17 qualified as schools under the new conditions. A school was defined as "a class or assembly of natives... conducted for not less than 120 days a year, and in which instruction is based on a code approved by the Director of Native Education and the Advisory Board."[23] As one might expect, investment in secular schooling by no means received a universally enthusiastic response among the White Fathers.[24] It came primarily from government pressure:

> La tyrannie de l'opinion, transportée jusqu'en nos villages nègres, veut que nous ayons de vraies écoles, et nous avons commencé, cette année, à en avoir sous l'impulsion, il est vrai, de nos gouvernants anglais.[25]

It appears that the situation at Chikuni was little different. If Moreau wanted government support, he had to follow government directives which he did not seem to entirely favour especially in the matter of teaching English. When one of the earliest Chikuni converts was asked why Fr. Moreau started schools, since, according to that convert, Moreau did not like education, he replied:

> When the area was just a mission, Fr. Moreau did not like education. When the British government came to the country they wanted education. Fr. Moreau had to follow the government. He had to start schools for he had no power over government.[26]

However, as already noted, the visit of Monsignor Arthur Hinsely to Africa in 1928 did much to promote the view of the school as an instrument of evangelisation. From Lagos to Dar-es-Salaam, Hinsley's often repeated message to the missionaries remained: collaborate with

---

[21] Garvey, "Colonial Schooling and Missionary Evangelism", p. 199.

[22] Annual Colonial Reports for Northern Rhodesia, no. 1410 for 1927 (CO 799-2: Public Records Office, Kew, London). Henceforth, P.R.L.

[23] Snelson, *Educational Development in Northern Rhodesia*, p. 151.

[24] Oger, *Where a Scattered Flock*, p. 57.

[25] Opinion even in the native villages demands that we should have schools in a true sense and this year we have started to do so under pressure, it is true, from our British governors. R.A. (1925/26), p. 119.

[26] Wilson Beenzu, Interview: 23 March 1984. Student at Chikuni from 1910-15.

the British administration in the work of education. This exhortation did not necessarily mean that the Catholic Church totally endorsed the British colonial administration's educational policy. In one of his African addresses, Hinsley noted that:

> there was a tendency of educating the African as part merely of a machinery for production of wealth for the benefit of others. The Catholic missions will support no such policy. Education, they believe, should aim at the uplifting of the whole of mankind, and development of the individual man for the sake of his temporal as well as eternal happiness.[27]

On July 5th, 1928, in a letter to Monsignor Guilleme of Nyasa, Hinsley stressed:

> L'école est, aujourd'hui, ce qu'il y a de plus important dans le Vicariat. Ma mission est d'insister pour que les missionaires concentrent leurs efforts sur les écoles. Le Saint-Siege considère que, sous bien des rapports, les écoles sont plus importantes que les églises. L'école est le vestibule de l'église: les sacraments sont administres dans l'église, mais à l'école vous vous assurez et vous préparez des sujets pour les Sacraments que vous administrez á l'église.[28]

Among the reasons given for choosing the school as the chief method of evangelisation included the desire of the local population for education which, if not satisfied by Catholics, would, it was felt, be met by government and Protestant sects. Promotion of an indigenous clergy remained a reason for adopting this new mode of evangelising.[29] In any event, after Hinsley's visit, the school became pivotal in the mission of the White Fathers. After a Church synod (meeting) in 1926, the administrator of the Bangweolo Vicariate wrote to his confreres thus:

> Le deuxième principe dont le Synode s'est inspiré, c'est celui-ci: l'oeuvre des écoles est actuellement d'une importance capitale. Déjà notre Directoire nous prêche la necessité de l'école: De la bonne marche de l'école dépend la bonne formation de la jeunesse, et on n'aura pas de chrétiente vraiment sérieuese, tant que la jeunesse n'aura pas reçue une

---

[27] *Fides Service* (October 1929) Archives of the Catholic Archdiocese of Westminster, London, Aaw Hi 1/139/3b.

[28] The school today is the most important work of the Vicariate. My mission is to insist that the missionaries concentrate on the schools. The Holy See considers that the schools are more important than churches. The school is the vestibule of the Church: the sacraments are administered in the Church, but the school supplies and prepares the candidates for the sacraments which the Church administers. *Petit Echo* No. 188 (May 1929), p. 87; See also: Hastings, *The Church in Africa*, p. 562.

[29] Ibid., pp. 88-90.

éducation profondement chrétienne.[30]

Nevertheless, despite the heavy official stress on the school and its importance, priests in the various parishes needed to be convinced that school work formed part of their mission. The newly appointed White Father director of education, Fr. Van Sambeek, wrote:

> La partie principale d'une école, au sens Catholique, n'est pas l'enseignement des sciences profanes. L'école bien comprise a pour but de dévelloper, d'éduquer l'homme tout entier, corps et âme; la fin première et principale de l'école est l'éducation religieuse et morale. It va donc de soi que l'oeuvre des écoles doit être rangée parmi les oeuvres d'apostolat du Missionaire.[31]

By 1930, the Education department was becoming happy with the White Fathers' schools:

> They (White Fathers) are now showing an increasing interest in education on the right lines and under Father Tanguy who is now in charge of their educational activities, good progress will be made.[32]

In the early 1930s, many of the White Fathers' missions became concerned with building a network of schools that would be academically attractive. It was no longer entirely a question of gaining new territory but of competing with the Protestant schools: "Avoir de bonnes écoles et avoir du succes dans l'évangelization, sont deux choses qui vont ensemble."[33] Not surprisingly, the education department did not always appreciate the White Fathers' method of competing as the following comment reveals:

> ...whilst maintaining that fair competition is a good thing, I would point out that with the White Fathers 'fair' competition often means definite attacks upon adherents of other missions and attempts to prevent children from attending schools of their own missions and make them come to those

---

[30] The second principle which inspired the Synod is this: the work of schools today is of utmost importance. Already, our director has preached the need for the school. On the good running of the school depends the proper formation of the youth, and one cannot have true Christianity unless the youth have received a profoundly Christian education. Lettre à Confreres, Chilubula, 1 Nov 1928. WFR.

[31] The primary purpose of a school, in the Catholic sense, is not the teaching of secular subjects. The school's function is to develop and educate the whole person, body and soul. The main aim of the school is religious and moral education. Thus it follows that the work of the schools should be among those of the missionary's apostolate. Van Sambeek, lettre à Confreres, 1 Nov 1928. WFR; See: Oger, *Our Missionary Shadow*, p. 27

[32] *African Education: Annual Report 1931*, p. 20.

[33] Having good schools and being successful evangelisers go hand in hand. R.A. (1936-7)

of the White Fathers.³⁴

At this time too the White Fathers stressed the need to have Catholic schools for Catholic children even when this tended to mean that a small village community would have two schools where one, if it could be inter-denominational, would have sufficed. In 1931, van Sambeek argued:

> One may be of the opinion that the school is something neutral and that it has nothing to do with religion. We, Catholics, are not of that opinion.... Were Catholics and Protestants in the same school, religious instruction should be undenominational. I think that undenominational religious instruction is à contradiction in terms.³⁵

However, in the mid-1930s, at the urging of the Department of Native Education, Fr. Tanguy who became Sambeek's successor, on advice from Rome, agreed that where there already was a Protestant school and not sufficient numbers to justify a second Catholic school, Catholic children could attend the Protestant school. However, they did not have to attend either Protestant prayers or religious instruction:

> ...ils ne doivent avoir aucune participation au culte hérétique, pas même a une simple prière, doivent s'abstenir d'assister aux instructions religieuses hérétique, pas même a une simple prière.³⁶

Thus, during much of the first decade after the assumption of responsibility for education by the colonial administration, the White Fathers worked hard to create a Catholic school system that would rival that of the Protestants to which, in many areas, much of the youth went.³⁷ By 1938, they appear to have succeeded very admirably for the report of the director of Native Education spoke of:

> the excellence of the work of the Bangweolo Vicariate which, under that inspiration of that broadminded man, Father Tanguy, has made great strides in remarkable harmony with the Livingstonia Mission.³⁸

---

³⁴ Letter from Superintendent, Native Education, to the Director, Native Education, Mazabuka, 8 February 1934. N.A.Z: Ed 1/5/36.

³⁵ Letter, van Sambeek to Mr. Keith, 5 May 1931. N.A.Z: Ed 1/5/3.

³⁶ They should not participate in any heretical cult, not even in a simple prayer. They should not attend heretical religious instructions, not even a simple prayer. *Petites Nouvelles* no. 61 (November 1933) series are kept at the White Fathers' Archives at Ilondola, Chinsali, Zambia; See also: Superintendent of Native Education to Director of Native Education, 26 February 1934. N.A.Z: Ed 1/5/36.

³⁷ R.A., (1934/5), p. 340; See: Hinfelaar, *Bemba-Speaking Women*, pp. 37, 47: Garvey, *Bembaland Church*, p. 105.

³⁸ Report of the Director of Native Education to Chief Secretary, Lusaka, 18 January 1938 (N.A.Z: Sec 1/550).

Although the White Fathers came to the Eastern part of the country only in 1924, they had thirty-six aided schools by 1938, together with a teacher training centre at Naviruli.

Undoubtedly, in the southern parts of the country, the Jesuits also endeavoured to build up better quality schools, even if the element of rivalry with Protestant groups did not appear so acute. In the early 1930s Fr. Zabdyr, a Polish Jesuit, lately arrived from Poland, did much to expand and improve the Jesuit schools. He developed and used a system of what was called village committees. In an attempt to interest the local population in schools and to encourage them to assume some responsibility for them, Fr. Zabdyr organised committees which basically consisted of a *kapitau* (captain), an orderly, and a *dokotera* or doctor. The *kapitau*'s main duty was to help the local headman to ensure regular attendance at school and church. The officer monitored general maintenance of the village while the doctor looked after the sick. This group had regular meetings with Fr. Zabdyr and on occasion with the headman or chief. Zabdyr's school system was so successful that it became a kind of model for the Education department. In his annual report the Director of Native Education wrote in 1934:

> The village committees inaugurated in the Monze area have made a promising start...In everything the aim is to secure the co-operation of the local authorities and results seem to point to the success of the scheme.[39]

Government, however, in concord with its policy of indirect rule, wanted to be assured that the authority of the chief was not in any way undermined. Zabdyr's method helped to increase the number of aided schools in the Chikuni area from seven in 1928 to 18 in 1937. Such steady, if not dramatic, progress resulted because of the assistance of some of the first graduates of the Jeanes school in Mazabuka, Antonio Monze and Paul Haakola. However, Mr. Rushbridger, superintendent of Native Education, was far from enthusiastic about the other Jesuit schools when, in January 1938, he wrote:

> Chikuni, Katondwe, Kasisi and Kapoche are four mission schools controlled by the Society of Jesus and all of them have been established for more than twenty years. Apart from Chikuni little of value has been achieved by this Mission.[40]

No sooner had the Capuchin friars entered Barotseland than did they begin schools. By 1937, they already had six aided schools and

---

[39] *Native Education: Annual Report 1934* (Lusaka: Government Printer), p. 41 as quoted in Carmody, *Conversion and Jesuit Schooling*, p. 33.
[40] N.A.Z. Sec 1/550.

twenty-nine unaided. A year later, the Capuchins established a normal school at Santa Maria, the name of the new mission at Lukulu.[41] In 1955, the Director of African Education, commenting on the Capuchin mission, wrote:

> Twenty years ago I had the privilege of steering the negotiations which led to their entering the mission field in Barotseland and two of the conditions agreed upon were that they should begin their education work in "empty spaces" not being developed by other agencies at the time and that quality and not quantity only should be the keynote of their work. In order to fulfil the second condition they agreed to engage only fully trained staff for all their educational work—managerial as well as teaching. These conditions have been faithfully carried out with the result that there has been no mushroom growth of useless "bush-schools" and no cut-throat competition with Protestant Societies but only a well planned expansion of schools of good quality. Considering their late entry into the field their achievements in Barotseland have been truly remarkable.[42]

In typical fashion of missionaries of the time, the Capuchins also were instrumental in creating a vernacular literature.[43]

Thus, in the wake of Monsignor Hinsley's visit, the Catholic Church in Northern Rhodesia co-operated closely with the colonial educational authorities in the provision of basic schooling. By 1937, the Catholic societies had 79 of the 413 or 19% of the aided primary schools in the territory and 597 or 36% of the 1,654 unaided schools. By 1945, the Catholic Church operated 33% of all primary schools. In 1954, it had 38% of the mission primary schools.[44]

---

[41] O. O'Sullivan, *Zambezi Mission: A History of the Capuchins in Zambia 1931-1981* (n.d), p.p. 54, 74; Snelson, *Educational Development in Northern Rhodesia*, p. 179; See also: Victor Muyatwa, *The Development of Catholic Education in Western Province, Zambia 1931-1995* (M.A. dissertation, Leeds University 1998)

[42] Notes on the Director of African Education's Tour in Barotse Protectorate, 4-18 December 1955. (Livingstone: Bishop's Archives)

[43] O'Sullivan, *Zambezi Mission*, p. 44; More specifically, the following are some of the main contribution of the Capuchins: *Katekisema ni Litapelo za Bakriste* (St. Louis, 1950); E. Daly, *Evangeli ya Mulen' a luna Jesu Kriste* (Livingstone:, 1957); A. Herlihy, *Litaluso za Katekisema*; *Litapelo ni Lipina* (St. Louis, 1960); *Litaba za Bibele* (Lusaka, 1961); *Katekisema*, (Lusaka, 1962); *Hymni et Cantici* (Lusaka, 1962); *Likuta leli Katoliki* (Livingstone, 1963); *Linyalo* (Ohio, 1963); *Katekisema* (Lusaka, 1967); *Vilombelo no Myaso* (Lusaka, 1963); B. Brown, *Buka ya Litapelo* (Mongu, 1971); *Litapelo za Missa* (Lusaka, 1973); C. Brady, *Litapelo za Lubasi* (Livingstone, 1974); *Litapelo za Kopano ya Pilu ye adoreha ya Jesu Kriste* (n.d); *Litoko* (Bulawayo, 1978); K. Shorten, *Katekisema* (Livingstone, 1985); *Buka ya Litapelo* (Livingstone, 1987); *Lusebeleze Mulimu: A Handbook for Leaders of Church Services* (Livingstone, 1990); O. O'Sullivan, *English-Silozi Dictionary* (Lusaka: Zambia Educational Publishing House, 1993).

[44] Henkel, *Christian Missions in Africa*, p. 128.

While the Catholic missions had done much to extend access to schooling in the rural areas, the children in the swiftly industrialising area of the Copperbelt initially had access to few schools or social services. The plight of these people formed a substantial part of the agenda of the Broken Hill General Missionary Conference in 1931. Four years later, the matter became ever more urgent after the riots that had taken place at Ndola. To meet some of the needs, a number of Protestant missions formed what became known as the United Missions in the Copperbelt (U.M.C.B.).[45] In subsequent times, they attempted to set up interdenominational schools, partly because the African Education Department would not permit churches to open their own schools. The organisation and maintenance of these schools provided an instance of rare inter-church co-operation. Although, as we have seen, there was no great openness among Catholics towards co-operation with Protestants at this time, they agreed to provide Catholic teachers for the Protestant-directed schools. Catholic teachers constituted about one-third of the teaching force in the early 1940s, providing schooling for about 6,000 children, many of whom were Catholic. This option to co-operate with Protestant Churches seems to have been taken out of necessity rather than because of its desirability. Nonetheless, the arrangement lasted until 1952 when the schools were handed over to government because of the increasing burden of administration.[46]

CONTROL OF CATHOLIC PRIMARY SCHOOLS

In Northern Rhodesia, the demand for state sponsored schools never appeared widespread, although native authorities had a tendency to request government schools. In the 1890s the Basuto evangelist, Mokalapa, started a non-mission school, which subsequently led to the opening of the Barotse National School in 1907. This represented the total B.S.A.C. contribution to African education during its term of control. As Snelson reminds us, it remained the only government school until the Jeanes school opened in Mazabuka in 1929. More widespread demands for non-mission schools occurred in other African territories and led to a number of government schools in countries like Kenya and

---

[45] The missions included: the London Missionary Society, the Livingstonia Mission (Church of Scotland), the Universities Mission to Central Africa, the Methodist Missionary Society, the South African Baptist Mission and the United Society for Christian Literature.

[46] Snelson, *Educational Development in Northern Rhodesia*, pp. 185-189: Weller & Linden, *Mainstream Christianity*, p. 147: N.A.Z.: Sec 1/550 Report on Mission Schools; Minutes of Ordinaries Conference Meeting, 1934. J.A.C.

Tanzania.⁴⁷ In the early 1930s, the government felt that the native authorities demanded non-mission schools because:

> Sometimes because they think it is modish and patent confirmation of their desire for progress and may ingratiate them with the "boma": sometimes because they think that the establishment of a government school will relieve them of the not infrequent and awkward responsibility of having to decide between two or more missions eager to open up schools in their area.⁴⁸

In any event, the Department did not have the resources to dispense with missionary provision of schools. After the arrival of Julian Tyndale-Biscoe as head of the Department of Native Education in 1937, the situation began to change. Tyndale-Biscoe favoured the establishment of native authority schools (N.A.S.). These schools were built and operated by the local authorities, receiving government grants for certified teachers, while meeting the cost of uncertified teachers from their own treasuries. Tyndale-Biscoe had experience of this type of school during his time in Tanganyika. In 1938, the first N.A.S. opened in Eastern Province and began to set the pattern for interdenominational co-operation with traditional indigenous authorities.⁴⁹ By 1945, there were twenty-three such schools in the territory. Although the number of these schools represented only about one percent of the total educational enterprise of the time, their appearance and subsequent promotion caused some concern to the missionary societies. In some cases, this initiative came to be seen as a move towards secular schooling or perhaps more precisely towards state-sponsored schools. From the minutes of the Catholic bishops' meeting in 1942, we read: "The whole tendency of Government regulations and legislation is clearly moving towards secularisation of education."⁵⁰ The Ordinaries (official church leaders) re-articulated the policy of the Catholic Church which remained "Catholic schools for Catholic children under Catholic management." They expressed opposition towards any form of secular school for Catholics because of what they termed a sad experience where Catholic children attended so-called "neutral" schools. ⁵¹

---

⁴⁷ Snelson, *Educational Development in Northern Rhodesia*, pp. 126, 204-5.
⁴⁸ Caldwell, "Report on Conference of British Governors of British East African Territories," (May 1934), as quoted in Ragsdale, *Protestant Mission Education*, p. 111.
⁴⁹ Ragsdale, *Protestant Mission Education*, pp. 138-9; D.M. Nguluwe, "The History of Religious Education in Zambia," (University of Birmingham: diploma essay, 1995), p. 3.
⁵⁰ Minutes of the Ordinaries Meeting of 1942. J.A.C.
⁵¹ Ibid.

In 1945, as part of an effort to develop African local government, the Education Department felt that the time was ripe for increasing the powers and functions of local education committees. The Christian Council reacted by stating that any transference of education from the missions should be gradual. Some time later, an ad-hoc advisory group called the Cartmel-Robinson Commission was set up to inquire into the possibility of African local government bodies assuming total responsibility for primary education in their areas. At a meeting between this Commission and the Standing Committee of the African Education Advisory Board on May 2, 1949, Cartmel-Robinson, the chairman, stated that a unanimous feeling had been expressed that Native Authorities should take over all education up to and including Standard IV. At the same meeting, which did not include a Catholic representative, the missionary societies agreed in a general way with the principle of devolving authority. The chairman, moreover, reported that the Catholics had been contacted and had also agreed. Missionary concern was more with the method and the timing than with the principle. However, at the following African Education Advisory Board meeting in June, 1949, the Catholic representative, Rev. Killian Flynn objected to the assumption that the handing over of schools to local government or Native Authorities was desirable. Nonetheless, he added that he was strongly in favour of giving more control to Native Authorities to secure their interest. At that same meeting, the African representative shared reservations:

> He doubted if there was as yet the necessary competence and feared that the interest of missions in education would fall away seriously if the Native Authorities took over mission schools. Missionaries would prefer to leave the Native Authorities to sink or swim and would probably not be displeased to see Africans fail...If the Native Authorities took over, the management of missionaries would be lacking and the schools would fail: the quality of building would also suffer. He thought the proposals premature and felt it essential to wait until chiefs and councillors understand what education really means. Teachers at present disliked service in Native Authority schools because the Native Authority over them was ignorant of the ends of education. A good religious grounding for children at school was necessary: this would be lost if the Native Authorities took over schools as they would not be interested in religious instruction but only in restricting the corporal punishment of pupils. He thought that the production of teachers would present considerable difficulty. [52]

---

[52] African Education Advisory Board Minutes (June 1949), p. 22; However, it needs to be noted that Africans may have been reluctant to criticise mission education in the

Similarly, a less than enthusiastic response to the handover of schools came from the Jesuit, Fr. Prokoph of Chikuni normal school, who had submitted a written memorandum stating that complete transfer of all elementary education in the immediate future seemed premature. He argued that, though central government wanted it and the younger generation were keen on it, the chiefs seemed unconvinced. Moreover, he considered that the performance of the native authorities so far in terms of responsibility for buildings and repairs had been unsatisfactory. In any case he stressed:

> As Catholics we would insist on the Catholic education of the children of our Christians and could hardly accept the proposal as it stands, i.e., indiscriminate transfer of Catholic schools to a mixed body with a common religious denominator, unless they could go on existing as Catholic schools under the African local authority as they work at present under Central Government. [53]

At their Conference in January 1951, the Catholic authorities expressed grave concern at the prospect of losing control both of their primary schools and of their teachers. This concern was expressed in the shadow of an impending Education Ordinance. The Conference resolved to protest "in the strongest terms against this grave danger to our Catholic schools."[54] As a follow-up they decided to organise a campaign to alert Catholic parents of the dangers now facing Catholic schools. They also decided to form a Catholic Association for teachers. In their memorandum to government, they asserted that they viewed with grave concern the tendency to reduce the direct influence of the missions on education, especially the tendency to have all primary education in the hands of Native Authorities. They proposed that any handover should be gradual and stated that they could not accept the posting, transfer and control of teachers in their schools to be outside their control. Training, posting, and transfer would have to remain under direct Catholic influence. Later in the year, on June 29th, the Apostolic Delegate, Archbishop Mathew, who was the supreme Catholic authority in the territory met government representatives with a further memorandum drawn up during the June session of the Ordinaries' Conference. The Ordinaries requested that teachers be assessed for employment in agency schools by the agency, that they be trained by the agency and that on completion of their course should supply agency requirements. The Ordinaries agreed to prepare more

---

presence of the missionaries. See: Ragsdale, *Protestant Mission Education*, p. 111.

[53] Ragsdale, *Protestant Mission Education*, p. 111.

[54] Draft Minutes of Educational items of Bishops' Conference, Lusaka, June, 1951. J.A.C.

teachers than they would need, if Government so desired. This memorandum appeared to present no difficulties to the government for the Administrative Secretary replied that he was in agreement with the proposals of the memorandum.[55]

With similar concerns, in September of the same year, a Catholic group of representatives met the Binns Study party who had been commissioned to undertake a survey of education in East Africa. The group expressed reservations about what they described as a dual system of Church and state schools that had developed in the territory. They wondered if the missions would be able to ensure that Christianity would be adequately taught in Local Education Authority (L.E.A.) schools. The Catholic group re-articulated the principle: "Catholic schools for Catholic children, where there were sufficient children." To this principle the chairman replied that he was very familiar with the sentiment as he had been an education officer in England where Catholic groups had frequently made this clear. The Catholics re-emphasised the desire of the voluntary agencies to retain the management of their schools, the training of their teachers and the appointment of their teachers to the agency as well as the payment of government salaries.[56] In their resolve to maintain control of their schools and teachers, the Catholic authorities took little for granted.

The draft Education Ordinance of 1951 authorised the L.E.A.s to take over existing government schools and any schools which the Native Authorities and Voluntary Agencies did not wish to continue to manage. The L.E.A. would also have authority to control the opening and closing of schools as well as to inspect schools, and would operate a system of school councils. The Ordinance moreover proposed the creation of a United African teaching service with parity of conditions for government and mission teachers. When the Ordinance was debated in the Legislative Council (Legco), the newly appointed Catholic Education Secretary General introduced significant amendments through the representative of African interests, Mr Nightingale, whereby church agencies should have two-third representation on the school councils on private property and one-third representation on school councils for schools established elsewhere.

The Director of African Education, Mr. Cottrell, passionately

---

[55] Draft Minutes of Educational items of Bishops' Conference, Lusaka, June 1951, appendix A: J.A.C; See also: Minutes of the Northern Rhodesian Ordinaries Conference, 9-15 January 1951, J.A.C.; Bishops' Memorandum to Government, 15 January 1951, J.A.C.

[56] Matters dealt with by the Binns study group session, held in September 1951. J.A.C.

opposed the Catholic Secretary General's amendment and was so determined to block it that he proposed that it should be reviewed by the Executive Council of Legco. This greatly worried the Catholic representative who complained to Mr. Wilson, a senior executive in government, that:

> The Missions do not trust Cottrell; that talk of partnership was a farce... and that the Missions would not stand for Cottrell's "fixed ideas of forcing State schools on the territory, whatever his crocodile tears about the poor Missions." [57]

Cottrell himself claimed that his opposition to the amended Ordinance arose out of his concern for the missionary contribution. In the Legislative Council Debate, he alleged:

> What I am trying to get my friend, Mr. Nightingale to understand is, above all, that his amendment is to the disadvantage of important mission institutions. [58]

The Catholic Ordinaries fought to retain substantial control of their schools, and, in this particular instance, won. One vicar-apostolic was to write:

> Grâce à l'attitude ferme des Ordinaires de la Rhodesia du Nord et grâce aussi à l'intervention heureuse de Son Excellence le Délégué Apostolique, la nouvelle loi scolaire a été modifiée en notre faveur: le contrôle des missions sur leurs propres écoles et leurs teachers est maintenu. [59]

Repeatedly, however, the Catholic leaders denied that they were opposed to having Africans assume control. To prove this, they cited their position on the promotion and education of Africans for the priesthood.[60] Indeed, by this time, a number of Northern Rhodesians had been ordained to special ministry or priesthood within the Church.

Many of the recommendations in the government policy document resulting from the Cambridge Conference and the Binns Commission of 1953, *African Education: A Study of Educational Policy and Practice in British Tropical Africa*, had been already introduced through the 1951

---

[57] Letter from Catholic Education Secretary General to Chairman, Bishops' Conference, 14 January 1952, J.A.C.
[58] Legco debates: 4th session of 9th Council, 10 November - 21 December 1951.
[59] Thanks to the determined attitude of the Ordinaries of Northern Rhodesia as well as to the welcome intervention of the Apostolic Delegate, the new schools' législation has been modified in our favour. The control of missions over their schools and teachers has been maintained. R.A. (1951-2), p. 113.
[60] Matters dealt with by the Binns study group, p. 3; See also: Catholic Education Secretary General, letter to the Ordinaries, 3 January 1952, J.A.C.

Ordinance. The report reinforced the policy of eventually granting full control of primary education to local authorities, and noted that:

> ...there was general agreement that effective control of education by a local authority or central government was bound to come. [61]

It was denied that this inferred that all education would eventually become secular. Education would continue to have a religious basis and this could only be assured if religious bodies were formally associated with government. Partnership between the voluntary agencies and central or local government bodies remained paramount.[62] The framework for such partnership in Northern Rhodesia had been set by the Ordinance of 1951.

Like the Northern Rhodesian Ordinance, the Cambridge Conference report envisaged the formation of a unified teaching service. In Northern Rhodesia, a unified teaching service was introduced in July 1953, whereby mission teachers received parity of service conditions with their government counterparts.[63] Though, as we already mentioned, the Education Department had approved many of the assurances requested by the Catholic Ordinaries, the Ordinance itself remained vague on the question of agency control of teachers. It allowed the agency to "impose special conditions not inconsistent" with the general Ordinance regulations.[64] The mission manager of schools would administer the United African Teaching Service (U.A.T.S) regulations at a local level.

In 1953, the Catholic Church was set for another period of partnership with government. However, the Catholic authorities had become more aware of the Department's orientation towards eventual state control of the schools. Meanwhile it had preserved sufficient autonomy to ensure the promotion of its interests, and took various initiatives to provide "Catholic schools for Catholic children." These included the production of a Catholic teachers' journal and occasional proposals to form a union for Catholic teachers.[65] Some other denominations appeared less satisfied with the new partnership and

---

[61] *African Education: A Study of Educational Policy and Practice in British Tropical Africa* (Oxford University Press, 1953), p. 143.

[62] Ibid.

[63] Ragsdale, *Protestant Mission Education*, pp. 151-53.

[64] African Education Ordinance (1951), sec 7, 3.

[65] The journal, entitled *The Catholic Teacher* was edited by Fr. Prokoph between 1950 and 1955. See also: Minutes of Northern Rhodesia Bishops' Conference, Lusaka, 20-22 November 1956; Minutes of Northern Rhodesia Bishops' Conferences, May, 1958; July 1959, March 1960.

within the next few years yielded up their schools, perhaps because of the perception that they were becoming more agents of government than partners in the educational system.⁶⁶ In some instances, Catholics were offered the management of schools surrendered by the Protestants. Their general unwillingness to accept such schools pivoted on the fact that what was then needed was quality not quantity in educational provision.⁶⁷ Partly because of many Protestant mission societies' surrender of their schools as well as the founding of new local education authority schools, in the years that followed there was a progressive increase in the number of L.E.A. schools. By 1963, 800 of the 2,100 were L.E.A. The rest were mainly agency schools 30 percent of which were operated by the Catholics.

Between 1953 and 1963, the Catholic Church, unlike a number of other churches, continued to view the school as an important means of conversion and church growth. In words taken from a meeting of the Lusaka regional Jesuit superiors in 1956: "The schools are a means to an end, that is, a means of bringing the Catholic faith to all."⁶⁸ In their determination to retain control of the schools, though not to over-expand, the Catholic authorities wished that all missionaries should pay special attention to the maintenance of high standards in the schools. Moreover, they regarded attempts at "democratisation of management" with great caution. If Africanization was necessary, it should be done at the beginning through having African priest managers. Later, headmasters could be considered but:

> The Conference accepted the above prospective steps be effected only with great caution, and the appointment made only of loyal and trustworthy lay folk.⁶⁹

By 1961, there were about 45 African managers and assistant-managers while the Chairman of the meeting of Education Secretaries noted that Catholic missions could not afford to hold their U.A.T.S. teachers back from management posts.⁷⁰ On the eve of Zambian independence, the Catholic Church remained steadfast in its mission to give Catholic children Catholic education ideally in Catholic schools even if this was ever more frequently proving to be impossible.⁷¹

---

⁶⁶ Ragsdale, *Protestant Mission Education*, p. 146.
⁶⁷ Education Secretary General to all Ordinaries. Ref. No: CAO/7/55. A.A.L.
⁶⁸ Minutes of Lusaka Vicariate Superiors' Meeting, held on 26-7 July 1956 (J.A.C.).
⁶⁹ Record of the XVIIth meeting of the Northern Rhodesia Bishops' Conference, 7-9 May 1958. A.A.L.
⁷⁰ Minutes of the Meeting of Education Secretaries held on 11-12 January 1961. C.S.A.
⁷¹ Record of the Archbishop of Lusaka's address to the Education Secretaries of East and

Despite the Church's magnanimous efforts to provide Catholic education in Catholic schools for Catholic children, many Catholic children had to receive their schooling outside Catholic schools. On the Copperbelt, the situation was worst because in 1958 it was estimated that about 10,000 Catholic children did not have access to any schooling.[72] By the end of the colonial era in Zambia, as we have already mentioned, the Catholic Church provided roughly 30% of the overall primary school places which included a significant proportion of schooling to Grade VI for boys and girls. In 1962, Catholic schools had 646 girls and 1640 boys in Grade VI classes, which represented 35% of all girls and 22% of all boys in Grade VI.[73]

CATHOLIC TEACHER TRAINING

As we have said earlier, one of the main objectives of the newly founded sub department of Native Education in 1926 was the promotion of normal schools. By 1943, Catholics had normal schools at Chikuni and Malole since 1933, Santa Maria in Lukulu since 1936, and at Naviruli in the Eastern province since 1938. In the early 1940s, Government decided to rationalise the numbers of mission normal schools that had multiplied. As part of its development plan, government proposed that the mission societies should co-operate in reducing the numbers of aided normal schools from twenty-one to six. The Catholic leaders, at their meeting in April 1945, welcomed the idea of establishing more centralised training centres. However, they felt justified in retaining their four centres, since each centre served a province. They also argued that they were educating roughly one-third of the school going children and so considered that they should have a third of the normal schools, which they reckoned should be reduced to twelve[74]

However, the Catholic authorities were determined that they should

---

Central Africa, dated: 31 July 1963. J.A.C.

[72] Minutes of the 17th Meeting of the Northern Rhodesian Bishops' Conference, 7-9 May 1958. A.A.L. It was estimated in 1967, that in Lusaka about 6,000 or roughly 55% of the 11,000 Catholic children were in Catholic schools (Minutes of Education Secretaries meeting held in Lusaka on 29 August 1966. J.A.C.

[73] See: Records J.A.C.; For overall figures, see: *African Education:* Annual Report (1962), p. 14.

[74] Minutes of the Meeting of Ordinaries of Northern Rhodesia, 10-13 April 1945. Archbishop's Archives, Lusaka. In 1946, it appears that the White Fathers, Jesuits, Capuchins, and Franciscans operated 369 of the 1,168 aided schools, 288 of the unaided schools.

not be left out of the teacher training endeavour, and that they should not allow themselves to be overtaken by the non-Catholic societies if the government insisted on only six centres. They speculated:

> If the Catholic body declined to co-operate wholeheartedly in the scheme and rigidly adhered to its Teacher-Training schools outside the centres (sic), then doubtless the centres would remain divorced from all Catholic influence, and the non-Catholics would be paramount therein. [75]

The Bishops' Conference clearly wished to present the Catholic Church as being ready to co-operate with the Development Plan. It sent a memo to government assuring it of Catholic co-operation provided that the Government would ensure that:

(a) A Catholic European educationist, nominated by the Bishop concerned, be appointed to the Central Teacher Training staff;
(b) A European "spiritual adviser" extra to the educationist be also accommodated at the Centre;
(c) Separate boarding accommodation be provided for their student-followers in the Catholic quarter;
(d) A chapel be attached for the use of Catholics.[76]

At this point the Catholics clearly sought government goodwill. However, other denominations reacted less favourably to the proposed plan. The Dutch Reformed Church, for instance, refused to co-operate in any scheme that appeared to favour Catholics. Catholics' unwillingness to surrender any of their training centres angered many of the non-Catholics who complained of the Catholic "intransigent" attitude.[77] It is true that the Protestant societies agreed to reduce the number of their centres to seven, while the Catholics seemed to feel justified in holding on to their four. Nonetheless, in reply to the Director of African Education on their unwillingness to cut down the number of their centres, the Catholic Ordinaries re-affirmed, in their eyes, the reasonableness of their position:

> Whilst we recognise the very large measure of rationalisation achieved by the Christian Council, it was pointed out that the Conference of Catholic Bishops had long anticipated the necessity for keeping to a strict maximum the number of our centres, by dissuading the Lwangwa (White Fathers) and the Ndola (Franciscans) missions from opening two extra training schools which for many years were, and still are, deemed a necessity in their

---

[75] Ibid.
[76] Ibid.
[77] Minutes of the Ordinaries Conference, 1945. A.A.L.

respective areas.[78]

This kind of logic failed to convince the non-Catholics who became less willing to co-operate in the face of Catholic "intransigence." The rationalisation process remained on the shelf.

Some years later, however, the Binns Commission raised the issue once more. At their meeting with the Catholic group in September 1951, the Commission stressed that if the missions were going to retain control of teacher training they would have to co-operate better to prevent uneconomical and inefficient centres. In its subsequent report, the Binns group advised mission societies that education would have to be thought of not only as preparation for religious life but also for the life of citizenship.[79] The Committee argued that such preparation could be best secured in large training centres:

> In a small college loyalties will be engendered to groups such as the tribe or the denomination which are very valuable in themselves but which may prevent the development of professional loyalty in the service of education in a territory, such loyalty is more likely to develop if training colleges are of a reasonable size and contain a good cross-section of the territorial community.[80]

The Commission envisaged an admission of not less than sixty yearly, making colleges of at least 120 students with a two year course.

In line with the Cambridge Conference recommendations, the Department of Education invited the African Education Advisory Board to consider the establishment of five colleges at its June, 1953, meeting. Surprisingly, there was general agreement on the need to set up five main colleges. The Roman Catholics and the Christian Council were invited to operate one major college each. A proposal to set up an interdenominational college was quickly rejected by Fr. Flynn, the Catholic representative, who stated that from the Roman Catholic point of view there was no point in debating the proposal, only a fully Roman Catholic College was acceptable.[81] Though, as we have seen, some years earlier the Ordinaries had felt obliged to reject any offer that would not allow them to have four colleges, they, like the Protestant representatives, accepted the Government's new offer of only one College in 1953, though it admittedly would be on a larger scale. They seemingly realised that they would have to respond to the government's

---

[78] Minutes of the Ordinaries Conference, 30 Jan-1 Feb 1947. A.A.L

[79] Ragsdale, *Protestant Mission Education*, p. 150.

[80] *African Education: A Study of Educational Policy*, p. 120.

[81] Minutes of the African Education Advisory Board Meeting, 23-26 June 1953. J.A.C.

terms or risk loosing out in an area that they considered to be of critical importance for their missions.

From the specifically Catholic perspective, a question of some internal conflict and controversy arose in connection with the siting of the proposed new Catholic College. The White Fathers and the Bishops favoured a site near Ft. Rosebery, where there were plenty of children and schools combined with the fact that it was a rural area which would benefit from such development. However, the Bishops decided that they would need to have English-speaking missionaries who would be well qualified academically according to British norms. They considered that the Irish Jesuits would be the most appropriate, for by then they were already operating a secondary school in the territory opened in 1949. While the Irish Jesuit Provincial was willing to commit himself to this important project, he was not in accord with the siting of the College in Ft. Rosebery. It appears that, since he was unfamiliar with the situation in Northern Rhodesia, he allowed himself to be unduly influenced by one or perhaps two of his advisors. In any event, he rejected the Ft Rosebery site, located in the middle of a White Father mission area, mainly because it:

> ...fails in respect of three requirements which I regard as of primary importance. First, it removes the Teachers' Training College from the centre of influence in Northern Rhodesia and thereby prejudices its future prestige and influence. Secondly, it leaves to non-Catholics and similar institutions the advantage of a central position and of proximate association with Government and educational administration. Thirdly, it does not take into account the contribution which such an institution as a Teachers' Training College can make to the social question which I suggest is destined to become a vital one here in this country in the near future.[82]

Instead, the Jesuit superior reasoned that such an institution should be along the line of rail or Lusaka, where it could be in a more socially influential position. The Education Department did not favour Lusaka since another teachers' College, Chalimbana, was already located there. Eventually it was decided to locate the College a mile distant from the secondary school at Chikuni. It is difficult to see how Chikuni, in a rather rural, backward, area, though admittedly on the line of rail, met the Irish Provincial's criteria much better than Ft. Rosebery. As he was supplying the staff to build and operate the institution, it appears that he had the final say.[83]

---

[82] Letter from Irish Jesuit Provincial to Msgr. Pailloux, 23 September 1954. J.A.C.
[83] However, as retired Bishop Adam Kozlowiecki remarked, the whole affair dampened what had been a good working relationship between the Jesuits and the White Fathers. Interview, Mpunde, Kabwe, 4 June 1996.

The controversy surrounding the siting of the College undoubtedly reveals friction among the Catholic bodies stemming perhaps from a certain degree of personality clash and poor communications. What is more significant is that there was a growing perception among certain groups of the need to be where the future action would be. The Jesuits envisaged such a territorial college not so much as a rural development centre but as a place where Catholics could be better integrated into the wider social development of the territory. Fr. Thompson, one of the people on whom the Irish Provincial seemed to heavily rely for advice noted that:

> Fr. O'Grady (Irish Provincial) said I want this college in an area of conflict. I don't want it set up in a Catholic area—we must deal with areas that are non-Catholic.[84]

Since the Irish supervisor had proved somewhat difficult in the negotiations, some Bishops reconsidered the desirability of having Irish Jesuits for this important undertaking. Thus, some of them and indeed some Jesuits had proposed inviting a Congregation of Brothers to undertake to build and operate the College. On reflection, the Jesuits decided that it was of such importance that they themselves should do it. One influential Jesuit administrator wrote:

> Proper Mission schools and teachers are of paramount importance and I think that it is true to say that the history of the growth of every Mission in Africa is the history of the development of its schools...There will be no Catholics unless there is a Catholic school and it is the teacher who has to do most of the work of teaching religion, holding prayers for the villagers every Sunday and so on. He must be trained not only professionally and academically, but above all morally. And I think too that he should be trained by priests, with whom and for whom he is going to work.[85]

Despite a certain degree of hesitancy about who would eventually manage the College, the Jesuits began work on its construction in 1957. The College had its first intake in 1959, under Fr. John Counihan S.J., as principal. During the following five years, the Jesuits built up and operated the new institution for men. In the meantime, smaller teacher training centres at Malole for men, Chilubula, Lukulu, Minga, and Chikuni for women continued to operate. Efforts to secure a second Catholic major teacher training centre in Kasama that would combine the efforts of Chilubula and Malole continued until the mid-1960s. However, this did not take place even though after Independence

---

[84] Fr. R. Thompson, Interview, Naas, Ireland. 24 August 1983.
[85] Letter from MacMahon to Irish Jesuit Provincial. J.A.D.

government opened its own co-educational college in Kasama. Similarly, when it opened a college in Chipata, Minga was phased out. In 1968, the women's teacher training centre at Chikuni became part of Charles Lwanga. Moreover, as we shall see, Lukulu relocated at Mongu in 1965 under the direction of the Holy Cross Sisters and in 1976 became co-educational with Fr. John Grace O.F.M. Cap as principal. Thus, by the early days of Independence, the Catholic Church operated two major teacher training colleges—Mongu and Charles Lwanga.

CATHOLIC SECONDARY SCHOOLS

In 1940, largely because of the outbreak of the Second World War in Europe, a Czech Jesuit, Fr. Maximillian Prokoph, decided to work in Africa. On arrival in Northern Rhodesia, he was sent to Chikuni. This was the place that had been chosen to be a normal school in 1926. Between then and 1934, when it had to be discontinued, many teachers had graduated there. In 1934, because of the departure of Mr. Harold Consterdine, the government recognised educationist, the school had closed. As Prokoph had studied pedagogy in London, he lost no time in re-opening the normal school and in the years that followed, he did much to raise the standards of Chikuni's schools.

Prokoph clearly brought new life and vision to Chikuni. Because of this, he was not entirely welcomed by the founder of the mission, Fr. Moreau. As we mentioned earlier, it appears that Moreau envisaged the creation of a prosperous peasantry and did not favour the urbanisation that was taking place. Consistent with this viewpoint, he did not greatly approve of providing facilities for higher levels of schooling. Unlike Moreau, Prokoph swiftly set the stage for higher learning. He began not simply to upgrade the teacher training but also to think of providing secondary schooling. When asked what he had had in mind, he stated:

> I was thinking primarily to have a place where you could prepare future seminarians for I did not believe in this second class clergy as did other denominations. [86]

However, the White Fathers already had a seminary, so why was it necessary to start a secondary school? To this, Fr. Prokoph replied:

> You needed a large body from which to select for the seminary. Seminaries by themselves were not too successful. We had our first priest in 1947 (the White Fathers had theirs in 1946 even though they had a seminary since

---

[86] Interview, Lusaka: October 1983.

1930).[87]

In the tradition of the Jesuits and the particular circumstances from which he had come, Prokoph was very much aware of the value of schooling as a means to promoting Catholic leadership. In the mid-1940s, he requested the Department of Education for permission to open a secondary stream at Chikuni. The reply that he received from the Director reads thus:

> We already have a secondary school at Munali for boys and are considering one for girls at Chipembi. If we open another one we shall create an intellectual unemployed proletariat.[88]

Nonetheless, the Education Department realised that some expansion would be needed so in the revised version of the Ten Year Development Plan of 1946, it proposed to assist two mission secondary schools which would have a higher teachers' course. One of the plan's suggestions included that:

> The Standing Committee of the Advisory Board be asked to make proposals for the establishment of two mission institutions which shall provide Junior Secondary Education (Forms I and II) and the T3 course.[89]

Though Prokoph was out of the country when the proposal was made public, the Ordinaries fully supported it and expressed their willingness to co-operate. Moreover, they argued that one such institution should be given to them, since they claimed, correctly it appears, that they controlled one-third of the total primary schools.[90] However, the controversy surrounding the rationalisation of teacher training institutions was still a burning issue, and so the Protestants were not endeared by what they termed Catholic intransigence. Hardly surprisingly, they strongly resisted any form of concession to the Catholics. The Anglican Bishop of Northern Rhodesia protested:

> The Roman Catholic Societies claimed one of these institutions (one of the two) and they suggested that the non-Roman Catholic missions should be satisfied with the other school. The suggestion was unacceptable to me and

---

[87] Ibid.

[88] As quoted in Carmody, *Conversion and Jesuit Schooling*, p. 73. It is to be noted of course that the General Missionary Conference (non-Catholic) had made a similar request in 1942. See: N.A.Z. Sec 1/556; "The Need for expansion of secondary school provision."

[89] (Development Plan Head LB (1947) Gov Zam E4 (058) 2 UNZA Special Collections Library); *Annual Report 1947*, p. 4 par 10.)

[90] Catholic Ordinaries Meeting Minutes: 4 February 1947. C.S.A. See also: *African Education Annual Report 1947*, p. 4.

most of the Protestant Missions were opposed to it.[91]

Refusing to countenance the Catholic proposals, the Christian Council argued that both centres should be interdenominational in character. They felt that to accede to the Roman Catholic claim would give the Roman Catholic Societies a privilege that could not be extended to other denominations. At the Standing Committee meeting of the Advisory Board in July 1947, Rev. Nightingale on behalf of the Christian Council requested government to take over all secondary schools for Africans. The Christian Council representatives suggested that in view of the attitude of the Roman Catholic Societies any new centres for junior secondary education that were to be established should be government schools (and that these schools should be so sited as to serve the needs of the whole territory.)[92]

However, at a subsequent meeting, Mr. Mason, the Acting Director of African Education, recommended that Government should start a school at Mazabuka while "a certain group of Mission Societies" who accepted the original offer should have their own secondary school. When the Protestant Legislative Council members realised that Mason had the Catholics in mind, two of them resigned from the Advisory Board and Standing Committees alleging that Mason had made "a private bargain with the Roman Catholics." Somewhat later, realising how petty and childish their action appeared, they withdrew their resignations claiming that they had misunderstood.

Despite such opposistion, the Catholic Ordinaries persisted in their demand that they should be allowed one centre for secondary schooling. They stated that any direct system of inter denominationalism was repugnant to the Catholic Church's principles.[93] As in the case of the teacher college rationalisation process, again, an impasse resulted. Fearing that this interdenominational rivalry might play into the hands of government, who might be happy to opt for government centres as they had already done at Munali, the Apostolic Delegate, Archbishop Mathew, sent a letter to the Governor, describing what he termed as "his personal approach." This so-called personal approach envisaged two schools for all denominations "under the wing of the administration" with special safeguards for the different denominations. He described his so-called personal approach thus:

---

[91] Bishop of Northern Rhodesia, "Education Development Plan," *Central Africa*, 65 (1947) as quoted in Ragsdale, *Protestant Mission Education*, p. 151.

[92] *African Education: Annual Report 1947* (Lusaka: Government Printer, 1948), p. 4.

[93] Minutes of the Conference of Ordinaries: 4 Feb 1947; *African Education: Annual Report 1947*, p. 4. para 10.

I have in mind two schools the chairmen of whose governing bodies would be appointed by His Excellency the Governor from among laymen of experience. The governing body would be composed of certain laymen nominated by the administration and representatives of the Christian Council and the Roman Catholic Conference in the proportion of three Christian Council to two Roman Catholics. I do not wish that either school have a Roman Catholic chairman. All that we require is a man of integrity in whose impartiality both sides had confidence.[94]

The Christian Council reacted positively to Mathew's proposal which was taken to supersede the Ordinaries' demand for a totally Catholic institution. However, at the Education Advisory Board meeting of July 8, 1947, the chairman stated that Government was not in a position to commit itself to Archbishop Mathew's proposal until certain points had been elaborated and details which were left in doubt had been clarified. At this juncture, Monsignor Flynn, the Catholic spokesman, put a spanner in the spokes, so to speak. He reported that he thought the meeting of the Mission Societies had been very divided on the Archbishop's proposal and confirmed the statement of the chairman that certain points of the Archbishop's proposal would need to be carefully elaborated and details clarified before the scheme could be put into operation.[95] Protestant groups rightly perceived that the Catholics were divided on the matter.

This show of apparent disunity greatly offended the Apostolic Delegate who, in a letter to the Prefect Apostolic of Lusaka, questioned Flynn's authority to make such a pronouncement. However, in 1996, Archbishop Kozlowiecki, who had been the Prefect Apostolic of Lusaka at the time, argued that Flynn's intervention proved both courageous and fortunate. Otherwise, Mathew would have jeopardised the bishops' efforts to secure a Catholic school.[96] Perhaps in order to save face as well as to clear up misunderstanding, Mathew quickly stressed that his approach was "a second line" and that his letter to the Governor contained the phrase "The Roman Catholic Bishop's Conference is placing their view (demanding a Catholic secondary school) before the Department of Education and personally I strongly endorse their request."[97] At about the same time, in reply to Canon Grace of the Conference of Missionary Societies in Great Britain and Ireland where

---

[94] Letter entitled: Proposed new secondary schools in Northern Rhodesia. Archbishop Mathew's personal approach. N.A.Z. Sec 1/557.

[95] N.A.Z: Sec 1/557.

[96] A. Kozlowiecki, Interview, Mpunde, Kabwe, 4 June 1996; See also: Letter from D. Mathew to B. Wolnik, 5 September 1947. J.A.C.

[97] Letter from Mathew to Ordinaries, Dec 1947. A.A.L.

the Canon expressed his confusion in the face of different Catholic reactions, Mathew unambiguously stated that he endorsed the Bishops' proposal. In retrospect, Mathew's proposal did little to advance the cause of denominational secondary schooling except to cause unnecessary confusion in an already difficult situation. However what Mathew's action perhaps does signify is the determination of the Catholic authorities to remain in the mainstream of educational provision in Northern Rhodesia. Partly for this reason, the Catholic Ordinaries decided not to start a private school as they felt in this way they might find themselves outside the mainstream:

> Il serait imprudent et probablement préjudiciable à la cause Catholique de vouloir instituer un enseignement secondaire Catholique indépendamment du Gouvernement.[98]

It also appears true that, at one point in the controversy, the government contemplated dispensing with the missionary bodies in the provision of secondary schooling. However much the concept of non-denominational secondary schooling may have appealed, government was not ready financially or otherwise for such a commitment.[99] Protestant reaction to Catholic secondary schooling in Northern Rhodesia was not unique, indicating the deep rivalry that existed at this time in history between Catholics and Protestants despite earlier attempts at co-operation through the Missionary Conferences. In some respects, what Fr. Moreau had feared about Catholic unwillingness to co-operate with non-Catholics in the early Missionary Conferences had proved accurate in that such behaviour had done little to foster inter-denominational endeavours.[100] Undoubtedly, as Oger suggests, the earlier Catholic aloof approach did not help, especially since the Protestants themselves were unable to unite in such an endeavour and so probably felt somewhat envious of the Catholic ability to undertake what they were unable to do.[101]

---

[98] It would be imprudent and possibly prejudicial to the Catholic cause to set up a secondary school independent of Government. *Petit Echo* 3 (1947), p. 112.

[99] N.A.Z. Sec 1/557; Letter from the Governor to the Secretary for Native Affairs, 25 September 1947.

[100] See: Chapter 1, footnote 21; On the more general Protestant-Catholic situation, see: David Abernethy, *The Political Dilemma of Popular Education* (Stanford University Press, 1969), p. 170.

[101] L. Oger, *Our Missionary Shadow*, p. 2; On the point of Protestant inability to unite on this matter, see: Letter from J.A. Cottrell to Sec. Native Affairs, July 1947. N.A.Z: Sec 1/557; For greater detail on the wider Protestant-Catholic rivalry, see: Abernethy, *The Political Dilemma*, p. 170.

After much delay, the Acting Director of Education, Mr. Mason, decided in favour of having a Catholic denominational secondary school but felt obliged to put his views at length before the Christian Council Executive in April 1948. He wrote:

> When a body of Mission Societies, sufficient in strength and in the scope of their work, seeks to justify from the educational and organisational standpoint, their being permitted to undertake the work of an aided secondary school, asks that they should be allowed to do so, I can see no reason, in logic, in equity or for educational reasons why their request should be refused...To deny them this opportunity would, in my view, lay me and all of us open to an accusation of bad faith. [102]

In response to Mason, the Executive of the Christian Council stated that it was grateful to the Director of African Education for his statement but added:

> It regrets that he feels obliged to insist on the denominational rather than the regional territorial approach to the problem.[103]

A new landmark had finally been placed, Northern Rhodesia had accepted the principle of denominational secondary schooling, which, as the Acting Director of African Education indicated, had already been established though not fully acknowledged through the opening of Chipembi in 1946.[104]

When permission was granted, the Catholic authorities opened their secondary school at Chikuni. They named it Canisius College after the famous European Jesuit educator, Peter Canisius, and it would be staffed by English-speaking Irish Jesuits who should be well qualified academically. The aim of the school would be:

> to provide general and vocational education above the primary stage permanently for boys and temporarily for girls, until similar facilities are provided for the latter under Catholic control elsewhere in the territory. [105]

The Ordinaries emphasised that, though non-Catholics could be admitted, the religious teaching would be that of the Catholic Church. Any non-Catholics would have to conform to the regulations, while the

---

[102] Statement made to the Christian Council Executive by the Director of African Education, giving his personal views on the question of mission secondary education and higher teacher training: 2 April 1948. J.A.C.

[103] Minutes of a meeting of the standing committee of the Advisory Board on African Education, Lusaka, 26 April 1948. N.A.Z: Sec1/550.

[104] Letter of J.A. Cottrell, A-Director of African Education, to Sec. For Native Affairs, July 1947. N.A.Z.: Sec 1/557.

[105] Minutes of a Conference on Catholic Secondary School for Northern Rhodesia, 1-4 July 1948. A.A.L.

"conscience clause" found in the Constitution of the Catholic secondary school in Zomba was omitted. All agreed that to admit non-Catholics in such numbers as would weaken or neutralise the Catholic atmosphere would defeat the school's purpose. Canisius was primarily set up to provide a Catholic secondary school for Catholic students.

In the years that followed, before Independence, Canisius provided secondary education at a time when such facilities were greatly limited. As an interim measure, Canisius provided limited facilities for girls until 1956, when St. Mary's secondary school opened in Livingstone. This had been a Catholic girls' primary school for many years known as Maria Assumpta under the direction of the Holy Cross Sisters. However, because of a lack of Holy Cross Sisters, the Franciscan Missionary Sisters for Africa assumed responsibility for running the new junior secondary school at the request of Bishop O'Shea O.F.M. Cap, the local Bishop.[106] This was the first Catholic secondary school for African girls in Northern Rhodesia, though of course the Dominican Sisters had provided such facilities for European girls from the 1950s.[107] While the Dominican Sisters had provided primary and later secondary schooling for Europeans at Broken Hill (Kabwe) from 1929, Ndola from 1936, Luanshya from 1941, Fatima from 1954, St. Mary's, Lusaka, from 1950, and Ibenga from 1963, they had not neglected African needs for schools. They started a school for African girls at Kasisi in 1924 and continued at Kabwe in 1929. This became a pivotal primary school in the area in subsequent years, while at the secondary level the Sisters pioneered non-racial schools in 1956 at Caritas and managed to have a multi-racial school at St. Mary's, Lusaka, in 1960, despite much opposition, given the colonial policy of colour bar. As the 1950s progressed, more Catholic secondary schools appeared so that by 1967, there were nineteen, nine of which were for boys and ten for girls. In that year the Catholic agency provided roughly 21% of all secondary school places, 16% for boys and 31% for girls in grant-aided schools.[108]

---

[106] Sr. Magdalene Sitondo, "Brief history of St. Mary's Secondary School, Maramba, Livingstone." (Long paper for H 910 course at the University of Zambia), pp. 3-4.

[107] On the beginnings of the Dominicans in Zambia, see: *In God's White Robed Army*.

[108] The Catholic secondary schools by 1966 with managers and date of founding included: For boys, Jesuits, St. Canisius, Chikuni (1949), Brothers of the Sacred Heart, St. Francis, Malole (1951), Marist Brothers, Chassa (1960), Marist Brothers, St. Paul's, Mulungushi (1960), Capuchin Fathers, Lukulu, 1962, Capuchin Fathers, St. John's, Mongu (1962), White Fathers, St. Clement's, Mansa (1964), Christian Brothers, St. Edmund's Mazabuka, (1964), Marianist Brothers, Matero (1966); For girls, St. Mary's, Maramba, Franciscan Missionary Sisters for Africa (1956), St. Joseph's, Chivuna, Religious Sisters of Charity (1961), St. Monica's, Chipata, Grey Sisters/Sisters of Charity

RESPONSE TO CATHOLIC SCHOOLING

As we have already seen, there was a gradual increase in the provision of primary schools in the territory. In 1935, mission societies operated approximately 397 aided schools. By 1963, 16 denominations operated 1,224 aided non fee paying schools, by which time 50% of all school age children were in school. Over the years, while the number of schools increased, their size and the quality of their instruction had also changed dramatically.[109]

Like other schools during this period, in concord with government directives, the Catholic schools had been upgraded and considerably expanded. In 1925, Catholic societies operated approximately 34% of the total number of schools in existence. As a result of the 1927 Ordinance, however, as we have noted earlier, the number of Catholic centres recognised as schools declined sharply in conformity with the more stringent requirements of the Education Department.[110] By 1935, the various Catholic societies operated 82 aided schools, approximately 20% of the country's aided primary schools and roughly 31% of the unaided schools.[111] In 1945, the number of Catholic aided schools had increased to 218, about 19% of the total number of such schools with about 34% of the unaided or sub-schools. Included in these figures were the contributions of the new Catholic societies that had started work in the territory in the early 1930s, the Capuchins of the Western Province and the Franciscans on the Copperbelt. In 1945, the Capuchins operated 66 aided and about 283 unaided schools, which was a remarkable contribution in a matter of about thirteen years.[112] By 1967, the Catholic societies, mainly the White Fathers, the Capuchins, and the Jesuits operated 588, that is, about 30% of all the primary schools.[113] Throughout the colonial period, it is thus safe to say that the Catholic

---

of Ottawa (1962), St. Theresa's, Ibenga, Dominican Sisters (1963), Holy Cross, Mongu, Holy Cross Sisters (1963), Roma, Lusaka, Religious Sisters of Charity (1963), St. Mary's, Kawambwa White Sisters (1963), St. Mary's, Luwitikila, White Sisters (1963), St. Theresa's, Chilubula, White Sisters (1967). In 1967, the nine Catholic boys' secondary schools educated 2,930 of the 18,376 boys in secondary school while the ten Catholic girls schools educated 2,496 of the total 8,167 secondary school girls. For greater detail, see: *Impact* no. 16 (1967).

[109] Henkel, *Christian Missions in Africa*, p. 128; Ministry of Education annual report (1964), p. 53; See also: Report on Schools 1963. J.A.C

[110] Snelson, *Educational Development in Northern Rhodesia*, p. 160.

[111] Henkel, *Christian Missions in Africa*, p. 128.

[112] O'Sullivan, *Zambezi Mission*, p. 53.

[113] Ministry of Education, Annual Report (1968), p. 32.

Bishop Dupont W.F.

Sr. Hedwig c. 1900

1890s at Kayambi

Chikuni 1905
Seated: F. Borgia, Hatontola.
From Left Standing: Bbinya, Jahaliso, Fr. Moreau, Fr. Torrend, Jojo

Chikuni Mission Church 1911

Kasisi School 1908

Rosa Church c. 1933

Fr. Van Sambeek W.F.

Mgr. John C. LYAMIBABA

St. Francis School Lusaka 1920

Malole College 1936

Elias Kasia
Catechist 1940-1970

Archbishop Chabukasansha (right) with President Kaunda, the Apostolic Pronuncio and Bishop Masombwe at installation of Archbishop Mutale 1973

Chilubula (photo 1996)

Fr. Walsh

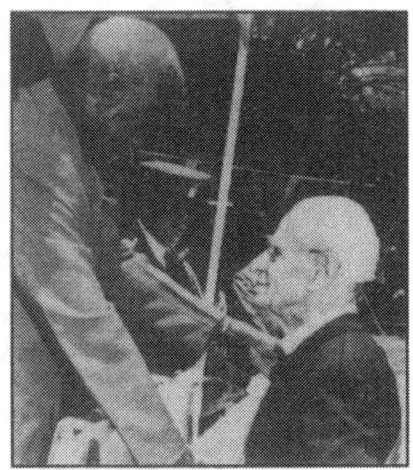

Fr. Prokoph being decorated by President Kaunda (1984)

Chilonga Church and teacher catechist L. Chikolokoso

St. Francis, Malole (photo 1996)

Dominican Convent, Ndola (photo 1996)

Ilondola (photo 1996)

Church maintained approximately one third of the primary schools of the country.

We will now examine how the local population responded to the Catholic provision of primary and later of secondary schooling. As we saw in the previous chapter, in general, children came in considerable numbers to the schools, even though regions differed somewhat in their responses.[114] A number of interrelated factors such as the setting up of government assisted teacher training centres, the 1927 Education Ordinance, and the visit of Mgr. Hinsley did much to promote the Catholic school as a place for secular as opposed to catechetical learning. The desire for secular learning, though crucial, varied considerably with place and time.

As we noted in the previous chapter, attendance at schools, though erratic, began to gain some momentum by 1924. Regular attendance appears to have been motivated both by interest in the religious message particularly at the White Fathers' missions, but progressively too by the prospect of wage employment. This had consequences for the type of schooling that was needed. As the preponderant interest became wage employment, more secular-type schools became necessary, providing special emphasis on proficiency in English. This entailed occasional conflict of interest between the missionaries and their students where the missionaries preferred more religiously focused learning whereas their students wanted what would empower them to gain waged employment. During this period in particular, perception of the opportunity structure remained a key factor in determining the response to missionary education. Where school graduates were well rewarded through the job market, desire for schooling increased.

After 1926, at Chikuni, the numbers increased rapidly with the opening of a normal school. At the outschools of the Chikuni area, the picture was far less encouraging. Parents' reluctance to send their children to school was one of the main reasons why Fr. Zabdyr initiated his village committee system. In 1934, he wrote:

> When one considers the uphill work of establishing schools and the point we have reached today he will realise that much progress has been made in spite of difficulties. Chiefs and headmen are often an obstacle instead of being a help.[115]

Even after schools or outschools had been set up, regular attendance proved to be an on-going difficulty. Much of Zabdyr's time and that of

---

[114] See: Chapter 1.
[115] Carmody, *Conversion and Jesuit Schooling*, p. 53.

the two Jeanes supervisors, Antonio Monze and Paul Haakola, who assisted him, was spent on persuading villagers of the value of education. Perhaps the fact that English was not taught in the first years of school was a factor as well as that villagers appear to have associated real education with European teachers:

> Another reason for irregularity of attendance is the parents' and pupils' feeling which is rarely absent, that village education is a poor substitute for the "real" thing, which in their opinion can only be got from Europeans in a boarding school.[116]

The struggle to secure regular attendance continued into the 1940s. As Fr. Prokoph recalled:

> It is safe to say that many missionaries spent as much time gathering children into school, persuading parents, headmen, chiefs and children in endless meetings, as they did in actual instruction.[117]

Among the White Fathers' missions in the Northern Province, the situation did not appear to be greatly different. In a report from the teacher training centre at Rosa, near Kasama, in 1930, we read:

> Sans doute la jeunesse des deux sexes est ardente pour apprendre à lire, écrire, calculer, voire même baragouiner un peu d'anglais, mais tout cela doit se faire rapidement et ne gêner en rein leur amour de la liberate et de la browse. Quant à accepter une discipline scolaire a jours et heurs fixes, non seulement des mois, mais des années, c'est une autre affaire. Dieu soit la peine que se donnent les Supérieurs de mission pour recruter les 25 a 30 élèves de leurs petits internats. Ce ne sont pas les enfants qui manquent, ce sont les écoliers.[118]

It was, however, largely the people's desire for secular-type schools that led the White Fathers to adopt the government aided school as an integral part of their mission:

> La jeunesse veut s'instruire pour avoir un emploi lucratif; elle va donc aux ecoles protestantes et partant nous echappe.[119]

---

[116] Ibid., p. 54.

[117] Ibid., p. 86.

[118] Undoubtedly both boys and girls are eager to learn to read, write and calculate and even to display a little English. Yet it all needs to be done fast and must not interfere with their love of the freedom of the bush. As for accepting the discipline of scholastic learning at fixed days and hours, not to mention, months and years, that is something else. Only God knows the pain which mission superiors experience in attempting to recruit 25 to 30 pupils in their small boarding schools. It is not so much children that are wanted as scholars. R.A. (1930-31), p. 245.

[119] Youth want instruction to gain lucrative employment; so they go to Protestant schools and thus we loose them. R.A. (1934-35), p. 340.

Generally Protestant missions had gained a good reputation for secular learning and so the White Fathers realised that in order to compete for converts, they would have to offer the type of schools that the local people wanted:

> Si nous voulons lutter avec eux (Protestants) il nous faut des écoles et surtout de bonnes écoles. Mais beaucoup de nos gens croient que seuls nos adversaires savent tenir une école; car il est bien difficile pour nous d'en ouvrir puisque pratiquement tous les villages sont pris par les Protestants.[120]

In the 1930s, an often repeated refrain from mission directors included: "fewer schools but better schools; fewer teachers but better teachers."[121] As these schools became more integrated into the government educational system, in many cases, their standards and reputations improved. Nevertheless, especially in rural areas, progress could be very slow even as late as the 1950s. As one of the mission teachers of those years recalled:

> At that time it was difficult. You had to persuade people to send children to school...When one went to the villages in the 1950s, it was difficult... Gradually people realised that education was much better. They saw young men who were educated, employed, and getting money...so it was worthwhile to send a child to school. To send a girl was a waste of time...it took time.[122]

In the late 1940s the numbers of students increased but, boys or young men continued to constitute the main student body. For instance in the Bangweolo area in 1937, there were 3395 boys and 848 girls in the schools.[123] As we have noted earlier, reluctance to send girls to school, especially beyond Standard II, remained widespread until the early 1950s. In 1938, of the 6,436 girls who entered Sub A (first school class at that time) only 18 survived to Std VI. By 1939, only six female students had completed Std. IV at Chilubula.[124] In 1944, there was one girl in Std II for every 20 in Sub A. Between 1940 and 1949, only 179 girls passed Std. VI, while approximately 3,000 boys had done so.[125] The attitude that still seemed to commonly prevail was:

---

[120] If we want to compete with the Protestants we must have good schools. Yet most people believe that it is only our adversaries who know how to run a school; thus it is very difficult for us to open schools since practically every village is already occupied by Protestants. R.A. (1937-38), p. 360.

[121] P.N. 42 (April 1932).

[122] Elias Kasia, born 1922, teacher from 1938. Interview, Kasisi, 5 June 1995.

[123] R.A. (1937-38), p. 355.

[124] N.A.Z.: HM42 Snelson Papers.

[125] Gadsden, "Education and Society in Colonial Zambia,", p. 119.

> L'ecole, disent ils, ce n'est pas pour la femme, elle n'a pas besoin de passer par l'ecole pour apprendre a tourner la bouillie de son mari.[126]

As a retired teacher who grew up in the 1940s explained:

> It was considered useless to educate a girl because when she knew how to read, she could get private letters ...Besides there were few women teachers in those days.[127]

In 1935, of the 1350 certified teachers, less than 100 were women.[128] Although the Department of Education did much to promote the education of girls, its vision remained rather narrow as we see from a report in 1937:

> The aim of all female education should be to educate girls for wifehood and motherhood...Mere academic education, undesirable for boys, is disastrous for girls.[129]

Progress in getting girls to remain in school remained slow particularly in the more remote areas.[130] A retired teacher from Eastern province recalled:

> In the 1940s we had to recruit the First Grade. We went about with chief's messengers, but as soon as a girl matured they looked for someone to marry her. School was considered to be a waste of time.[131]

It should however be noted that even where girls desired advanced schooling, oftentimes there was a very limited number of places. Moreover, not all missionaries of this time showed enthusiasm for the more advanced education of girls. For instance, Mary Chilala (later Sr. Agnes) recalled that in the early 1940s, Fr. Moreau of Chikuni wanted all girls to return home after Std II. She herself was counselled in this way by Fr. Moreau.[132] However, Moreau's successor, Fr. Prokoph encouraged her to remain in school and laboured hard to establish the

---

[126] They say that school is not for the woman. She has no need to go to school in order to learn how to cook for her husband. R.A. (1937-38)

[127] Mr. L. Chikolokoso, born 1932, served as teacher from 1949. Interview, Chilonga, Mpika, 9 July 1996.

[128] Report of Proceedings of the meeting of the Central Advisory Board on Native Education 1935 (N.A.Z: Sec 1/444).

[129] *Northern Rhodesia, Department of Education: Report of Sub-Committee on Female Education 1937* (Lusaka: Government Printer, 1938), p. 1.

[130] F. Gadsden, "Patriarchal Attitudes," *Zambia Journal of History* nos. 6/7 (1993/94), pp. 25-45: "Education and Society in Colonial Zambia," p. 107.

[131] Yambani Phiri, Teacher and later Manager of Schools, Interview, Chipata, 15 June 1996.

[132] Sr. Agnes, H.B.V.M., interview, Kabwe, March 1984.

only Catholic upper primary school for girls and boys in Southern, Central, and Copperbelt provinces until the late 1940s. At Prokoph's death in 1990, it was recalled that:

> More than forty years ago, he saw the potential of women in Zambia's development. During that time teaching was still regarded as a man's domain, as were many other ventures. But he persuaded a group of girls to take up the profession.[133]

Prokoph himself felt that the arrival of African Sisters did much to promote the desire for schooling among girls. The African Sisters perhaps provided new role models. In the Chikuni area, Prokoph related:

> Not until 1940 was a girl found to have the courage to continue beyond Grade 4. The breakthrough came in 1943. In 1942, I had been to Rhodesia where Bishop Chichester took me round the schools where African Sisters did such admirable work in classes full of girls. I asked him whether he could lend us a couple for a few years as an object lesson of what African girls could do. Not only was that the beginning of the Handmaids, but the number of advancing girls steadily increased from then onwards.[134]

It appears clear that the presence of African, as opposed to European, sisters had a significant impact on local girls' aspirations to religious life. As a sister of another congregation and another region of the country recalled:

> I admired the White Sisters but when I saw the Sisters of the Child Jesus (first Zambian Congregation) I knew it was possible to become a Sister.[135]

Seeing Zambian women in professional roles no doubt had a similar effect on girls aspirations' for other ways of life.

Scudder and Colson, in their discussion of education in the Gwembe valley, parts of which are rather remote, considered that certain Council regulations opposing child betrothal and limiting puberty seclusion helped the regularity of girls' attendance in school. In the 1950s, bursaries became more widely available.[136] When the first fruits of investment in girls' schooling became apparent with the

---

[133] "Pioneer leaves indelible mark," *Times of Zambia* (15 June 1990), p. 6.

[134] M. Prokoph, "Our Mission and Education," p. 3. J.A.C.

[135] Sr. Genevive Masase, S.C.J., interview, Chilubula, 16 July 1996. Sr. Genevive was one of first girls from the Northern part of the country to go for secondary schooling at St. Mary's, Livingstone in 1956.

[136] Thayer Scudder & Elizabeth Colson, *Secondary Education and the Formation of an Elite: The Impact of Education on Gwembe District, Zambia* (New York: Academic Press, 1980), pp. 64 ff.

possibility not only of girls becoming sisters but of securing jobs as teachers, nurses, and secretaries, the general attitude to investment in schooling for girls seemed to change.[137] As one teacher of the period commented:

> In the early days, girls did not see the value of school. For example, there were no women teachers or women in offices. But this changed when women were seen to have responsible jobs with salaries.[138]

It would seem that the early 1950s revealed a new perception of the opportunity structure. With the guarded expansion of secondary schooling in the early 1950s, opportunities for better forms of employment appeared. Many began to perceive schooling as the gateway to white-collar employment. As one student of the late 1950s recalled:

> The main reason I admired the Jesuits was for their education. They had what I wanted. I could see that educated people were promoted for I had grown up in a mining town where one knew that education gave access to highly paid jobs.[139]

What Ogbu found elsewhere seemed especially true in this situation, namely: "Achievement motivation and behaviour are determined to a large extent by the prevailing system of social mobility."[140]

With the formation of the African National Congress (A.N.C.) in 1946 and the subsequent imposition of the Federation with Southern Rhodesia and Nyasaland in 1953, Africans' frustration reached a high pitch. Howsoever, Federation served as a rallying point for A.N.C. under the leadership of Harry Nkumbula and Kenneth Kaunda. By 1958, when Kaunda broke with A.N.C. to form Zambia African National Congress party (Z.A.N.C.), which later became the United National Independence Party (U.N.I.P.), nationalist hopes for independence were high. With the prospect of Federation's collapse in the late 1950s, the elimination of the caste-like society that had existed through the so-called colour bar became a possibility. Many students of Northern Rhodesia at this period were not only alive to the nationalist sentiments for independence but were also very conscious of the

---

[137] Janet Nyeko, "The Development of female education in Northern Rhodesia 1925-63: the case of Central Province." (Masters thesis, U.N.Z.A, 1983), pp. 33, 38,

[138] Jonas Sokoni and Henry Chakobe, Interview, Ilondola, 11 July 1996; Yambani Phiri, Manager of schools, 1959-64, inspector, 1965-70. Interview, Chipata, 15 June 1996.

[139] Raphael Mulenga, Student at Canisius, 1957-9. Interview, Lusaka, 15 June 1984.

[140] John Ogbu, *Minority Education and Caste* (New York: Academic Press, 1978), p. 18; R. Clignet and P. Foster, *The Fortunate Few: A Study of Secondary schools and students in the Ivory Coast* (Evanston: North-western University, 1966), pp. 15, 143.

importance and value that academic qualifications would have for them in the new order. This explains the rapid increase in the number of secondary schools and in the sharply rising numbers of both boys and girls desiring secondary education between 1950 and 1964.

Partly in response to their students' aspirations, the staff of Canisius College, the first Catholic secondary school, did much to provide a good academic programme. The other Catholic secondary schools also created and maintained a similar tradition of providing good academic facilities, enabling their students to perform well in public examinations. A complaint sometimes heard more from the staff than from the students was that there probably was an over-emphasis on academics.[141]

At the beginning, the primary schools proved to be very effective instruments of gaining access to sections of the population and eventually leading them into the orbit of the mission through Baptism. In the 1950s, the secondary school provision became a further key means of securing the support and loyalty of those who, in a sense, had opted for modernity. As noted earlier, the provision of access to more advanced education through Catholic upper primary and secondary schools, for both boys and girls, dramatically increased in the early 1960s.

THE SCHOOL AND CONVERSION

The period between 1924 and 1964 represents a period when the Catholic Church in Northern Rhodesia moved from being a series of mission stations operated by two major missionary societies to securely established Church structures with a Zambian bishop by the time of Independence in 1964.

Today, one might speak of this newly formed Church as being predominantly institutional, emphasising such things as Sunday attendance at Mass, regular reception of the sacrament of Confession or Penance, as well as Baptism of children, Extreme Unction (Anointing of

---

[141] Carmody, *Conversion and Jesuit Schooling*, p. 70; As elsewhere and up to the present, popular demand focused on general, academic-type rather than on vocational schooling. Br. Keating who spent many years as principal of the Choma Trades Institute re-affirmed this. (Interview, Choma, 16 July 1997). It is of course true that Catholic schools included skills training and work in the fields as part of their programmes even at the secondary school level. However, students wanted English based, academic, schooling as the pathway to more lucrative employment. On this see: A.R. Thompson, *Education and Development in Africa* (New York: St. Martin's Press, 1981), pp. 33-44; Mwanakatwe, *The Growth of Education in Zambia*, pp. 90-106; Carmody, "Jesuit Mission School: Ally of Zambian Nationalism?" *Zambia Journal of History* no. 5 (1992), p. 49.

the Sick), and Matrimony, while paying scant attention to such things as laity formation, community development, and social commitment. Moreover, from 1935 onwards, the Church held territory-wide Conferences of Ordinaries or later of Bishops, from which came the main directives to the local churches.

During this period, the primary schools and teacher training institutions were seen as pivotal means of Church growth. The boarding schools, particularly at the secondary level, became very significant. However, we have seen that the school became progressively more secular, creating a certain degree of ambiguity for its students. While the Catholic Church attempted to create a Catholic ethos, to what extent were both the Catholic Church and the Catholic school alien to their African clientele?

It could perhaps be said with some justification that, during this time, the Church stressed loyalty and obedience to its norms more than critical questioning and personal responsibility. As one person was to comment:

> People believed without proof. They did not examine to find out how true the new religion was compared with the traditional religion.[142]

The position and authority of the priest was paramount. Leadership, on the whole, seemed to be in the hands of the bishops and priests who, as the case of Emilio Mulolani illustrates according to Hinfelaar, had little readiness for any form of real dialogue.[143] Instead, the main, official, response to this movement appears to have been that the bishops "deplored the lack of obedience of some Christians to Episcopal authority."[144] It appears true that devolution of authority even to faithful and long-serving teachers was gradual and cautious. For instance, at their Conference in 1958, some of the Bishops expressed fear of any form of "democratisation" of management of schools and hoped that African priests could be introduced as managers to maintain sufficient

---

[142] Edward Chisengalumbwe, "The Repercussions of Colonial Religions in Independent Africa." Address to the Historical Association of Zambia, Lusaka, 12 November 1976.

[143] Hinfelaar, *Bemba-Speaking Women*, p. 169; For greater detail on the movement, see: Clement Mweemba, "Bana Ba-Mutima Church 1954-1985," (dissertation, University of Zimbabwe, 1986), a copy of which is held at the Special Collections section of the University library in Lusaka.

[144] As quoted in Mweemba, "Bana Ba Mutima," p. 18. However, before this official and somewhat veiled reply, much had been done to accommodate some of Emilio's ideas at a parish and unofficial level, but Emilio did not appear to be too responsive. Fr. Vincent Cichecki, who had been parish priest at Matero, recalls that on a number of occasions efforts were made to accommodate Emilio but he proved uncooperative. Letter from Vincent Cichecki, 9 March 1997. J.A.C.

church control.¹⁴⁵ It is true that lay organisations such as the Legion of Mary and Actio did much to help the growth of the Church.¹⁴⁶ Actio or Catholic Action, originally an Italian movement, appeared in Zambia in 1934. Although its aim was far from clear, it was designed to involve laity in conducting prayer services and supervising Catholic practice in the local setting. Legio or the Legion of Mary had been founded in Dublin in 1922 and was brought to Zambia in 1945. It, too, helped to involve the laity, particularly women, in leading prayer services and monitoring the community's practice of Catholicism. This movement had about 2,000 members in the Kasama area alone in 1962 and did much to counteract the destructive influence of the Lenshina movement in those years. Both groups operated more as appendages of the priest or bishop than as having identity and contribution of their own.

In concord with seeing the bishop and priest as pivotal in the growth of the Church, much attention was given to the promotion of vocations and the formation of a native clergy. Progress on this remained slow initially. When one considers the enormous change of lifestyle which becoming a priest, brother or sister entailed, this is hardly surprising. Oftentimes, such a choice entailed radical and painful separation from friends and families who for the most part, especially in the case of girls, did not support their children in their choice of this foreign way of life. As Isichei wrote:

> Each religious vocation represented the most radical renunciation, in cultures where children are cherished above everything.¹⁴⁷

The radical nature of the religious vocation and the pain it could cause can be gleaned from the letter of a devout Catholic teacher in the 1960s

---

[145] Record of XVII Meeting of Northern Rhodesian Bishops Conference, Lusaka, 7-9 May 1958. J.A.C.

[146] For more detail on these movements, see: Garvey, *Bembaland Church*, pp. 151-5.

[147] Isichei, *A History of Christianity*, p. 241. This is confirmed through interviews with: Sr. Agnes Chilala, H.B.V.M. (Chikuni 1941-43), the first Handmaid Sister and first girl to go to Standard IV at Chikuni, interview, Lusaka, December 1983: Sr. Teresa Mulenga, H.B.V.M., interview, Lusaka, December 1983; Sr. Fidelina Mooya, H.B.V.M., interview, Lusaka, December 1983; Sr. Alfreda Michelo, H.B.V.M., interview, Lusaka, December 1983; Sr. Helen Mwalye, S.S.F., interview, Livingstone, June 1995; Sr. Leona Chintu, L.S.M.I., interview, Lusaka, December 1983; Sr. Faustina Mulenga, L.S.M.I, interview, Lusaka, December 1983; Sr. Genevive Masase, S.C.J., interview, Chilubula, July 1996. On a wider context see: Garvey, *Bembaland Church*, p. 148; Isichei, *A History of Christianity in Africa*, p. 241; For more detail on the various vocational institutes in Zambia, see: Weller & Linden, *Mainstream Christianity*, pp. 159-61; Garvey, *Bembaland Church*, pp. 135-9, 146-9; Ogez, *Where it all began*, pp. 82-4.

who wrote to his daughter who had entered the convent pleading thus:

> My desire to stop you is increasing day by day and will tell you to stop continuously till you STOP(sic). I withdraw my permission for you to be a sister. Come home when you finish school. Our Lord was obedient to His parents and why not you?[148]

Nonetheless, by 1968, the country had 100 local sisters, eight brothers, and 48 priests the first of whom, Fr. John Lyamibaba, was ordained in 1946.

Undoubtedly, the Catholic authorities of the Northern region were surprised by the large number of defections to the two major religious movements of the region in the 1950s, that of Alice Lenshina and that of former Catholic, Emilio Mulolani, whom we have mentioned above.[149] Speaking of the effects of the Lenshina movement at Ilondola, located near the centre of where the movement originated, one missionary in 1967 wrote:

> At the beginning of the movement most catechumens went over. Some came back; others joined...The movement of conversion slowed down and because of the Lumpa Church and the possibility of political unrest, in the mission (Ilondola) where I was working up to 1958, we lost 900 baptised Christians and most of the catechumens in some quarters.[150]

Perhaps one positive outcome from its encounter with these movements was that the Church began to pay more attention to such things as the use of Bemba melodies and musical instruments in the ecclesiastical ritual of its liturgy at a time when the Catholic Church world-wide stressed uniformity of language, rite and ritual. It was often said as a kind of indication of the Church's universality that the Mass was the same whether you attended in Tokyo or Mazabuka. In the administration of the sacraments, the priest had very clear and definite rubrics, which he had to observe with fidelity.

Even though, as we have noted, the Catholic Church had made a significant commitment to schooling, one could ask if this was done primarily to foster evangelisation or did it also include national development? Unquestionably, the early missionaries primarily aimed to build up a Christian community. Somewhat belatedly and in some cases,

---

[148] Letter written in the mid-1960s. J.A.C.

[149] For details on the Lenshina movement, see: J-L. Calmettes, "The Lumpa Sect, rural reconstruction, and conflict." (M.Sc. thesis, University of Wales, 1978); VanBinsbergen, *Religious Change in Zambia*, pp. 266-316; Garvey, *Bembaland Church*, pp. 159-79; Oger, *Where a Scattered flock*, pp. 148-61.

[150] Letter from Fr. L. Oger to A. Roberts, 22 February 1967 (W.F.L. Box MH 28).

especially after the visit of Mgr. Hinsley, they reluctantly engaged in secular-type schooling. Despite a somewhat slow start, however, the Catholic Church became a major partner with government in the provision of schooling that provided secular subjects in the curriculum during the early days of the colonial era. Eventually, in the 1950s, when other denominations began to withdraw from the administration of primary schools, the Catholic authorities remained set to continue and even to expand their commitment. In the 1940s, the Catholic Church advocated denominational secondary schooling and by 1964 was making a significant contribution at that level. It had assumed responsibility for secondary schooling not only to provide religious leadership but in addition to form an educated Catholic laity.

It appears true that the Catholic Church's commitment to the emergence of a new type of socio-political system came slowly. In the early days, the Catholic missionaries concentrated on the rural populations even when many of their converts went for employment to the urban centres. As we have noted, Catholics opened almost no schools on the Copperbelt. As commitment to running aided schools and higher education institutes grew, widespread missionary support for engagement in secular schooling appears far from unambiguous, as the conflict of vision between that of Fr. Moreau and Fr. Prokoph illustrates. At Chikuni, where the first Catholic secondary school came to be located, Fr. Moreau's view of creating a prosperous peasantry was superseded by that of Fr. Prokoph. His vision appeared more attuned to the demands of economic growth, and, in some ways, the desires of the local population, particularly those who began to have wider social contacts than those of the neighbourhood or village.[151] Nonetheless, until the late 1940s, Catholic schools in urban settings remained few, though in Lusaka they led the way.[152] When Catholic authorities began to rectify this situation, they felt government resistance. As an education secretary of the time recalled:

> Government had some kind of policy pushing missions to the rural areas

---

[151] H.E. Peters, *Education and Achievement* (Lusaka: Institute of African Studies, 1976); Henkel, *Christian Missions in Africa*, pp. 138-41: A.M. Mhoswa, "A Study of the educational contribution of the Jesuit Mission at Chikuni and the Adventist Mission at Rusangu, 1905-1964" (M.Ed. thesis, University of Zambia, 1980); B. Carmody, "Secular and Sacred at Chikuni 1905-1940," *Journal of Religion in Africa* XXI, 2 (1991), pp. 139, 144.

[152] In Lusaka, there were Chibolya (1919), St. Francis (1923), Regiment (1939), while there were European schools for girls operated by the Dominican Sisters (1939), which later was transferred to Woodlands. M. Prokoph, "The Involvement of the Churches in Education." J.A.C.

and leaving the towns for government. Some of the thinking was that the towns were more pluralistic and less monolithic religiously so that the towns could have mixed schools. [153]

Another education secretary with wider knowledge of the period added:

> In general we received little or no opposition from government. However, from the official point of view they were interested in seeing that the school served a population area not just a church school. In that way, they may have preferred L.E.A. schools.[154]

This concurs with a statement from an administrator of the period who noted:

> Over and over the administration was British and until the 1960s you rarely had Catholics in the administration so you were looking at education with a Protestant or agnostic approach and for them religion was something to be tolerated, but really they wanted as much secular approach as possible.[155]

In fact, attempts were made by government to 'take over' urban Church primary schools in the 1950s.[156] Catholic attention to urbanisation and its consequences for schooling in Zambia came perhaps mainly through the vision of people like Monsignor Flynn and Fr. Prokoph. However, it had come late, when government felt better prepared to direct the process through non-denominational schools.[157]

Politically, the Church maintained a safe distance from controversial issues, particularly up to the early 1950s. The Church co-operated with the government on educational matters and appeared careful to maintain a good general working relationship to the point of having a Catholic priest represent African interests between 1948 and 1955 in Parliament or Legco as it was called. For much of its existence

---

[153] Fr. John Counihan, interview, Chikuni, 1 January 1984.

[154] Fr. Colm O'Riordan, interview, Monze, 12 January 1984.

[155] Dominic Mulaisho, Permanent Sec. in the Ministry of Education after Independence. Interview, December 1983.

[156] Fr. Vincent Cichecki, S.J. Written comment dated 22 March 1997, where he noted that in 1956, when St. Francis primary school was being transferred to Matero, he sought parents' signatures so that the school should remain in Catholic hands.

[157] This is not to underestimate what was done. By 1974 there were 8 major Catholic primary schools in Lusaka serving 30% of the boys and 35% of the girls. These included: Matero (1954), Regiment (1954), St. Patrick's, Kabwata (1957), St. Monica's, Matero (1959), Chibelo (1964), Kizito (1965), Mutambe (1969) and Olympia Park (1969). Moreover, by 1966, there were two Catholic secondary schools in Lusaka, Roma (1963), and Matero (1966) as well as the Dominican Convent in Woodlands which was private until 1978.

under the British colonial administration, the Catholic Church was conscious of its outsider status in that its missionaries were preponderantly non-British, as the frequent requests for English-speaking missionaries indicates. However, even the securing of English-speaking missionaries often did not preclude the possibility of outsider status as is clear from the presence of the Irish, who though in general spoke English as their first language, rarely identified themselves as British nor would they have been so regarded by the colonial administration. This did not mean that the Catholic missionaries never criticised the colonial administration. In matters of unfair taxation and land issues, they did, but, as Freund put it, they did not challenge the overall political and economic imperatives of the colonial system.[158]

With the imposition of Federation in 1953, the Catholic Church's acceptance of the overall system came under strict scrutiny. Catholic authorities appear to have been aware of African opposition to the idea of Federation so that when the Anglican Church proposed having a day of prayer for the Federation, the Catholics declined saying: "...to call for a special day of prayer would probably do more harm than good, and this should be avoided."[159] However, given the colonial setting and the Church's links with the settler community, it hesitated about coming out clearly on the issue. Instead, the Bishops claimed that it was a political matter and so it was not something in which the Catholic Church should be directly involved. In the context of Federation, the main representative of the Catholic Church, the Apostolic Delegate, wrote:

> Provided there is no question of principle involved it is the practice of the Catholic missionaries to take no part in advocating or opposing contentious political solutions...On the other hand, Catholic missionaries can be trusted to use their influence against any unconstitutional action.[160]

As a result of this desire to remain neutral, the Catholic authorities decided not to make a public statement at the imposition of Federation. This swiftly led to misunderstandings as the Bishop of Abercorn noted:

> Catholic Africans are reproaching us for not taking up their defence in the

---

[158] B. Freund, *The Making of Contemporary Africa* (Bloomington: Indiana University Press, 1984), p. 157; See also Garvey, *Bembaland Church*, p. 180.

[159] Letter from Chairman, Bishops' Conference to Anglican Bishop of Northern Rhodesia in reply to an invitation to have a special day of prayer. 8 October 1953. (Bishop's Archives, Mansa).

[160] Letter from Apostolic Delegate, Mombasa, to Sir Thomas Lloyd, Colonial Office, London. 28 July 1952 (Bishops' Archives, Mpika). See: L.H. Gann, *A History of Northern Rhodesia: Early days to 1953* (London: Chatto & Windus, 1964), p. 422.

struggle, and some even take this attitude as a sign that we are pro-Federation. The more so as quite a number of Protestant missionaries has declared themselves openly against Federation in a public letter to the Press, mostly Church of Scotland and London Mission Society.[161]

It seems true that in the Northern part of the country at any rate, the neutral attitude of the Catholic authorities contrasted with the active political involvement of the Church of Scotland.[162] Moreover, some Protestant schools were perceived to be considerably more subversive of the colonial state than those of the Catholics. Referring to the handover of the Church of Scotland schools, the local Catholic bishop wrote:

> Government is certainly pleased with it (handover) because they are fed up with the kind of education this body is giving, turning out strong politicians for African Congress.[163]

As the 1950s advanced, the Catholic Church became more openly critical of the government. The Bishops firmly resisted the recommendation of the Education Advisory Board that mission teachers should be barred from taking part in politics[164]. Through the Bishops' public statement in 1958, their criticism of the status-quo became clearer, even if they were still ambivalent towards the nationalist movement.[165] Nevertheless, Colin Morris, Protestant missionary and close ally of some of the nationalists was to write:

> In January 1958, the Northern Rhodesian Bishops issued a joint pastoral letter which is one of the most important statements of race relations ever to be made in the Federation.[166]

In the name of Christian charity and justice the letter advocated a multi-racial society where the rights of all would be respected and where forced segregation and all forms of discrimination on the basis of colour

---

[161] Letter from Vicar Apostolic, Abercorn, to Apostolic Delegate, Mombasa. (Bishop's Archives, Mpika); The Seventh Day Adventists in the south had a similar dilemma with their African members. See: W. Hazemba, "The Seventh Day Adventist Church and State in Zambia: 1905-1990," (RS 400 research essay, 1996); M. Dixon-Fyle, "The Seventh Day Adventists (S.D.A.) in the protest politics of the Tonga Plateau, Northern Rhodesia," *African Social Research* 26 (December 1978), pp. 453-67.

[162] Ipenburg, *All Good Men*, p. 219.

[163] Letter from Vicar Apostolic, Abercorn, to Education Secretary General, Lusaka, 17 June 1955. (Bishop's Archives, Mpika).

[164] Garvey, *Bembaland Church*, p. 181; See also: Minutes of Northern Rhodesia Bishops' Conference, 20-22 Nov 1956. C.S.A.

[165] See: Carmody, *Conversion and Jesuit Schooling*, pp. 91-3; Haynes, *Religion and Politics in Africa*, pp. 61, 64.

[166] Colin Morris, *The Hour after Midnight* (London: Longmans, 1961), p. 154.

should end.[167]

More forthright support for the nationalists followed somewhat later through the appearance of newspapers like *The Leader* and *The Star*, inspired by the Irish priest Fr. Patrick Walsh S.J. who had been a founder member of an interracial club in Kabulonga, Lusaka, and had developed friendship ties with such nationalists as Harry Nkumbula and Kenneth Kaunda. When asked if *The Leader* or *The Star* helped the Independence campaign, Dr. Kaunda replied:

> Yes. Because they were about the only papers which could express the feelings of the – if I may call them – black masses in those days.[168]

Moreover, on numerous occasions in later years, Dr. Kaunda was to speak with affection about Fr. Walsh's support in those times. At the Golden Jubilee of Lusaka's Regiment Church, he recalled with emotion that:

> Father Patrick Walsh was very much a man who identified with the hopes and aspirations of the Zambian people at a time when these hopes and aspirations were in the process of formation...At times during the Independence campaigns in this country when our movements were restricted he visited me and brought me books in prison. Furthermore, Father Walsh helped ease my responsibilities by arranging school places for my children.[169]

The interracial club which Walsh helped to establish provided a forum for some dialogue between African and European:

> In the years between 1953 and 1962, it was about the only place that Africans and Europeans could meet and talk. Father Walsh, along with Mr. Harry Franklin, was founder of the organisation[170]

Even if support for the nationalist cause by the Catholic authorities remained guarded, they were very much concerned that this movement would not become unduly influenced by communist ideology and eventually go the way of China in 1949.[171]

---

[167] Joint Pastoral Letter of the Bishops of Northern Rhodesia. 6 January 1958. J.A.C. See also: "Catholics have not always been vocal," *Times of Zambia* (1 Feb 1999); "Catholics were vocal against colonialists." *Times of Zambia* (24 Feb 1999).
[168] Dr. K.D. Kaunda, Interview, Lusaka, 19 February 1999.
[169] Speech by His Excellency the President, Comrade Dr. Kenneth D. Kaunda, at the Golden Jubilee Celebrations of Regiment Church, 26 November 1989.
[170] *Northern Star* (4 June 1964) J.A.C.
[171] See: Hastings, *The Church in Africa*, p. 571. It is also worth noting that Fr. Walsh had been a missionary to China earlier while the Irish Jesuits were very alert to what happened in China since they had many confreres working in nearby Hong Kong.

This gradual shift to greater criticism by the Catholic leaders of the colonial administration and their more open support of the nationalist cause did not entirely save the Church's schools and teachers from nationalist attack. On the parish level, perhaps Oger's description of Ilondola would be fairly typical. He noted:

> It can be said that the missionaries at Ilondola did not take any political action, respected lawful authorities but silently sided with the people against injustices or lack of Christian charity. This policy of non-involvement was not appreciated by the colonial government.[172]

It is not clear that the policy was appreciated by the nationalists either for many Catholic schools and, in a number of cases, churches became the target of nationalist, mainly UNIP, protest. Moreover, teachers in the schools were often perceived by the nationalists to be traitors. As one teacher related: "We were civil servants and UNIP regarded us as informers...They were anti-Church".[173] Another teacher recalled: "Political cadres intimidated us. We'll burn your house, they would say. We were a class apart. We were treated as spies."[174]. Mr. Jonas Sokoni, a Catholic teacher from Ilondola, who took Kenneth Kaunda's place as a teacher in Mufulira noted:

> As teachers we were afraid. I remember we asked Kaunda and Kapepwe not to visit the school. I took Kaunda's place at Mufulira. Politicians thought we were siding with the colonial government.[175]

At Ilondola, in 1953, so as to create an impression that the teachers were on the nationalist side, a teacher wrote to the newspaper to say that more than fifty pupils had joined A.N.C. and that those who had no money borrowed from the teachers.[176]

As the Federation's collapse neared, secondary schools seem to have been used as instruments of nationalist protest especially through instigating strikes. In this context, strikes at Catholic institutions like Canisius secondary school, St. Francis, Malole, St Paul's, Mulungushi, St. John's, Mongu, formed part of a more general anti-colonial strategy. In March 1960, the headmaster of St. John's, Mongu, wrote:

---

[172] Oger, *Where a scattered flock*, p. 229.

[173] Abel Mutale, Teacher. Interview, Chilubula, 16 July 1996.

[174] P. Mumpangwe, Teacher, Interview, Mansa, 23 July 1996.

[175] Jonas Sokoni, Teacher. Interview, 11 July 1996, Ilondola. Similar sentiments were expressed by Henry Chakobe, Ilondola, (11 July 1996) and Chikolokoso, Chilonga (8 July 1996).

[176] See: *African Eagle* (3 March 1953); Letter from Vicar Apostolic to P.E.O., Kasama, 15 March 1953; Headmaster to *African Eagle* (15 March 1953). (N.A.Z. Ed 1/5/47).

> The present policy of African politicians seems to be aimed at causing trouble in all the secondary schools in the country. So many of the present leaders of agitation have failed academically but they apparently want to see nobody doing well at school. Besides they know that expelled schoolboys are the best source of recruits for their organisations.[177]

There is little evidence to suggest that Catholic secondary schools were any more supportive of the colonial hegemony or that they predisposed the elite to acceptance of alien suzerainty than others. In fact, in the case of Canisius and St. John's with their Irish element in terms of Irish Jesuits and Capuchins, there is some indication that they were perhaps less loyal to the system than others.[178] As in the case of the attacks on the Catholic primary schools and rural churches, the strikes in these institutions were not directed against the Catholic Church so much as against the overall colonial set up. In fact, at least one mission offered a hide-out for the freedom fighters.[179] It is of course possible that in some cases personal antagonism or denominational rivalry could have contributed to the attacks on the missions.[180]

Through its commitment to schooling of a more secular type at the primary and later at the secondary level, one might say that the Catholic Church had begun to identify with the new men and women, who on the whole were urban-oriented. Although the Church had started its days among the peasants of Kayambi and Syantumbu, it had also accompanied many of the emerging elite to the Copperbelt towns as well as to Lusaka and Livingstone through its schools and urban parishes. Moreover, many of its school people were among State House staff when Zambia gained its Independence in 1964 even if, in the words of one of them:

> I suppose it is the Catholic fatalistic ascetic view of life which made our school products not really interested in going into politics and yet those

---

[177] Letter from Headmaster to Education Secretary General, 22 March 1960 (Bishop's Archives, Livingstone). Canisius was operated by Irish Jesuits and St. John's by Irish Capuchins.

[178] B. Carmody, "Jesuit Mission School: Ally of Zambian Nationalism?" *Zambia Journal of History* No. 5 (1992).

[179] Hinfelaar, *Bemba-Speaking Women*, p. 146; This was confirmed in an interview where Fr. Hinfelaar told me that he himself was one of the missionaries involved in giving refuge to the freedom fighters. (Interview, Lusaka, 17 March 1997).

[180] Garvy, *Bembaland Church*, p. 183. This was confirmed by Dr. Kaunda who stated that the U.N.I.P. never had an anti-Church campaign. It could have been individuals who did this but it was not policy. K.D. Kaunda, Interview, Lusaka, 19 Feb 1999. On the general strikes of the era, see: *Northern Rhodesia: Report of the Commission of Inquiry into disturbances in certain African schools* (Lusaka: Government Printer, 1960).

who went into politics were so committed that they got into the top positions and were very loyal.[181]

Reflecting on the overall political involvement of the Catholic Church in the colonial era, a prominent Catholic noted:

> I don't think they (Catholic Church leaders) impressed me in any way by the issues they championed, but they did impress me with the sense of personal care they showed to us as students and to the villagers.[182]

Similarly, when Dr. Kaunda, former head of state and leader of U.N.I.P., was asked if he felt that the Catholic Church should have been more in the forefront of the critique of colonialism, he reported:

> I will not hesitate to say yes. They should have been more involved, but I think that the weakness of the Church as a whole was taken care of by what individual priests did.[183]

Like other secondary schools in the colonial period, the Catholic schools provided an intertribal setting where inevitably a transtribal consciousness began to take shape. The Catholic schools generally included only Catholics where, as one student remembered:

> Going to Chikuni (Canisius in 1950) was more than going to Tongaland... You went to a mission where you belonged. It was the first time all the Catholic students throughout Zambia met there as secondary school students and thus learned to recognise and know each other under the roof of the Church. I think that was the most important experience I had there.[184]

The Catholic schools helped to give their students a sense of being Zambian Catholics rather than Bemba or Lozi Catholics, thus paving the way to national consciousness. While the school system fitted the British pattern with sports, houses, prefects, and Cambridge certificates, it is unclear to what extent such schools were designed to prepare an elite for participatory politics as Hastings argued.[185] Frequently, such

---

[181] Dominic Mulaisho, Teacher 1953-57, lecturer Charles Lwanga College, 1960-62. Interview, Lusaka, 13 December 1983.

[182] Elias Chipimo, interview, Lusaka, 12 December 1983: Lusaka, 9 March 1997.

[183] Dr. K.D. Kaunda, Interview, Lusaka, 19 February 1999.

[184] Elias Chipimo, interview, Lusaka, 12 December 1983. See also: Berman, *African Reactions*, p. 42; Moreover, according to Colson, at this time there was little objection to using English as a common language. ("Bantu Botatwe," p. 67.); J. Wakeford, *The Cloistered Elite* (New York: Praeger, 1969); Abernethy, *The Political Dilemma*, pp. 256-7; J.S. Coleman, *Nigeria: Background to Nationalism* (Berkeley: University of California Press), p. 104.

[185] Adrian Hastings, "The Churches and Democracy: Reviewing a Relationship" in Gifford, *The Christian Churches and the Democratisation of Africa*, pp. 15, 40: See also J.W.

institutions had highly autocratic administrations while the education itself focused more on passing exams than on personal development. Moreover, the education provided had an almost exclusively Catholic focus which would not have been particularly favourable to preparing its recipients for life in a multi-denominational state.

The Catholic Church gained many converts throughout Zambia during this era. One may ask: To what extent were they converted? This is difficult to assess. To what degree the reception of the sacraments really touched the inner life of the converts remains obscure. What is clear is that the nature of the conversion process stressed understanding and acceptance of foreign ways rather than emotional and critical assimilation. In many instances, this led to the Sunday Catholic mentality, where people attended church on Sunday morning but accused their neighbour of witchcraft that afternoon and had a secret second wife. As one Catholic put it:

> Up to now we in Africa have been faced with the concept of double think—the power of holding two contradictory beliefs simultaneously, and accepting both of them.[186]

While the cognitive dimension of conversion was strongly emphasised, especially in the religious education programmes, there was some affective appeal especially in the liturgy, even though Gregorian chant and the celebration of European saints' feasts had little immediate resonance.[187] Nonetheless, devotional practices like school retreats, pilgrimages, novenas and Benediction did seem to appeal. Perhaps there was an informal indiginization where in the words of one student of the day "We had naturalised Mass in the sense in which we were singing vernacular hymns."[188] However, there was little attempt at an official

---

De Cruchy, *Christianity and Democracy* (Cambridge University Press, 1995), p. 169; David Kamens, "Education and Democracy: a comparative institutional analysis," *Sociology of Education* vol. 61, 2 (1988): 120.

[186] Chisengalumbwe, "The Repercussions of Colonial Religions." See also: A. Shorter, *African Christian Theology* (New York: Orbis Books, 1977), p. 10; Desmond Tutu, "Whither African Theology," in E. Fashole-Luke, ed. *Christianity in Independent Africa* (London: Rex Collings, 1978), p. 366.

[187] The catechism was the main instrument of instruction. From the 1950s, the Bishops were generally concerned not about the method but about the need to standardise catechisms. See: Minutes of Ordinaries' Conference, 30 July 1954; Minutes of Northern Rhodesian Bishops' Conference, 20-22 November 1956; Minutes of Bishops' Conference, 13-14 October 1959; Minutes of the Plenary Meeting of the Northern Rhodesia Episcopal Conference, Lusaka, 9-10 July 1963. C.S.A. On the need to form a nuanced interpretation of this point, see: D. O'Loghlen, review article in *Studies* (Autumn, 1992), pp. 344-46.

[188] E. Chipimo, Interview, 9 March 1997; Adoption not just of vernacular words but of

level to integrate such devotional practices and experiences with the Mass and the central mysteries of faith in a way that truly moved the people. The following reflection may help clarify this phenomenon:

> When I was there (at a Catholic school between 1950 and 1954), catechism was the way...We had to accept without questioning...Yes we had retreats which were deep and rewarding...Today, I don't just accept everything from Fr...I could have been described as an adult with infant faith (my faith was not deep). After two or three years in the Charismatics, this changed...God used to be so distant when the priest said Mass in Latin...There was a sense of awe. God is no longer distant. The idea of a loving faith has become important to me. [189]

Another older Catholic, when asked how he found the changes in the Church reflected:

> I am happy with the changes in Church. You know when we prayed and sang at Mass, we didn't understand what it meant. We were like gramophones but now we enjoy Mass. [190]

The Church to which African converts were introduced through the schools was psychologically distant. It is hardly surprising therefore that Catholicism became like an overcoat, hardly touching the underlying reality of the Zambian personality especially in issues connected with witchcraft.[191] This is not to infer that the missionaries like Moreau, Dupont, and countless others failed to touch the inner lives of the people. They did this especially through their work of translation and familiarity with the vernacular languages. The Tonga, for instance, regarded Moreau as one of their own and so wanted to accord him a traditional funeral, which many Tonga felt he would have appreciated.[192] However, few of Moreau's generation were in a position to inculturate the liturgy which remained alien to the new converts.

Furthermore, the school through whose doors many entered the church appeared alien and the instrument of an alienating political system. To use McLaren's terminology, the student state with its emphasis on instructional rituals, monochromatic time, punctuality, hard work and large-scale acceptance of an alien suzerainty and ideology

---

music and rhythm in the 1970s greatly enhanced the inculturation effort. Frank Wafer, S.J. Interview, Chikuni, 19 July 1997.

[189] Silverio Lwiindi Chimuka, Lusaka, 21 June 1984.

[190] Elias Kasia, Interview, Kasisi, June 1995. Mr. Kasia was well over seventy years old at the time of the interview. He had converted to Catholicism as a young man in 1938.

[191] L. Oger, *Our Missionary Shadow* (Lusaka, n.d.), p. 21, 24,32.

[192] B. Carmody, "Secular and Sacred at Chikuni 1905-1940," *Journal of Religion in Africa*, 21 (1991), p. 134; See also: Hastings, *The Church in Africa*, p. 590.

dwarfed the fragmentary attention dedicated to the sanctity, street corner, and home states, which constituted the bulk of what rendered life meaningful.[193] Catholic authorities seem to have done little to indigenize the school curriculum, particularly after the establishment of the Education department in 1925, even though they were represented on the Educational Advisory Board. As one Jesuit ex-headmaster of Canisius commented:

> The church did not participate enough in changing the system—it was too busy running it. Even religious education was from very out-dated books.[194]

Despite this double source of alienation from both church and school, Zambians gained some means with which to carve their destiny, both personal and social, in the new world of modern life.[195] Ideally, the Church demanded more personal investment and assimilation of its message than the school. However, even here, as Fisher has noted, many Catholics probably moved from what he has termed the quarantine to the reform stage without going through the mixing stage.[196] The overall result seems to have been that there were, as Oger, a long time Catholic missionary among the Bemba, put it:

> two levels of thinking, from below, the unconscious intuitive and inborn level, from above, the intellectual and mental level.[197]

Until such time as the mixing stage would occur both levels would

---

[193] McLaren, *Schooling as a Ritual Performance*, pp. 83-112.

[194] R. Cremins, S.J. Interview, Lusaka, December 1983; See also: C. MacKenzie, "Demythologising the Missionaries: a reassessment of the functions and relationships of Christian missionary education under colonialism," *Comparative Education* Vol. 29, no. 1 (1993), p. 54; On this topic of alienation in schools, see: R. Zimba, "Education for Authentic African Development." (n.d.); A.J. Simpson, "Religious Formations in a Postcolony: an ethnographic study of a Zambian Mission School." (Ph.D. dissertation, University of Manchester, 1996); Francis Carey, "Conscientization and in-service Education of Zambian Primary School Teachers," (Ph.D. dissertation, University of London, 1986).

[195] Melville J. Herskovits, *The Human Factor in Changing Africa* (New York: Vintage Books, 1957), p. 223.

[196] See: H. Fisher, "Conversion Rediscovered: Some Historical Aspects of Religious Change in Black Africa," *Africa* XLIII (1973), pp. 27-40; "The Juggernaut's Apologia: Conversion to Islam in Black Africa," *Africa* 55, 2(1985), pp. 153-73. See also: B. Carmody, "Conversion to Roman Catholicism in Zambia: Shifting Pedagogies," *African Christian Studies*, vol. 4, 2 (June 1988), pp. 12-13. When I state that I think Fisher has overstated the case, I had in mind that devout Catholics often became victims of witchcraft so that at a subconscious level there must have been some mixing.

[197] Oger, *Our Missionary Shadow*, p. 32; Carey, "Conscientization and in-service Education." Tutu speaks of schizophrenia in the new converts. See: D. Tutu, "Whither African Theology?", p. 366.

remain not only quite distinct but separate in the person, with little conscious attempt to integrate them.

CHAPTER THREE

CONVERSION AND SCHOOL: 1964-1995

In 1964, at Independence, the Church in Zambia had one archdiocese, Lusaka, and seven dioceses. As in other parts of Africa, it was white-led.[1] All the bishops were expatriates. This situation was quickly to change. In 1965, a Zambian priest, Fr. Chabukasansha was appointed Bishop of Kasama. The process of Zambianization continued. In 1969, Pope Paul VI ordained Fr. Emmanuel Milingo as Archbishop of Lusaka. He replaced Archbishop Adam Kozlowiecki who had been bishop there since 1950. In 1971, two other Zambian priests, Frs. Medardo Mazombwe and Elias Mutale were ordained bishops in the dioceses of Chipata and Mansa, for in July 1970, Bishop Courtemanche of Chipata and in February 1971 Bishop Pailloux of Mansa resigned. Three years later, when the diocese of Kasama became vacant with the resignation of Bishop Chabukasansha, Bishop Mutale moved there as Bishop, while Fr. James Spaita took his place in Mansa. Thus, ten years after Independence, five of Zambia's nine bishops were Zambian. In July 1972, Bishop Mazombwe of Chipata became the first Zambian to chair the Zambian Episcopal Conference (Z.E.C.).

Although the top leadership was swiftly Zambianizing, by 1966 only 12% of the 374 priests, 4.5% of the 135 brothers, and 21% of the 528 sisters were Zambian. Nonetheless, the situation was changing for in 1968 there were 430 seminarians throughout the country, while the novitiates of both the brothers and sisters received large numbers of candidates. In April 1973, the national seminary shifted from Kachebere on the Malawian border to Kabwe. By 1984, 16% of the 515 priests, 18% of the 161 brothers, and 39% of the 731 sisters were now Zambian. In that year, seven of the nine dioceses had Zambian bishops or archbishops. In 1996, 33% of the 200 diocesan priests, 42% of the 864 religious men, and 62% of the 1135 religious women were Zambian. What needs to be kept in mind, however, is that in those years since Independence, the Catholic population had increased from 571,208 in 1965 to 1,626,608 in 1983, and to 2,136,000 or approximately 24% of the total population in 1996.[2]

---

[1] Hastings, *African Catholicism*, p. 122
[2] *Impact* 102 (March 1984); *Catholic Directory* (1996).

Even though the bishops were encouraged by the numbers of seminarians and candidates for the religious life, at their meeting in February 1971 they stressed the great need for lay leaders from local communities. This stress on lay local community leadership gained momentum in the years following when the idea of Small Christian Communities (S.C.C.) became more pivotal in the Zambian Church. This had begun in South America and essentially meant breaking down large groups into more intimate prayer focused communities. In 1973, the Study Conference of the Association of Member Episcopal Conferences in East Africa (AMECEA) concluded that the Church in Africa would succeed only in the measure to which the entire community was involved. By 1976, a number of Zambian dioceses had adopted the Small Christian Community pastoral approach. In 1984, the Zambian Church was singled out by Rev. Oscar Hirmer from the Lumko Educational Institute of the South African Bishops' Conference for special praise because of the headway it had made in the establishment and development of Small Christian Communities. Over the years, the Small Christian Communities method of evangelisation has become a very central part of the Zambian Church. In 1996, Zambia was reckoned to have about 8,704 Small Christian Communities.

In 1967, the Catholic Church operated 644 primary schools, which represented 20% of the overall primary schools in the country. For reasons that we shall discuss, the Catholic Church handed over these schools to government in 1974. However, between 1964 and 1995, the Catholic Church's investment in secondary schools increased considerably and in 1967, Catholic schools had approximately 21% of all secondary school students in their care. By 1995, of the 150 government and grant-aided schools offering schooling at Grades 10-12, 17% were Catholic-managed. These schools provided secondary facilities for 13% of all the boys and 31% of all the girls in secondary schools of this category. In all, they provided roughly 14,000 or 6.5% of total secondary school places.[3] At the teacher training level, the Catholic Church developed and maintained two of the nine teacher colleges, catering for approximately 700 students annually.

CATHOLIC PERSPECTIVES ON SCHOOLING

On May 17, 1959, Pope John XXIII designated a commission to prepare for a major ecumenical Council. This came to be known later as

---

[3] Ministry of Education, *Educating our Future. National Policy on Education* (February 1996), p. 50.

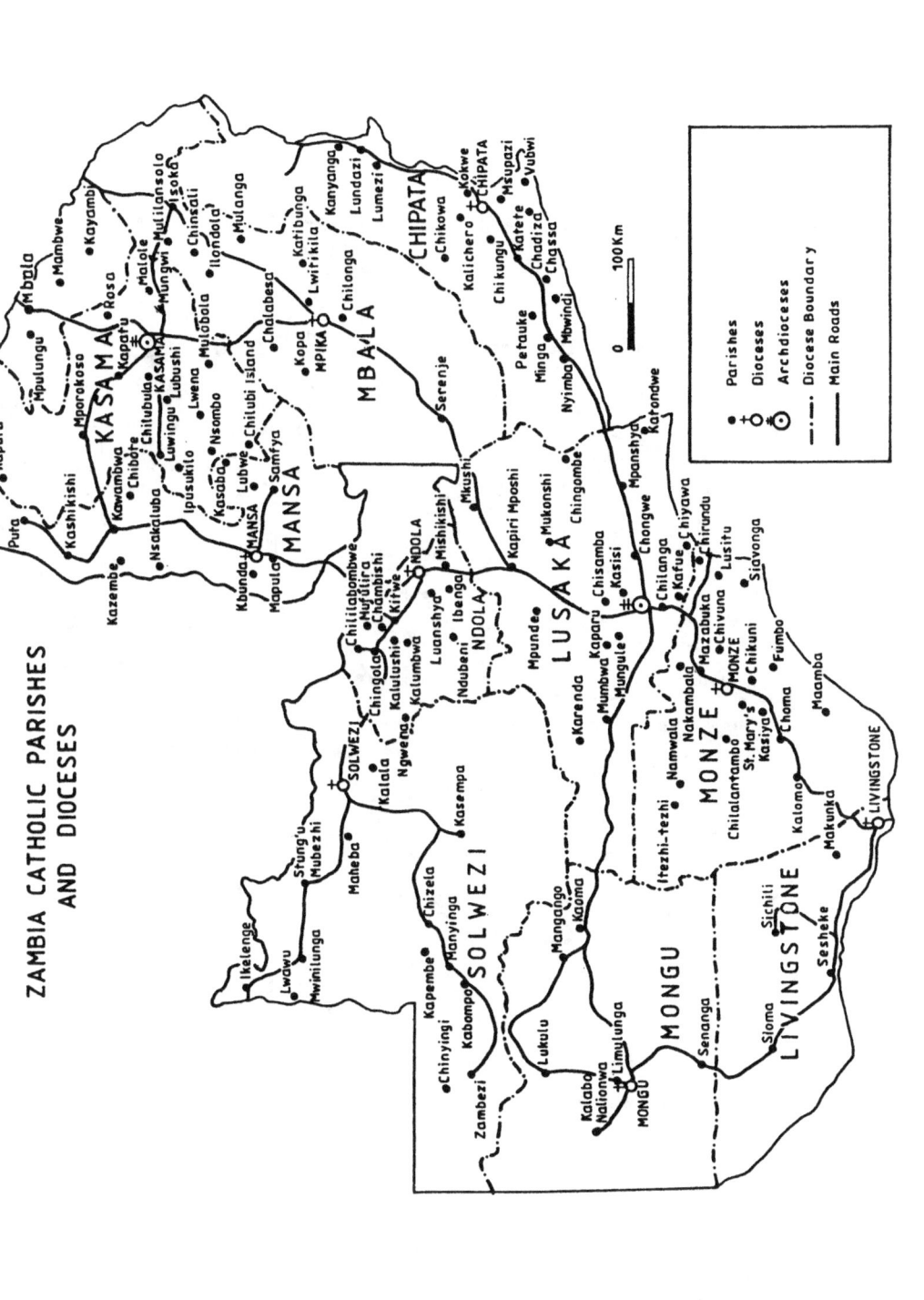

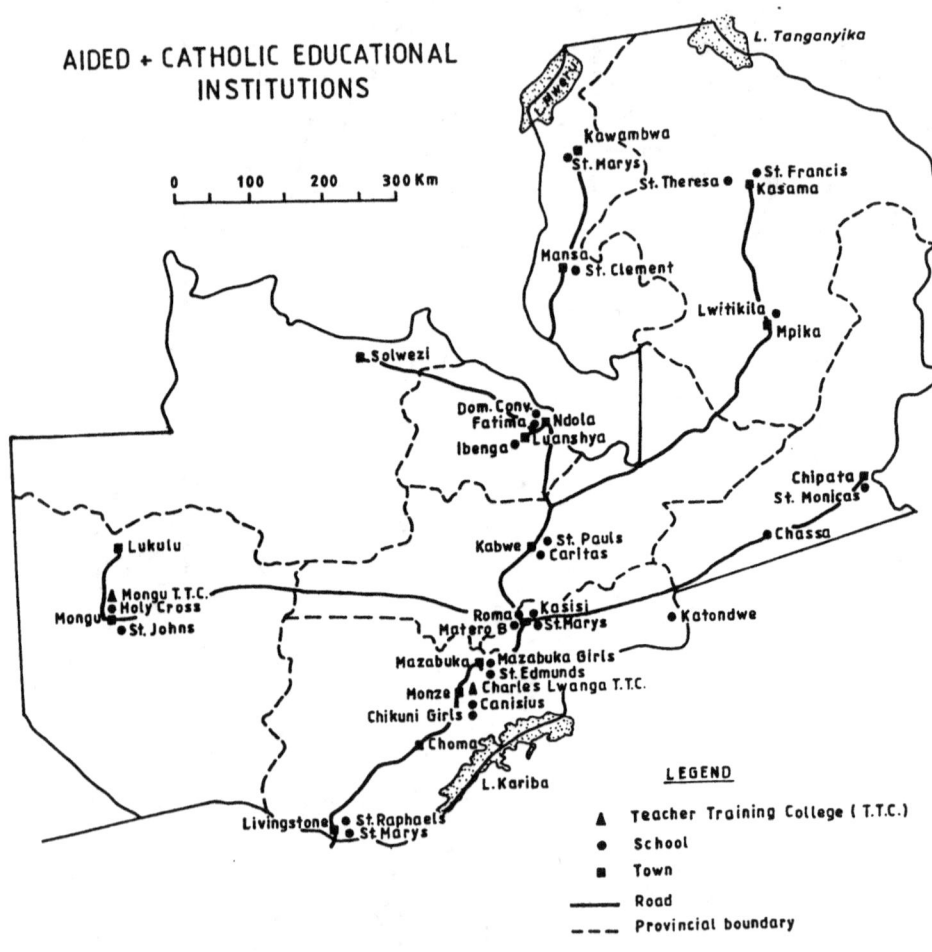

the Second Vatican Council. It was held in Rome between October 11, 1962 and December 8, 1965. Four hundred years after the Council of Trent, this world-wide meeting of Catholic bishops was to have a very significant impact on the subsequent direction of the Catholic Church.

When the Council ended in 1965, earlier Catholic emphases on the conversion of pagans to Catholicism and the need to build up the institutional church remained. One of the major Council documents, "Lumen Gentium," focused on Christ as the light of all peoples. This document presented the Church of Christ, the true Church, subsisting in the Catholic Church. The Church of Christ and the Catholic Church no longer appeared co-terminal. It was thereby admitted that other churches and religious traditions could form part of the Church of Christ.[4] This more open attitude to other religious traditions marked a significant milestone in the subsequent direction of the Church. Thus, it was considered that those who had not received the Gospel could know Christ through their consciences.[5] The Council did not intend this to mean that the Church was unnecessary for salvation. Rather, the Council members wished to emphasise that non-Roman Catholics could also form part of the community of salvation.[6] The Council stressed that all peoples are called to belong to the Church of Christ, which is constituted by different groups who share, in varying degrees, in the unity of Christ.[7] The document went on to describe how this might be true:

> This holy Council first of all turns its attention to the Catholic faithful. Basing itself on scripture and tradition, it teaches that the Church, a pilgrim now on earth, is necessary for salvation, the one Christ is mediator and way of salvation, he is present to us in his body which is the Church.
> Fully incorporated into the Church are those who, possessing the Spirit of Christ, accept all the means of salvation given to the Church together with her entire organisation, and who by the bonds constituted by the profession of faith, the sacraments, ecclessial government and communion are joined in the visible structure of the Church of Christ, who rules her through the

---

[4] "Lumen Gentium," sec 8, in Walter M. Abbott, ed. *The Documents of Vatican II* (New York: Guild Press, 1966); See: David J. Bosch, *Transforming Mission* (New York: Orbis, 1994), pp. 371-2; R.J. Schreiter, "Changes in Roman Catholic attitudes towards Proselytism and Mission," in J.A. Scherer, S.B. Bevans, eds. *New Directions in Mission and Evangelisation* 2 (New York: Orbis, 1994), pp. 116-125.

[5] Ibid., sec 16. On this point, see: Karl Rahner, "Anonymous Christianity and the Missionary Task of the Church" in *Theological Investigations* (New York: Seabury Press, 1974), Vol. XII, pp. 161-78. Translated by David Bourke.

[6] "Missions," sec. 1; "Ecumenism," sec 3, in Abbott, *The Documents of Vatican II*.

[7] "Lumen Gentium," sec. 8, 13-16.

Supreme Pontiff and the bishops.[8]

The document noted how those Christians who do not profess the Catholic faith in its entirety are joined with Catholics. The decree stated:

> These Christians are indeed in some real way joined to us in the Holy Spirit for, by His gifts and graces, his sanctifying power is also active in them.[9]

Jews, Moslems and people of other religious faiths also form part of the Catholic faith.[10] While the Council proclaimed the uniqueness of Christ who is the way, it rejected nothing of what is true and holy in other religions.[11] As a result of this way of perceiving other Christian Churches and religious traditions, new attitudes towards traditional mission work ensued. One might ask if the Council considered it legitimate to "convert" people to Christ? In its decree on religious freedom, the Council declared: "...the human person has a right to religious freedom based on the dignity of the human person".[12] Although the Council maintained the uniqueness of Christ as revealed through the Catholic tradition, it clearly rejected any methods of conversion that implied coercion.

Respect for the dignity of the human person underpinned the decree "Gaudium et Spes," leading to a strong emphasis on the need for a more just and humane world order.[13] This aspect of Catholic thought had been stressed by Pope John XXIII, but Pope Paul VI's encyclical, "*Populorum Progressio*," articulated it more thoroughly.[14] This concern for a more just world persisted throughout the period under discussion. It was clearly reflected at the Medellin Conference of Bishops in 1968, as well as by repeated Papal exhortations to transform the structures of society. Pope Paul VI, in "*Evangelisation in the Modern World*," noted that:

> The Church considers it to be undoubtedly important to build up structures that are more human, more just, more respectful of the rights of the person, and less oppressive and enslaving.[15]

---

[8] Ibid., sec. 14.
[9] Ibid., sec. 15.
[10] Ibid., sec 16.
[11] "Ecumensim," sec. 2.
[12] "Declaration on Religious Liberty," sec. 1.
[13] "Gaudium et Spes," secs. 9, 12, 15, 16, 17, 23, 27, 29.
[14] Pope John Paul VI, "*Populorum Progressio*," in Joseph Gremillion, ed. *The Gospel of Peace and Justice* (New York: Orbis Books, 1975), pp. 387-415.
[15] Pope Paul VI, "*Evangelisation in the Modern World*." (Washington D.C.: U.S. Conference of Bishops, 1976)

Continuing this tradition, in his post-Synod address of 1995 to the Church of Africa, Pope John Paul II endorsed this tradition when he stated:

> Integral human development—the development of every person and the whole person, especially of the poorest and most neglected in the community—is at the very heart of evangelisation and human advancement—development and liberation—there are in fact profound links.[16]

In the same exhortation, the Pope further observed:

> It is impossible to accept that in evangelisation one could or should ignore the importance of the problems so much discussed today, concerning justice, liberation, development and peace in the world.[17]

As Hastings remarks, the Catholic Church in contemporary Africa was profoundly affected by the Second Vatican Council. The image of opening windows coincided excellently with African countries struggle for Independence.[18] However, perhaps except in South Africa, the Church in the years following Independence tended to adopt a cautious approach to local politicians as well as to the Roman Curia.

In the late 1980s, the Catholic Church seemed for a brief moment to take a more unusually prophetic stance in the context of what Gifford called Africa's second liberation where the peoples tried to throw off the post-independence political systems that had served them so badly.[19] In Zambia, the Catholic Church, like other Christian Churches, conscious of her former alliance with the colonial government attempted to maintain good relationships with the post-Independent government. Undoubtedly, the Church took a strong and ultimately victorious stand against Scientific Socialism, but was ineffective as the conscience of the nation in the Termination of Pregnancy Act of 1972. As Lungu argued,

---

[16] Pope John Paul II, "*Post Synodal Apostolic Exhortation Ecclesia in Africa of the Holy Father John Paul II to the Bishops, Priests, and Deacons Men and Women Religious and All the Lay Faithful on the Church in Africa and its Evangelising Mission Towards the Year 2000.*" (Vatican City, 1995), para. 68. Future reference will be to Ecclesia in Africa.

[17] Ibid. See also: C. McGarry, "Ecclesia in Africa," *Hekima Review* 14 (January 1996), pp. 57-63; Brendan Carmody, "Conversion to Roman Catholicism in Zambia: Shifting Pedagogies," *African Christian Studies* Vol. 4, 2(1988), pp. 13-15.

[18] Hastings, *Catholicism*, pp. 125, 126, 136.

[19] Paul Gifford, "Some Recent Developments in African Christianity," *African Affairs* 93 (1994), p. 513; Paul Gifford, "Christian Fundamentalism, State and Policies in Black Africa," in D. Westerlund, ed. *Questioning the Secular State* (London: Hurst, 1996), pp. 198-215; Paul Gifford, ed. *The Christian Churches & the Democratisation of Africa* (Leiden: E.J. Brill, 1995), pp. 1-13; Haynes, *Religion and Politics in Africa*, p. 117.

this working relationship was maintained through employing a language style at once laudatory and occasionally critical of some aspect of government policy. Even after the food riots of 1990, the Catholic Church's criticism, though clear, maintained much of the style that Lungu described as characterising the earlier period. After acknowledging the complexity of the problem underlying the food riots, the Bishops' statement pointed to Zambia's achievements and then asked, among other things, why the economic system benefited the rich at the expense of the poor.[20]

While the Catholic Church at Vatican II had assumed a more ecumenical outlook towards other religious traditions and had decided to take a more forthright position aimed at transforming the world for the better, its view of the role of the Catholic school remained almost exclusively denominational and apolitical. In the document, "The Catholic School," published in 1977, the Sacred Congregation for Catholic Education unambiguously stressed the need for, and the value of, the specifically Catholic school.[21] However, the document was far from clear on the specific nature of the Catholic school. Rather, it is spoken of as a meeting place for those who wish to express Christian values in education: "The Catholic school, far more than any other, must be a community whose aim is the transmission of values for living."[22] It would lose its purpose without constant reference to the Gospel and a frequent encounter with Christ. It should not be divisive and should avoid any one-sided proselytism.[23] Nonetheless the document's authors tended to presume that students and teachers at Catholic schools would be almost totally Catholic. It was envisaged that the school would contribute to the formation of a more egalitarian society:

> Since it is motivated by the Christian ideal, the Catholic school is particularly sensitive to the call from every part of the world for a more just society, and it tries to make its own contribution towards it. It does not stop at the courageous teaching of the demands of justice even in the face of local opposition, but it tries to put these demands into practice in its own

---

[20] Gatian Lungu, "The Church, Labour and the Press in Zambia: The Role of critical observers in a one party state," *African Affairs* Vol. 83, 340 (July 1986), pp. 385-410. "Economics, Politics and Justice: Pastoral Statement of the Bishops of Zambia." (Catholic Secretariat, July 1990).

[21] *"The Catholic School."* (Office of Publishing Services: U.S. Catholic Conference, Washington D.C.), para. 3, 8, 12, 14, 24, 75, 77.

[22] *The Catholic School*, para. 53.

[23] Ibid., para. 57, 19.

community in the daily life of the school.[24]

Quoting the "Declaration on Christian Education," from Vatican II, the document clearly affirmed the need for Catholic schools to offer their educational services to "the poor or those who are deprived." It cautioned:

> ...if the Catholic school were to turn its attention exclusively or predominantly to those from the wealthier social classes, it could be contributing towards maintaining their privileged position, and could thereby continue to favour a society that is unjust.[25]

In this post-Vatican II period, then, the Catholic Church had significantly extended its mission. It still aimed to increase its membership, but it further endeavoured to struggle for a more just and humane world. In continuing to develop and maintain its schools, the Church wished to emphasise both the need to educate Catholic youth and to help create a better world.

ZAMBIAN GOVERNMENT AND SCHOOLS

At Independence in 1964, Zambia had a very limited pool of educated labour. There were only 110,000 living persons who had received six years of schooling by 1963. A total of 32,000 Africans had completed the full primary school course of eight years. Only 4,420 had passed the two-year Junior Secondary Course (Form II) and a mere 961 were known to have passed the Cambridge School Certificate (Form V). Zambia could only count 1,200 Zambians with full secondary school certificates.[26] As the *Zambian Manpower Report* of 1965 put it: Zambia was less prepared (for Independence) than most African countries.[27]

To Zambianize (place Zambian nationals in positions of leadership) the new state, an immediate and extensive linear expansion of the existing educational system appeared imperative. This was needed not only to fuel growth but also, and perhaps just as importantly, to consolidate control and legitimise the new government's own position in

---

[24] Ibid., para. 58.
[25] Ibid.
[26] John Mwanakatwe, *The Growth of Education in Zambia since Independence* (Lusaka: Oxford University Press, 1968), p. 37.
[27] *Manpower Report*, p. 1, as quoted in John Saxby, "The Politics of Education in Zambia" (Unpublished Ph.D. thesis, University of Toronto, 1980), pp. 235, 297; See also: Edward Murphy, "Changing Educational Policy of the Catholic Voluntary Organisations with reference to Zambia," (Essay for the Post Graduate Certificate of Education at the University of Zambia, 1972), pp. 8-12.

a fragile situation where tribalism remained a potential hazard.[28] Understandably, therefore, the new government set out to correct the colonial legacy in education. Indeed, the colonial neglect had fuelled the nationalist cause as championed by the United National Independence Party (U.N.I.P.). This party that had gained political power had placed education as one of its key policies. Their 1962 policy statement read:

> Everyone has a right to education. Education shall be free, at least in the elementary and fundamental stages. The state shall require that all children receive a certain minimum education.[29]

A further cardinal U.N.I.P. policy pivoted around the need to desegregate. Included, to some extent, in this desire to desegregate the schooling system was a parallel wish to abolish denominational barriers. These, as we have noted, reached back to the first days of Christian evangelisation of the country.[30] The U.N.I.P. manifesto had declared that education should be compulsory, free, and in no way subject to the individual's creed, colour, or sex.[31] As Saxby commented, the educational policy of the new government may be described in essence as "the massive expansion, elaboration and desegregation (i.e., Zambianization) of existing colonial structures." [32]

Massive expansion of the educational system certainly followed in the early years of Independence, particularly after the abolition of school fees in 1965.[33] Intake to Form I increased from 4,639 in 1964 to 19,254 in 1974. The rapid increase in secondary school provision included the expansion of all existing schools and the building of many others. In 1966 alone, the country doubled its secondary intake:

> thereby creating in one year more new secondary opportunities for Africans than had been supplied in the whole seventy years of Company, colonial, and Federal rule.[34]

The years that followed witnessed even greater expansion at the secondary school level.

At the primary level, the Addis Ababa Conference resolutions of

---

[28] Saxby, "The Politics of Education," p. 294; See: Elizabeth Colson, "Bantu Botatwe," p. 69; A.R. Thompson, *Education and Development in Africa*, pp. 49, 51, 54.

[29] United National Independence Party Policy, p. 4, as quoted in Saxby, "The Politics of Education", p. 237.

[30] Murphy, "Changing Educational Policy", p. 34.

[31] U.N.I.P. as in Saxby, "The Politics of Education", p. 238.

[32] Saxby, "The Politics of Education," p. 260.

[33] Mwanakatwe, *The Growth of Education in Zambia*, p. 70.

[34] Ministry of Education, *Annual Report* 1966 (Lusaka: Government Printer, 1967)

1961 advocated universal primary education by 1980. This objective needs to be seen in the context of the 1960s. In 1963, the record figure of 342,105 primary pupils was reached, which nevertheless only represented 62% of the boys and 45% of the girls who should have been in primary schools.[35] Between 1964 and 1978, the number of children in primary school increased from 378,417 to 964,475. By 1980, primary school enrolment as a proportion of the nominal primary school age group (7-14 year olds) was 83.7% as opposed to 58% in 1966.[36]

Parallel developments took place at the Teacher Training level. In 1966, the overall number of teachers employed was 10,864. In the context of the expansion envisaged, it became necessary to embark on an intensive teacher training campaign with the extension of existing facilities and the opening of two new primary Teacher Training Colleges. These opened at Ft. Jameson (currently Chipata) and Kasama. They replaced the Catholic mission colleges at Chilubula and Minga and the Dutch Reformed College at Katete respectively.[37] The number of students in primary teacher colleges increased from 1,603 in 1966 to 2,146 in 1970.[38] Meanwhile, secondary teachers' colleges were opened, Nkrumah in Kabwe in 1969 and Copperbelt Teachers' College at Itempi near Kitwe in 1974 to supply, together with the University of Zambia, Evelyn Hone College in Lusaka, and Luanshya College the teachers that would be needed for this dramatic expansion.[39] Howsoever, from the time of embarking on the school expansion programme until Zambian teachers would be ready for service, it was necessary to employ teachers from outside Zambia. In 1966 alone, over 560 primary and secondary expatriate teachers were recruited. In 1971, 84% of the teachers in the secondary schools and training colleges were non-Zambian, but by 1984, 82% of the total secondary teaching force was Zambian.[40]

Expansion of the system in accord with political promises

---

[35] Mwanakatwe, *The Growth of Education in Zambia*, p. 23. On the wider issue of universal primary education, see: Abernethy, *The Political Dilemma of Popular Education: An African case*, p. 4.

[36] *Educational Statistics 1983* (Lusaka: Government Printer, 1987), p. 43; *Statistical Profile of Zambian Education 1977/78* (Lusaka: Government Printer, 1978); Educational Statistics 1980 (August 1982), p. 31; Saxby, "The Politics of Education", p. 412.

[37] Ministry of Education, *Annual Report 1966* (Lusaka: Government Printer, 1967), p. 21.

[38] Saxby, "The Politics of Education", p. 345.

[39] Michael J. Kelly, *Education in a Declining Economy: The Case of Zambia, 1975-1985* (Washington, D.C., 1991), p. 135.

[40] Saxby, "The Politics of Education in Zambia", p. 237; Kelly, *Education in a Declining Economy*, p. 137; B. Sanyal et al. *Higher Education and the labour market in Zambia: Expectations and Performance* (Uncesco Press, 1976), p. 60.

characterised the early years after Independence. By the late 1960s, however, cracks began to manifest themselves. Securing universal primary schooling proved more difficult than anticipated. In 1969, only 66% of the seven year old children were in school and only 42% of the Grade I places were filled by seven year olds. Both under and over-aged children occupied the remainder.[41] Estimates in the early 1970s indicated that as many as one third of the primary age children in urban areas was not in school.[42] Moreover, in rural areas the proportion of students advancing from lower to upper primary school dropped dramatically.

At the secondary level, there was also a decline in the proportion of Grade VII leavers entering secondary school. As Saxby reported:

> For many Zambians, the ironic corollary of the early growth in educational opportunity proved to be a frustrating and abrupt exclusion from the middle and upper levels of the system.[43]

As we have noted, the government aimed to provide universal primary education as a right for each Zambian and so its attainment was an imperative. There was no such clear-cut rationale for secondary schooling. Among other things, a central objective of the secondary schools was to select a Zambian administrative cadre. In the late 1960s, the school was frequently viewed by governments as the means for achieving national unity, political legitimisation, and equity.[44] Underlying this viewpoint lay what is called the human capital approach to education, which basically maintained that schooling increased peoples' productive capacities. At a national level, investment was seen to enhance economic productivity. By the early 1970s the human capital approach had come under fire. Its ability to create a more equitable and prosperous society became progressively more suspect. In September 1971, the World Bank, after examining the situation at the end of the decade noted:

> Not only is (education) not directly revenue producing; in the present state of our knowledge its economic return is not accurately measurable.[45]

---

[41] Saxby, "The Politics of Education", p. 432.

[42] Ibid., p. 432.

[43] Ibid., p. 436.

[44] Philip H. Coombs, *The World Crisis in Education: The View from the Eighties* (New York: Oxford University Press, 1985), pp. 66, 213, 215ff; A.R. Thompson, *Education and Development in Africa*, pp. 48, 49, 54, 56, 96.

[45] Thompson, *Education and Development*, p. 104; See also: Brendan Carmody, "Denominational Secondary Schooling in post-Independence Zambia: A case study," *African Affairs* Vol. 89, no. 355 (April 1990), pp. 260-1;

In the Zambian situation, by 1970, this selective system of education in operation had already excluded 50,000 children at the Grade VII level who failed to go to Form I. Even in 1969, about 60,000 primary school pupils would fail to obtain a place in Grade V or Form I.[46] Meanwhile, to gain any kind of decent wage employment it was necessary to have secondary schooling. Thus in the Second National Development Plan, we find:

> The annual output from schools, especially from primary schools, far exceeds the growth of new wage-earning jobs. This means increasing numbers of boys and girls must be prepared in the best possible way for self-employment.[47]

Even if the numbers of Zambians in waged employment grew from 269,000 to 384,000 between 1964 and 1970, the numbers of unemployed school leavers increased greatly. In this context, President Kaunda, at the First National Education Conference in 1969 made "a call for serious reform of our educational system."[48] However there followed no immediate or systematic move to reform. Instead, the Second National Development Plan tended to reflect consolidation of planning. It was not until 1973 that reform assumed some momentum. If Saxby is correct, the critical impetus for reform and ideological sanction for a socialist redirection of the economy came from President Kaunda. The socialist dimension had been taking shape for some time previously but in 1974 it became more openly part of the political picture. Kaunda then spoke of socialism as a means, perhaps the means, of preventing the emergence of an elite "whose thoughts and actions are couched in terms of the very rapine system which Humanism was meant to combat."[49]

Between 1974 and 1976, the Ministry of Education engaged itself in the task of re-designing the Zambian educational system. As a result of much consultation and research, a draft proposal appeared in 1976 entitled: *Education for Development*.[50] This proposal outlined ways in

---

[46] Ibid., p. 496.

[47] As quoted in Saxby, "The Politics of Education", p. 447; On a wider context, see: R. Dore, *The Diploma Disease* (Berkeley: University of California Press, 1976), pp. 4-6.

[48] Report on the First National Education Conference held at Evelyn Hone College, Lusaka, 30 September – 2 October 1969, pp. 9, 26-30.

[49] Saxby, "The Politics of Education", pp. 507-10; Kenneth Kaunda, *Humanism Part II* (Lusaka: Government Printer, n.d.), p. 6; Carmody, *Conversion and Jesuit Schooling in Zambia*, p. 107.

[50] *Education for Development: Draft Statement on Educational Reform* (Lusaka: Ministry of Education, 1976).

which the Zambian education system could be transformed to suit the more socialist aspirations of the President. One of the proposals of the draft document included the possibility of increased access to the educational system, especially at the lower levels, which, as we have noted, had become a growing problem. The proposals attempted to break the fast-growing link between higher wages and certification.[51] As we have earlier indicated, government employment policies had exacerbated this problem that was not new. Its roots stretched to the colonial days and extended far beyond Zambia.[52] As the 1970s progressed, more certificate devaluation occurred as the job market began to shrink, leaving Zambia with more and more "educated unemployed."[53] Clearly, the linear expansionist approach to education in national development needed to be reviewed.

However plausible many of the ideals of *Education for Development* may have been, it was quickly superseded by a more conventional document, *Educational Reform*.[54] The reasons for this sudden shift of emphasis still remain far from evident but the political and practical unrealism of the original proposal probably contributed. In Saxby's view:

> Education for Development advocates socialist ideas or principles, but divorces them from any analysis of the reality—the social relations of economic and political power.[55]

Those who were in positions of economic and political power had been propelled there by a system which they were now being asked to dismantle. Such an outcome was unlikely.

What emerged from *Educational Reform* were directives aimed to continue the pre-reform direction of the educational system. The

---

[51] Kenneth Blakemore and Brian Cooksey, *A Sociology of Education for Africa* (London: George Allen and Unwin, 1980), pp. 40-42; R. Dore, *The Diploma Disease*.

[52] Carmody, *Conversion and Jesuit Schooling in Zambia*, p. 108; Thompson, *Educational Development*, p. 84.

[53] Ibid. See also: Coombs, *The World Crisis*, p. 179.

[54] *Educational Reform: Proposals and Recommendations* (Lusaka: Ministry of Education, 1977)

[55] Saxby, "The Politics of Education", p. 651; On the reform movement in Zambia, see: R. Clarke, "Policy and Ideology in Educational Reform in Zambia 1974-78," (M.A. dissertation, University of Lancaster, 1978); Y.G.M. Lulat, "Political Constraints on Educational Reform for Development: lessons from an African experience, *Comparative Educational Review* 26 (1982), pp. 235-53; D.J. Alexander, "Problems of educational reform in Zambia," *International Journal of Educational Development* 3 (1983), pp. 203-22; T. Draisma, *The Struggle against Underdevelopment in Zambia since Independence: what role for education?* (Amsterdam: The Free Press, 1987), pp. 229ff; E.M. Chipimo, "Statement of Education Reforms—An Irrational View," *Zango* No. 2 (April, 1977), pp. 49-71.

document reflected large-scale acceptance of the highly selective, white-collar, credentialist, academic orientation of the educational system in pursuit of a more egalitarian society. This hardly appeared feasible since the educational system that had made reforms necessary was hardly the tool needed to reverse the inegalitarian thrust of the society.

With the progressive decline in copper prices in the late 1970s and the increased school-going population, the educational system inevitably suffered. Nonetheless, expansion of provision continued.[56] In its pursuit of nine years basic education for all, communities were encouraged to add on to primary schools the physical structures needed to enable pupils to continue to Grades 8 and 9. These schools became known as basic schools. Given the expansion programme in the context of diminishing resources, it is not surprising that the quality of the education deteriorated.

Despite the great effort that was made to reform the educational system, little real progress was made in changing the nature and thrust of what was and is being provided even today. Issues of relevance of the curriculum for large numbers who cannot complete the school programme each year has not been systematically addressed. Instead, the education remains highly academic, even when employment opportunities for University graduates are quickly shrinking. While many of the educational reform proposals have been quietly shelved, the concern for equity that they had articulated returned in a 1986 report.[57] This report's somewhat blinkered emphasis on seven years basic education for every child and the consequent implications for secondary and higher education in a situation of shrinking resources, though not radical, manifests some desire for a more equitable order. As Coombs asked:

> How appropriate and useful to the vast majority of primary and secondary school pupils is an education designed primarily to get a tiny minority into the university?[58]

Nonetheless, as in Tanzania, the demand for expansion of secondary school provision continues as the dramatic increase in the number of private schools and Academic Production Units illustrate.[59]

---

[56] Kelly, *Education in a Declining Economy*, pp. 16-25, 27-29.

[57] E.R.I.P., para 1, 5, 7; See: T. Draisma, *The Struggles against Underdevelopment* p. 426; Kelly, *Education in a Declining Economy*, pp. 164, 197.

[58] Coombs, *The World Crisis*, p. 214.

[59] Joel Samoff, "School Expansion in Tanzania: Private Initiatives and Public Policy," *Comparative Education Review* 31, 3 (August, 1987), pp. 333-60; *Focus on Learning* (Lusaka: Ministry of Education, 1992), p. xxi.

Unfortunately, however, the increasingly urgent major issue that the educational reforms were to address still persists. The question remains: how to create an educational system that promotes the welfare of all Zambians, not simply that of a minority?

CATHOLIC RESPONSE TO POST INDEPENDENCE EDUCATIONAL NEEDS

As we noted, after Vatican II, the Catholic Church continued to view schooling as part of its conversion mission. It is hardly a surprise then that the Catholic Church in Zambia remained willing to co-operate with the new government in its efforts to develop the nation. Moreover, for its part, the new nation showed no immediate signs of wishing to dispense with the services of the churches in education. In an address in September 1964 to the staff and students of Canisius College, one of the first secondary schools in the country, the President elect of the Republic of Zambia, Dr. Kenneth Kaunda, commented:

> In coming out to Chikuni, my colleague, the Minister for Education, and I were still and are very conscious of the importance of the contribution to the growth of the country this College makes, and this College has been making, and that this College no doubt will continue to make.[60]

Some years later in an address to the Synod of the United Church of Zambia, President Kaunda clearly articulated his high regard for the contribution of the churches. He noted:

> In the past, as of now, we have been grateful for the work the missionaries did in the field of education. This is exemplified by the fact that most, if not all, members of my Central Committee and indeed the Cabinet, have gone through mission schools at some stage during the course of their schooling[61]

The expression of appreciation for what the churches had done appeared genuine and opened the way to continued co-operation.

Although the government invited co-operation, it left little ambiguity concerning who was in charge. Through the Education Act of 1966, which became effective on September 2, 1966, the Ministry of Education and Culture outlined its sphere of control. Henceforth, the Ministry would not only direct the school calendar, syllabus, and subjects of instruction, but would assume control over appointment of

---

[60] President Kaunda, Address to staff and students of Canisius secondary school. 29 September 1964. Jesuit Archives, Chikuni.

[61] President Kaunda, Talk to the Synod of the United Church of Zambia. 4 April 1967. JAC.

staff, admission of students, punishment, conditions of suspension, expulsion, and transfer of students.[62]

Having set out some of the terms of partnership, we will now examine how this continued church-state co-operation worked out in the three principal areas of primary schools, secondary schools, and teacher training institutes.

CONTROL OF PRIMARY SCHOOLS

After Independence, African countries tended to nationalise their primary schools.[63] As noted earlier, the issue of government's securing control of the primary schools had a long-standing history in Zambia. In the 1950s, a number of denominations had handed over control of what had been their schools. At their meeting on September 3, 1964, one month before Independence, the Northern Rhodesia Episcopal Conference discussed their policy on the administration of the primary schools. According to the minutes, they unanimously concluded that:

> The Northern Rhodesia Episcopal Conference would continue as heretofore to administer primary schools pending the enactment of a new education ordinance, due for discussion at the next meeting of the Education Advisory Board in mid-October...[64]

One month later, the Minister of Education stated:

> ...the problem of management of schools has been a live issue this year. I must emphasise that voluntary agencies will not be compelled to surrender management of primary schools. Nevertheless, it is government policy to assume responsibility for the management of primary schools when voluntary agencies express a willingness to transfer them to local authorities.[65]

Given the somewhat cryptic assurance by government that it did not intend to force a take-over of the primary schools, the Catholic authorities had some doubts about the wisdom of maintaining control, especially since the other major Church groups, the Christian Council of Zambia and the United Church of Zambia had handed over their schools at Independence as a sign of confidence in the new

---

[62] *Education Act* (1966)
[63] Adrian Hastings, *A History of African Christianity 1950-1975* (Cambridge: Cambridge University Press, 1979), p. 188: Haynes, *Religion and Politics in Africa*, p. 115.
[64] Minutes of the Administrative Board Meeting held at the Northern Rhodesia Catholic Secretariat on 3 September 1964. JAC.
[65] Minister's Speech at the Advisory Board Meeting. 13 October 1964. CSA.

government.[66] On August 29, 1966, at a meeting of Catholic Educational Secretaries, the question was posed: To what extent has there been pressure from the local population on the Church to hand over the schools to the direct control of Government? The answer was that there was virtually none. It was noted:

> Apart from some local politicians, the Secretaries agreed that the local expression against the Church agency schools was not universal and certainly not sufficiently acute to present a change of policy by the Church.[67]

While there appeared to be relatively little pressure from people in general for a hand-over of the Catholic schools, Catholic teachers in some areas were unwilling to teach in mission schools. In Fort Jameson (Chipata today) 75% of the 1965 newly trained Catholic teachers opted to work in L.E.A. schools.[68] Moreover, it became clearer that many missionaries appeared to have lost interest in maintaining the schools. Nonetheless, the Bishop Director of Education for the Zambian Episcopal Conference, stressed that the Second Vatican Council favoured the maintenance and promotion of Catholic schools.[69] The participants seriously debated the value of holding on to the Catholic primary schools, but ended by re-affirming their commitment. One reason against a handover at this time was that there was no proper provision in the Education Act for the teaching of Religious Education. The Act was perceived to be somewhat negative in that it included provisions for having children excused from taking Religious Education. When questioned on this issue, the Minister of Education replied:

> Although religious instruction is not specifically mentioned in the Education Act, in fact it is one of the most important subjects which will continue to be taught in our schools.[70]

Since the Religious Education in Catholic schools at this time was Catholic, non-Catholics could not be forced to attend. Moreover, in many L.E.A. schools, there was little provision for the Catholic instruction of Catholic children. In Lusaka, for instance, it was estimated that 5,000 of the 11,000 Catholic school children were in L.E.A. schools. In the Northern Province, the proportion of Catholic children in L.E.A. schools, in some areas, was as high as 70%. As a

---

[66] "Education Minister boobed," Letter from M. Prokoph, *Times of Zambia*, 23 April 1984.
[67] Minutes of Education Secretaries' meeting held in Lusaka on 29 August 1966. JAC.
[68] Ibid.
[69] Ibid. See also: Murphy, "Changing Education Policy," p. 10.
[70] Radio Zambia Broadcasting Interview. 27 September 1966. Transcript at JAC.

result, one education secretary felt that solving the issue of Catholic instruction for Catholics in L.E.A. schools should be resolved before opening the doors to new problems by handing over the schools.[71] Evidently, different regions felt differently about a handover. It appears that Fort Jameson, Kasama, and Mbala favoured an immediate handover while Lusaka, Livingstone, and Monze wanted to retain the schools for some time at any rate.[72] Ft. Jameson, Kasama and Mbala were under the control of the White Fathers who, as a group catering for the largest number of schools, decided that the burden of so much administration had become an obstacle to more direct pastoral work. Finally, it was resolved that "it is generally accepted that the handing over to the L.E.A. of our Catholic schools at the present time would involve lowering of standards as regards Religious Education and Moral Training."[73] While continuing to operate primary schools, the Bishops wished to make it clear that they supported the new government. In a letter to the Minister of Education in 1967, they stated that they feared "withdrawal might be seen as disengaging from responsibility for education when the newly Independent Republic needed all possible assistance."[74] That year, the Catholic Church operated 644 primary schools throughout the country. This represented roughly 20% of the total number of primary schools. As the Catholic Church continued to co-operate with government in the provision of primary schooling, problems persisted. In 1968, an administrative working party was established in order to examine aspects of the teaching service. Eventually, this group produced what became known as the Rogers Report. One important recommendation from the report that was to undermine the authority of the Church through bypassing its managers of schools was: "headmasters must be prepared to manage their own schools."[75] The headmaster would henceforth deal directly with the Chief Education Officer, thereby ignoring the manager. As self

---

[71] Minutes of Education Secretaries' meeting held in Lusaka on 29 August 1966. JAC; "Chilubula Memo," dated 23 September 1969. (Kasama Archdiocesan Archives, henceforth K.A.A.). In 1972, it was calculated that the following numbers in L.E.A. schools were Catholic: by diocese: Ndola 25%; Mongu 10%; Lusaka 40%; Kabwe 40%; Mbala 50%; Kasama 65%; Chipata 30%; Solwezi 10%; Livingstone 19%; Monze 15% "Primary School Statistics 1972" J.A.C.

[72] See: Letter from Courtemanche to Chairman, Zambia Episcopal Conference, 17 November 1966; Bishop of Kasama, memo 7 December 1966; Bishop of Mbala to Education Secretary General, 24 November 1966. K.A.A.

[73] Ibid.

[74] Episcopal Conference Minutes May 1967, Appendix III. A.A.L.

[75] *Education in Transition* (Lusaka: Government Printer, 1969), p. 16.

managers, the headmasters would deal directly with the Chief Education Officer, referring only to the Education Secretary of the Voluntary Agency for financial support, supplies, and general policy.[76] This led to certain anomalies. As one Education Secretary of the time recalled:

> In my time (roughly 1967-69) there was less (than previously) contact with the teachers. This was done through the managers. There was little control of discipline, staffing of primary schools, and no control of promotions. By 1969 it was obvious that the primary schools were going to be given over.[77]

As a result of increased difficulty and less control over the system, the dioceses of Livingstone and Monze officially protested:

> That agencies are superfluous bodies in a more streamlined system, often becomes apparent in the ways in which agencies are bypassed. Important information may not be communicated—dates of meetings, funds available, upgrading etc. [78]

By way of conclusion they added:

> The period where voluntary agencies were required has come to a close. This phasing out of agencies has been something that was always regarded as a thing that would happen in the course of development.[79]

This letter was copied to the Chief Education Officer, Livingstone. Although it was signed by only the Education Secretary of the Monze diocese, in essence it probably expressed the feelings and sentiments of many Education Secretaries, even if one Education Secretary felt that the tone was inappropriate. He noted:

> Most of the points are valid but I think the peeved confrontation with government is uncalled for. Kind of attitude—we are being ill treated so take them. The schools will go. But I think we could do it in a more co-operative spirit.[80]

A somewhat similar memorandum from the Education Secretaries of Lusaka and Kabwe stated:

> Suppression of the post of manager of schools, as from January 1, 1973, and refusal to appoint for the Agency any corresponding officers will paralyse

---

[76] Murphy, "Changing Educational Policy," p. 25.

[77] Fr. John Counihan, Education Secretary for the Monze diocese. Interview, Charles Lwanga, 2 January 1984.

[78] Education Secretary, Monze diocese, to Education Secretary General, Catholic Secretariat, Lusaka, 31 January 1972. JAC.

[79] Ibid.

[80] Letter to Bishop of Livingstone, from Education Secretary. Bishop's Archives, Livingstone.

our administration, or, at least, render it less efficient.[81]

Similar sentiments were voiced by the authorities in Kasama and Mansa. The Education Secretary of the diocese of Mansa wrote:

> The position about our participation in the management of primary schools under the present system of decentralisation is still the same...Experience has shown that with the introduction of the decentralised system, our participation in the running of primary schools has become less and less effective and efficient.[82]

In 1972, the Catholic schools in most areas were predominantly staffed by Catholic teachers even though the number of Catholic children in these schools was only about 60%.[83] It is not so clear that this group of about 2,500 Catholic teachers strongly supported the Catholic Agency. Loyalty to the Agency in some cases was undoubtedly ambivalent. On this issue the Monze Education Secretary wrote:

> While teachers might say that they world prefer the agencies to remain, the fact that they have rubber stamps remade with "Ministry of Education," and have Ministry of Education inscribed on the signposts to their schools, is indicative of their true statements.[84]

Among the teachers there was an expectancy that their conditions of service under government management would improve. This was especially true in terms of teachers' perceptions of rapid promotion. In other instances, government take-over was welcomed because of the freedom from certain disciplinary sanctions, particularly polygamy, that it would bring. As one ex-teacher, when asked in 1995, if he was happy when the government took over the schools replied:

> Most of us were happy because there was no risk of being dismissed over a small thing—unless a teacher (male) was going out with a school girl. But there was no problem if you were going out with anybody outside the school. One could even bring two women to the school. You only had to tell them that they were your wives.[85]

Another long-serving teacher from the Monze area recalled:

---

[81] Memorandum from the Education Secretaries, Lusaka and Kabwe. n.d. JAC.

[82] Letter held in K.A.A.

[83] *Impact* 47 (February 1973); More specifically, the numbers in the dioceses were thus: Ndola 50%; Livingstone 33%; Mongu 80%; Monze 50%; Lusaka 64%; Kabwe 65%; Mbala 50%; Kasama 78%; Chipata 60%; Solwezi 20%. (Document held at J.A.C.).

[84] Education Secretary, Monze, to Education Secretary General. 31 January 1972. CSA.

[85] Andrew Chisopa. Teacher in Northern Province, 1943-70. Interviewed by Kennedy Mwamba, 1995.

> Teachers welcomed (the government take-over) because of indiscipline. Under agency, teachers were expected to keep families well—one wife and good behaviour. When the handover came, a teacher could be drunk early in the morning or could absent himself. Those were the people who welcomed the handover of the schools.[86]

Frequently in the interviews, former male teachers repeated the desire for freedom as a prime reason for teachers' tendency to welcome the handover of schools. At least one teacher felt that the government had been very ungrateful:

> The take-over of the schools was unfair. The government was very ungrateful despite that many of the leaders had been brought up and educated by missionaries. Those of us who wanted to leave the influence of the missionaries wanted to be polygamists. Of course few missionaries knew us for what we really were. We always pretended.[87]

On the other hand, many women had misgivings about the handover because they felt that the missionary conditions of service helped the stability of their marriages. As one such teacher stated:

> Most of us women liked those rules (missionary regulations) very much because they were safeguarding our homes. They were good rules because our husbands were afraid of loosing their jobs if they went for other women.[88]

Furthermore, as the years progressed, it appears that many missionaries grew less enthusiastic about the value of such secular engagement as the administration of primary schools:

> The missionaries, especially those of the Northern and Eastern dioceses, feel that our schools are a failure...that they do not produce real Catholics, that they involve us in so much material expense and administration...they are of the opinion that by handing the schools over to the government we can still have the same, or even bigger Catholic influence in all the schools without the burdens of administration.[89]

In the midst of much debate and some soul-searching, the Zambian Episcopal Conference made clear:

---

[86] Stephen Malambo, Former Teacher, Manager of Schools, and District Education Officer. Interviewed, Chikuni, 13 June 1995.

[87] Nicholas Muyowe, Former Teacher. Interviewed, Pemba. 23 March 1984.

[88] Woman teacher, Kasama, Interview by Kennedy Mwamba, (June 1995). This point whereby missionaries' emphasis on monogamy helped the emancipation of women is developed by Hinfelaar, *Bemba-Speaking Women*, pp. 45, 132.

[89] Fr. Vincent Cichecki, "The Catholic Schools in Zambia," (manuscript, n.d.), p. 12. JAC.

that the Zambia Episcopal Conference has no desire to make a last ditch stand over the issue (of holding on to the schools).[90]

What seemed of paramount importance to the Episcopal Conference was that the handover of the schools would be without acrimony. By achieving a somewhat cordial conclusion of this long-standing issue, it was hoped that favourable conditions could be secured. These would include the right of entry to schools by ministers of religion, that a reasonable proportion of Catholic teachers would still be posted to former Catholic schools and that Catholic religious instruction would be maintained until such time as a common syllabus would be produced.[91]

As dissatisfaction increased with the administration of the schools, an outward show of mutuality continued. At their meeting in January 1972, the Catholic Education Secretaries declared that, in the light of the implementation of the Rogers Report of 1969, it was only a question of time until practically all effective control would have passed from the agency to the government.[92] With this inevitable handover of the schools in view, at this meeting, the Secretaries considered three possible options: (1) for the Agency to resist encroachments and insist upon its rights, (2) for the Agency to take the decision to hand over all responsibility immediately, or (3) for the Agency to go along with the process of being eventually phased out of this area of activity. After lengthy discussions, they agreed to recommend the third option to the Zambia Episcopal Conference. They further recommended that in all dioceses the Bishop and the Education Secretary should meet the Chief Education Officer of the region to discuss the best procedure for handing over. They reiterated the Catholic Church's position which remained that it was willing to assist in so far as its assistance was required.[93]

As the end of a long saga drew near, the Education Secretary General, Fr. Colm O'Riordan, wrote to the Permanent Secretary at the Ministry of Education and Culture on July 31, 1973, indicating the Catholic Church's intention to withdraw. While the letter's tone remained cordial, it explained that this decision to hand over the schools was precipitated by government's action in terms of its implementation of the Rogers report.[94]

---

[90] Zambia Episcopal Conference. Administrative Board Meeting, Catholic Secretariat, Lusaka: 11-12 February 1970.
[91] Ibid.
[92] *Impact* 47 (February 1973).
[93] Ibid.
[94] Letter from Catholic Education Secretary General to Permanent Secretary, Ministry of

For many, the outcome was unsatisfactory. The first archbishop of Lusaka who had retired by the time of the handover stated: "I felt it was all done too quickly and without sufficient fight."[95] In 1996, he still regretted the handover that he judged to have been a mistake. He recalled:

> When I returned after a year's leave after my resignation as archbishop, I found that the Bishops had accepted to hand over. I know that two bishops wanted to retain them...I was very unhappy that they had agreed...As a result, here today at Mpunde, I don't know any of the pupils even though the school is on mission property.[96]

A somewhat similar sentiment was expressed by the first Zambian principal of Charles Lwanga College who wrote:

> In 1974, the running of primary schools was handed over to government. Unlike other Churches, the Seventh Day Adventists for example, the Catholic Church surrendered all its primary schools to government even schools like Chikuni and Charles Lwanga primary which are on mission property. This was a step backwards.[97]

At stages in the process leading to the handover, the possibility of retaining control of the schools on mission property had been suggested. Bishop O'Shea of Livingstone wrote:

> We feel it would be unnecessary to phase out these schools (schools on mission stations) at the moment. Too, it might be unwise, as we might have second thoughts later. However should difficulties arise, or should the Ministry feel strongly about these exceptions, we would willingly go along.[98]

However, with few teachers enthusiastic to take employment in mission schools, this possibility became less and less feasible. Among the reasons why many teachers were unwilling to work in mission settings were the strict code of discipline operative in Catholic schools as well as expectations that government employment would result in better working conditions which, in some instances, remained true for a time.

Moreover, it would appear that the concern to conclude this period cordially which we have mentioned earlier won the day, confirming the comments of Bishop Kozlowiecki and Mr. Haambote regarding the

---

Education and Culture, 31 July 1973. CSA.
[95] Archbishop Adam Kozolowiecki. Interview, Lusaka, 28 November 1983.
[96] Interview, 5 June 1996. Mpunde, Kabwe.
[97] B.M. Haambote, Letter to Proprietor, Charles Lwanga College. 10 July 1981. CSA.
[98] Letter from T.P. O'Shea, Bishop of Livingstone, to Bishop James Corboy, Bishop of Monze. 3 March 1973. Monze diocesan archives; in 1967, the number of station schools was 70.

absence of any real bargaining. In some respects, the Catholic authorities seemed to have grown weary of the demands connected with control of the primary schools, but had shaped no alternative vision as a backdrop to an agreement. As one influential educationist later reflected:

> To my mind, even at the time of handing over there was the possibility then, with some sacrifice, to appoint chaplains, organisers, motivators of the teachers for the primary school sector and to save them for the work of the Church. The Church personnel seemed to have become tired with the educational effort and the result was the practical alienation of the mass of the primary school teachers from the Church.[99]

Nonetheless, despite an outwardly friendly face, perhaps as Fr. Prokoph was later to comment: The Bishops "grudgingly handed over all primary schools to government."[100] In 1996, the Archbishop of Kasama noted: "We were forced out of the schools. We never decided to pull out. Government made it impossible."[101]

The handover of the primary schools thus rather unsatisfactorily ended a long era of Catholic Church involvement in Zambia's primary schooling. In 1996, when asked why many schools and some hospitals had been taken over by government during his Presidency, Dr. Kaunda replied: "I don't think it was the right decision."[102]

CHURCH STRUGGLE FOR SCHOOL CURRICULUM

Soon after the handover of the primary schools, the Catholic Church, along with other churches entered upon a somewhat ambiguous relationship with government as Zambian Humanism became socialistic. This on-going tension with government lasted from roughly 1974 until when U.N.I.P. lost power in 1991. Unlike the outcome of the struggle on the issue of control of primary schools, the Churches appeared to gain the upper hand in the ideological duel as we shall see.

From the Catholic educational point of view, the socialist ideal,

---

[99] Vincent Cichecki, "Towards Teachers' deeper Involvement," Reflection paper, n.d. JAC; As far as Fr. Colm O'Riordan, Education Secretary General at the time, was concerned, some dioceses were awaiting a graceful way out of the heavy responsibilities that the administration of the schools had produced. Interview, Monze, 15 January 1984.
[100] M.A. Prokoph, Letter to *Times of Zambia*, 23 April 1984.
[101] Interview, Kasama, 16 July 1996.
[102] Dr. Kenneth Kaunda, Interview, as reported in Casmir Chanda, University of Zambia: Essay for RS312 (October, 1996), p. 5.

proposed by the new version of Zambian Humanism initially received some acceptance. For instance, in a paper given to principals of Catholic colleges and secondary school headmasters, it was stressed that openness was needed when evaluating the document, *Education for Development*. The presenters of the paper stated:

> Christians should surely rejoice at the draft on educational reforms. Anywhere where there is denouncing of unjust structures of community and society, protest against barriers between people (such as discrimination according to colour, class, etc.) there, in that denouncing, the Gospel of God's salvation is being prepared in its denouncing aspect, God's grace is at work. The draft denounces such unjust structures. We, as Christians, should be the first to join in this denunciation, but the draft is far from merely denouncing injustice, it proposes a remedy, an educational system geared to bring about a just society. The Churches should recognise God's hand at work in this humanist socialist attempt to build a more fully human community. We should be the first to recognise the values of the reforms, the first to show ourselves willing to join in the great effort that will be needed to put the reforms into practice.[103]

The presenters clearly wanted to encourage co-operation with the reform movement and appeared prepared to downplay the fact that religious education was omitted from the document:

> Of course we must be concerned that there be scope and place in the new system for explicit teaching of religion. We must ensure that the new system is not atheistic. But, as the saying goes, let us not fail to see the wood for the trees. We all know of countries near to us, such as South Africa, where Jesus is preached about even in schools, where churches are "taken over" for use as schools and yet the whole structure of society and its institutions such as its educational system work against God's saving plan and activity.[104]

In a meeting with Ministry of Education delegates, the Bishop of Livingstone's response to the reforms was: "They are long overdue."[105] In a sense, this was the general tone, even if the Catholic delegation stressed that the omission of religious instruction in the draft was not satisfactory. The Ministry's representative however assured the meeting that:

> ...there was no intention to leave out religious education in the schools. If you keep seeds from a pumpkin, it is a sign you are interested in more

---

[103] Zambia Episcopal Conference: Meeting of Principals and Heads of Catholic Colleges and Secondary Schools, 5 November 1976. CSA.
[104] Ibid., p. 6.
[105] Ibid.

pumpkins. Further, there are now inspectors of religious education, and at Nkrumah Teachers' College, Kabwe, religion was included in the curriculum.[106]

The individual Catholic institutions reacted more restrainedly to the reform proposals. The staff of Charles Lwanga for example expressed reservation about the ideology of socialism and wanted more clear definitions of Zambian Humanism and political education as mentioned in *Education for Development*.[107] Moreover, they called for explicit inclusion of Religious Education in the curriculum. They wrote:

> We are surprised that there is not a single reference to Religious Education as a subject in the whole draft statement. We would like to know whether this omission was by accident or by design.[108]

Other criticisms included the danger of neglecting academic standards. Mongu Teachers' College followed a somewhat similar pattern of praise followed by criticism. Its representatives voiced support for the idea of basic education for all though, as in the case of Charles Lwanga, they disagreed with the extra pressures which would come upon teachers if the proposed reforms were implemented. Moreover, they too stressed the need for high academic standards in institutions of learning:

> We do not wish to cut ourselves off from the world, and to lose all international recognition as far as our certificates are concerned, especially at the higher educational level. For University and Teacher Training Colleges our people want qualifications that the world will recognise.[109]

Many of these concerns seem to have been noted for, as we have said, the later draft was significantly different. It included Religious Education and the document, *Educational Reform*, had far less marxist jargon. It retained certain ideas such as political education, which in subsequent years was to become part of the Teacher Training curriculum. It was then claimed to be a non-teaching subject and followed a syllabus entitled: "Political and Ideological Education."[110] Catholic authorities were apprehensive about this but they adopted a "wait and see" attitude.

The early years of Scientific Socialism rhetoric coincided with the

---

[106] *Impact* (October 1976).

[107] B. Haambote, "Education for Development," letter to Education for Development Committee, Lusaka, 25 November 1976. JAC.

[108] Ibid., p. 9.

[109] Mongu Teacher Training College: Staff Meeting 18 June 1976. CSA.

[110] "Social Education," *Impact* (March 1983).

Zimbabwean guerrilla war, which may explain the atheistic tone and the apparent wholesale acceptance of Soviet block propaganda. The communist bloc was more and more heralded as partners and friends while the United States and the Western countries were more or less identified as neo-colonial oppressors. As a result of increasing antagonism towards Western countries and anything associated with them, the Churches felt under increasing attack. In 1979, when leaders began to state clearly that they saw no contradictions between Christianity and Scientific Socialism, the Churches decided that they had better take a clear stand perhaps before it might be too late. In 1979, the main churches which included the Zambia Evangelical Fellowship issued a statement, called "Marxism, Humanism and Christianity."[111]

Government never publicly and clearly reacted to such criticism. Privately, the Church leaders were all summoned to State House where a stormy meeting took place.[112] However, soon afterwards, political education was introduced into the colleges and primary schools. Eventually, this led to the organisation of a seminar on the topic of Scientific Socialism in educational institutions by the National Council of Catholic Women where they advised that:

> The authority should realise that teaching of Scientific Socialism at an early age is dangerous because children are too young to understand and balance the implications.[113]

Some days later, President Kaunda met Church leaders at Mulungushi Hall where he stated that no decision had been made to give the party a Marxist ideology:

> Scientific Socialism will be taught in all schools in future as part of political education...It will not replace religious education.[114]

---

[111] This was published in August 1979, and signed by all the Catholic Bishops and by representatives from the Christian Council of Zambia and the Zambia Evangelical Fellowship. Gifford notes how unique this kind of co-operation was. See: Paul Gifford, "Christian Fundamentalism, State and Policies in Black Africa," in Westerlund, *Questioning the Secular State*, p. 210; See also: Lungu, "The Church, Labour, and the Press."; Clive Dillon-Malone, *Zambian Humanism; Religion and Social Morality* (Ndola: Mission Press, 1989); Draisma, *The Struggle Against Underdevelopment*, pp. 337-347; "Roman Catholics and African Politics," *Pro Mundi Vita Dossiers* 7/8 (March 1979).

[112] Bishop Denis DeJong, Interview, Ndola. 29 July 1996.

[113] Notes on the seminar held at Evelyn Hone College, 13 March 1982. CSA; See: Kelly, *Education in a Declining Economy*, pp. 113-4.

[114] K. Kaunda, "Humanism and Development," Presidential Address to Church Leaders, Lusaka: 18-19 March 1982. (J.A.C.).

Reflecting back on this meeting in 1999, Dr. Kaunda had this to say:

> It was a very heated meeting. Thank God He helped me to calm the situation. I was quite sincere about this. There was no way we could go atheistic ourselves. No way at all. But some of those young members of the Party were putting pressure on us.[115]

In response to the deliberations at Mulungushi Hall, the Church leaders resolved that they were willing to accept Zambian Humanism as a vehicle to organise Zambian society, but affirmed that they totally rejected Scientific Socialism.[116] This did not signal the end of Scientific Socialism in the schools and colleges as party cadres went regularly to Eastern Europe for training. Open and direct attacks on Christian Churches diminished, but several attempts were made to covertly introduce what Catholic authorities identified as atheistic literature. In general, this included textbooks in history, social studies, or civics which employed a fairly unrefined version of Marx's dialectical materialism. On April 20, 1982, for instance, the Bishop of Livingstone wrote:

> I wish again to express my deep concern over the atheistic literature that was sent to the College (Mongu Teachers) without prior consultation of the proprietors. Mongu Teachers' College is a Catholic Educational Institution and as such we cannot accept that such literature be freely distributed among the students.[117]

Further protests came from the Catholic Education Secretary General in 1984 when a book, authored by an inspector of civics and history and recommended by the Permanent Secretary of the Ministry of Education and Culture, was unofficially introduced into some Catholic secondary schools. The Secretary Education General not only criticised the book for equating Zambian Humanism with Scientific Socialism but also for the clandestine manner in which it was introduced.[118]

Despite the protests, Scientific Socialism continued to be part of the dominant rhetoric of U.N.I.P. to the time of its catastrophic fall from power in November 1991. After the mid 1980s, however, at the school level, the methods used to advance the cause seemed somewhat ineffective. In conclusion, one might say that the Catholic Church, sometimes in union with other Churches, played a cautious but

---

[115] Dr. K.D. Kaunda, Interview, Lusaka, 19 February 1999.

[116] Kelly, *Education in a Declining Economy*, pp. 113-4.

[117] Bishop of Livingstone, letter to Permanent Secretary, Ministry of Education and Culture. Bishop's archives, Livingstone.

[118] Fr. Vincent Cichecki, letter to The Permanent Secretary, Ministry of General Education and Culture. 19 November 1984. CSA.

determined role in keeping political education in check while it secured a central place for Religious Education in the schools' curricula. Church leaders realised the wisdom of acting together. They feared that government would try to isolate them and in that way render their protest less effective.[119] After the handover of schools, the issue of Scientific Socialism became one of the most pervasive issues between the U.N.I.P. government and the Churches in administering the Teacher Colleges and secondary schools.

TEACHER TRAINING COLLEGES

As we have already mentioned, Charles Lwanga Teachers' College opened for student intake in 1959 and was completed in 1962. It then accommodated 250 male students. At this time there were a number of smaller colleges that catered for Catholic women trainee teachers. These included Chilubula and Minga, and Lukulu from 1959 to 1965. In 1965, Catholic colleges supplied 31% of all primary teachers.[120] Until this time, the Catholic authorities had hoped that they would be enabled to open a major teachers' college for women equivalent to Charles Lwanga for men. However, government became more concerned to provide regional rather than denominational colleges and so they started such colleges at Kasama and Chipata. Meanwhile, the smaller women's college at Chikuni became part of Charles Lwanga in 1969, and the Lukulu college relocated at Mongu in 1965 under the direction of the Holy Cross Sisters, providing facilities for women teacher trainees, with both a domestic science and academic curriculum. In 1976, Mongu became co-educational, with Fr. John Grace, O.F.M. Cap., as principal. In the post-Independence years, both Charles Lwanga and Mongu Teachers' Colleges have provided approximately 25% of all primary teachers for the country.

Unlike Mongu Teachers' College which never had a preponderance of Catholic students, from its inception in 1959, Charles Lwanga had almost an entire Catholic staff and student body. Teaching of Catholic doctrine and morality had a central role. The College aimed to supply Catholic teachers for the Catholic schools. When asked about the Catholic atmosphere of the College in the 1960s, one past student replied:

It was very much a Catholic College. Attendance at Mass was obligatory.

---

[119] Bishop D. De Jong, Interview, Ndola, 29 July 1996.
[120] Ministry of Education, *Annual Report* (1965), p. 70.

There was Benediction. Attendance was expected. Sundays were obligatory. In those days non-Catholic students were few.[121]

By the 1970s, the Catholic ethos of Charles Lwanga had declined in the sense that many more non-Catholic students were admitted than had been the case previously. This happened to some degree because, under the new government, these Colleges were meant primarily to serve regional rather than denominational interests. Though this was the stated policy of the Ministry of Education, it was not strictly imposed. Each College retained autonomy over intake which was usually decided by a College committee, who often gave high priority to academic qualification and local applicants. As a principal of the time recalled:

> There was always freedom of intake of students but we were always open to non-Catholics. When there were only a few Colleges, the students were selected from all over the country but when other provinces had their Colleges this was not such an issue so there was concentration on Tonga (local) students at Charles Lwanga which meant that many of them were not Catholic.[122]

This is not to imply that the authorities were unaware of the need to maintain a large percentage of the student body as Catholics. However, ecumenical considerations in the wake of Vatican II combined with the leading state ideology of "one Zambia—one nation" contributed to a rather relaxed approach to the issue. Somewhat later, in the late 1970s and early 1980s, the number of Catholic staff began to dwindle. The government's Zambianization policy meant that as Zambian staff recruited from various institutions were posted to the Colleges, fewer Grant Aided Educationists (G.A.E.s) and particularly Lay Missionary Associate Teachers (L.M.A.T.s) were needed.[123] Many of the Zambians were non-Catholic. Although the Catholic Secretariat, the Catholic agency for staff recruitment, could theoretically select the staff, in

---

[121] Patrick M. Haamujompa. Student at Charles Lwanga 1959-61. Later Dean of the School of Education at the University of Zambia. Interview: 7 December 1983.

[122] B.M. Hambote. Principal of Charles Lwanga College 1973-81. Interview, 21 March 1984.

[123] Grant Aided Educationists, usually priests, brothers or sisters, received a token salary towards their maintenance without any further benefits. Of the 360 teachers in Catholic institutions in 1969, 33% were G.A.E. See: *Impact* 24 (April 1969). In 1996, of the total 722 teachers in Catholic institutions 7% were G.A.E. For 1996 statistics, I contacted Fr. Thomas McGivern, Education Secretary General. L.M.A.T.s were men and women usually Catholic and recruited from outside Zambia. They received salary and extra benefits. In 1968, there were 186 L.M.A.T.s, 37% Irish, 31% British, and 26% Indian. *Impact* 18 (April 1968); In 1996, 3% of the staff of Catholic institutions were L.M.A.T. (Fr. Thomas McGivern).

practice this did not really happen. It is not entirely clear if this happened by accident or if there was some covert design operating. In 1982, the proprietor of Mongu Teachers' College wrote to the Permanent Secretary:

> As the Proprietor of the College I am extremely worried about the lack of consultation between the Episcopal Conference Office (the Catholic Secretariat) and your office, in the appointments of lecturers at the College.[124]

As the Zambianization process gained momentum, Zambians replaced L.M.A.T.s and, in some cases, G.A.Es, in that missionaries' numbers began to decline or they chose more pastoral occupations. This became a source of special concern to the Principal of Mongu Teachers' College in the 1980s, when he pleaded with the Provincial of the Holy Cross Sisters thus:

> The mere presence of the clergy amongst the laymen, be they staff or students, means quite a lot in controlling the morals—there is great need for the presence of clergy—priests and sisters amongst us. This is not merely my feeling but that of the majority of the staff.[125]

The decline in the proportion of Catholic staff and students meant that a large percentage of College staff and students were non-Catholic. This situation was in accord with Vatican II's emphasis on ecumenism. Another factor that had a strong ecumenical element at this time was the newly designed interdenominational Religious Education syllabus. This had started at Charles Lwanga in 1970. Until then, Catholics spoke of a Catholic syllabus for their Catholic schools, though it appears to have been a poorly taught subject. However, the Ministry of Education pressed for some kind of common, interdenominational syllabus in the late 1960s. With the prospect of a handover of the primary schools becoming ever more likely, the idea of a specifically Catholic syllabus became less realistic.

In this context, Fr. Thomas O'Brien, a lecturer at Charles Lwanga, took the initiative in 1970 and formed a group who helped create a common syllabus. As lecturers in a setting where many were non-Catholic, they perhaps felt the need to have religious lessons that all could accept. Inevitably, this entailed reducing some of the Catholic content. Their position hinged on a distinction between religious education and catechesis. The business of the College included religious

---

[124] Letter from Bishop of Livingstone to Permanent Secretary, Ministry of Education and Culture, 20 April 1982. Bishop's Archives, Livingstone.

[125] Letter from the Acting Principal to Mother Provincial, 24 July 1980. CSA.

education while catechesis belonged outside the College. From the beginning, this project was strongly opposed by people like the director of the Monze diocesan catechetical centre, who claimed that the new syllabus was too fundamentalist, overstressing the historical Jesus, without a clear denouement and lacking sufficient attention to the need for commitment.[126] This critique possibly reflected some major concerns from more conservative Catholic quarters where Catholic understanding of the Eucharist and Sacraments would be part of the curriculum. It was also uneasy with a use of scripture that tended to neglect or downplay tradition in its interpretation. Twelve years later, in 1983, when the present writer conducted research on this issue, one of the main supporters of the new approach pleaded with him to try to explain the rationale behind the new syllabus to those with whom he would be in contact. Even in the 1990s, the R.E. syllabus continued to be perceived in some quarters as a dilution of the Christian (Catholic) message.[127] While, among the more informed, there was some awareness of the distinction between "religious education" and "catechesis," the distinction was generally far from clear or acceptable.[128] Fr. O'Brien recalled:

> Monze diocese wanted their own syllabus. The Bishop did not see the interdenominational syllabus fulfilling the need he had in mind. It is true that our first meeting at Charles Lwanga had the approval of the Bishop, but it was clear whose side the Bishop was on.[129]

Some twelve years down the road, the same Bishop acknowledged that Fr. O'Brien and the group had greatly contributed to the Religious Education programme as it then operated in the schools. He further admitted that they deserved more support than they had received.[130]

After the introduction of the common syllabus, teachers at the Catholic colleges were no longer trained to teach specifically Catholic doctrine. Whatever Catholic teaching was given came through membership of clubs or from the Church services. At Mongu, however, there had always been a special Catholic programme, since as we have noted, Catholics were never a majority in the college.[131] At Charles Lwanga, it took some years before the then Catholic chaplain perceived

---

[126] Fr. Frank Keenan, Interview, Chelston, Lusaka. December 1983.
[127] Clement Katulushi, "Religious Education in a Secular Institution: A Case study of Nkrumah Teachers' College, Kabwe, Zambia," (M.A. dissertation, Leeds, 1996), p. 18.
[128] See: A.B. Smith, *Interdenominational Religious Education in Zambia* (Leiden: 1982).
[129] Fr. Thomas O'Brien, Interview, Lusaka, 5 December 1983.
[130] Bishop James Corboy, Bishop of Monze, 1962-1992. Interview, Monze, 1 March 1984.
[131] Sr. M. Dympna, H.C. Interview, Lusaka, 27 May 1996.

the need for a Catholic programme. Thus, with the approval and encouragement of the Principal, Mr. Haambote, the College chaplain, Fr. Anthony Geoghegan, set up groups known as Confraternity of Catholic Doctrine (C.C.D.). In these voluntary clubs, Catholics could learn about their Catholic faith. The two main architects of the common syllabus at the College, Mr. Freeburn and Sr. Josephine Clarke, opposed the formation of such societies, presumably because they viewed them as some form of rejection of the new syllabus. Over the years, a division had grown between the Catholic syllabus advocates and those who had designed and implemented the new syllabus. At Charles Lwanga these C.C.D. groups met in the evenings but remained somewhat peripheral to the main College programme. In 1981, for reasons of discipline rather than because of a more integral Catholic vision, these groups began to meet on the afternoon of some class day, while non-Catholics also could meet at the same time. A system of this kind had been in operation at Mongu for some time where the newly appointed vice-principal, Mr. Bruno Mwiinga, had experienced its efficacy.

In the late 1970s, Sr. Aileen Waldron, a lecturer at Charles Lwanga, initiated a programme which was linked to the C.C.D. Each Sunday, she arranged that a group of Catholic students should teach in the local parish catechumenate programme. She felt that this provided a good training ground even if it was limited in that they needed an opportunity to prepare services and at that point Masses were always provided on Sundays in the parish. In her view, having Mass each week did not give a realistic preparation for students who, once they graduated, would frequently be in locations that did not have a priest and where Mass would be rare.[132] Sr. Aileen's programme lasted for some years, but after her transfer and different ideas about the value of this initiative, it eventually was dropped. Sr. Dympna O'Leary in Mongu set up a similar programme, but it also was dropped because of different theological perspectives of parish clergy.[133] Other initiatives to enlist the assistance of Catholic teachers in the Catholic teaching of children over the years have included the establishment of a Catholic Association for Religious Education (C.A.R.E.) in the Livingstone diocese by Fr. Herlihy O.F.M. Cap.

By the early 1980s, the Colleges began to reawaken to what being Catholic meant in a situation where many of the factors which had constituted a Catholic college had disappeared. No longer was there a

---

[132] Sr. Aileen Waldron, R.S.C. Interview, Chikuni. 8 March 1984.
[133] Sr. Dympna O'Leary, H.C. Interview, Lusaka, 27 May 1996.

preponderance of Catholic students and staff, daily Mass, and a Catholic religious education syllabus. From then onward, there was some concern to maintain a certain percentage of Catholic students and staff. At times this led to some fear on the part of non-Catholic staff who felt that they were not really welcome.

Over the years, Charles Lwanga and Mongu Colleges gained good reputations for the kind of professional training they provided. As one ex-student from Charles Lwanga and later Dean of the School of Education at the University of Zambia put it: "Charles Lwanga was an all men's college. It instilled a sense of responsibility. We got a sense of professional training and basically a good foundation."[134] In the early post-Independence years, the entry level of students remained rather low but by the 1980s, when secondary school graduates began to have difficulty finding employment, they turned more and more to teacher training. By 1983, the entry level had been raised to successful completion of secondary school with O level passes in English language and Mathematics or a single Science subject.[135] In the years following, it appears that many students tended to view primary teacher training as a stepping stone to some more desired occupation. This undoubtedly affected students morale and commitment.

From the earliest times, the Catholic colleges maintained a strict code of discipline which was on occasion compared to that of a secondary school. However, from the early 1980s, when graduates from secondary schools constituted much of the student intake, such strict discipline became less appropriate. At Charles Lwanga in the mid 1980s, one of the lecturers seriously questioned the kind of discipline operating at that college. He noted:

> As a teacher training college there should be more emphasis on leadership training than there is. These people are not in secondary school. For many it is the end of their education, so there should be an attempt to introduce self discipline. At present the place is more conductive to a spirit of detention which students bear while they are here but what lasting effect will it have?[136]

Although the discipline at Charles Lwanga resembled that of a secondary school, it was not the subject of major complaint from former

---

[134] C.P. Chishimba, Student at Charles Lwanga in early 1960s. Later lecturer and Dean of the School of Education at the University of Zambia. Interview, 8 December 1983.

[135] Kelly, *Education in a Declining Economy*, p. 131. In 1984, only 35% of the staff of primary teachers' colleges had educational qualifications at the same level or superior to the students they were required to train.

[136] Mr. Nkomo, Tutor and acting-principal at the time of the interview, April 1984.

students surveyed in 1984. When 100 of Charles Lwanga's past students were asked, 92% described the discipline of their time as reasonable, while 21% noted that it was strict. In the same survey, when asked if they felt that they had been treated like children as students by the administration or by the tutors, 90% claimed that they had felt treated as adults.[137]

By the late 1980s, then, the Catholic colleges had moved towards creating some kind of new identity in a context of swiftly changing circumstances, especially in their role as grant-in-aid institutions.

SECONDARY SCHOOLS

As we noted, in the years after Independence, the need for educated labour proved urgent in view of the government's rapid Zambianization agenda. The Catholic Church not only welcomed Zambia's Independence but wished to contribute to the creation of an educated population. An immediate need was to increase provision of secondary schooling.

The first Catholic secondary school, Canisius College near Chisekesi, opened in 1949. This was followed by Malole in 1951, Maramba for girls in 1956, and fourteen others by the time of Independence which together then catered for approximately 15% of the boys and 30% of the girls in secondary schools.[138] Immediately after Independence, many existing facilities were extended while a number of new secondary schools were built. Between 1968 and 1971, the number of classes in Catholic agency secondary schools increased from 189 to 252.[139] In subsequent years, the number of Catholic aided schools continued to increase so that in 1995, there were 26 Catholic grant-aided schools or approximately 4.5% of the total number of schools offering some form of secondary schooling and 17% of those which provide facilities to Grade XII.[140]

Because of its commitment to secondary schooling in the colonial days, the Catholic Church found itself in the happy position after Independence of having a high percentage of Catholics who were

---

[137] Survey mailed randomly to past students in 1984.

[138] *Impact* (December 1967).

[139] *Impact* (February 1968).

[140] National Policy on Education (June 1995). The country had 589 government and aided schools with an enrolment of 199,081 pupils, 122,756 boys and 76,325 girls. There were approximately 150 schools that offered schooling to the Grade XII level. These estimates do not include Katondwe secondary school nor the minor seminaries.

educated. In 1966, for instance, the Catholic chaplain to higher institutes of learning reckoned that they had about 33% Catholics in their student bodies. Of the women at such centres, 40% were Catholic.[141] He felt that in the light of the fact that about 16% of the total population of the country was then Catholic, such numbers at higher centres of learning indicated a remarkable achievement.

Over the period since Independence, the Catholic Church has continued to contribute to the secondary schooling endeavour. As can be seen, the magnitude of this contribution has been somewhat dwarfed by the enormous expansion of provision which has resulted particularly at the Grade VIII level through the introduction of basic schools. Today, the Catholic Church is concerned not so much with linear extension of provision but with maintaining quality in the education it offers. One sign of the Catholic authorities' concern with quality is the close eye they keep on annual results of the Grade XII examinations. Each year, the newsletter, *Impact*, of the Catholic Secretariat publishes these results. Over the years, they have been impressive, when compared to the overall performance in the country. In this way, many of the Catholic secondary schools have gained reputations for being "good" schools which generally means that their results in the examinations have been high. In Catholic schools the average passing rate has not only been high but the number of upper division results have remained higher than in the other schools, with the result that a larger proportion of students from Catholic managed schools have gained entry to the University of Zambia.[142] In 1972, for instance, 37% of all students at the University of Zambia were Catholic while 30% had completed their schooling in Catholic managed schools. That year, 68% of girls selected for University courses came from Catholic-run schools.[143] In 1975, it was found that 68% of all students at the University of Zambia had done all or part of their secondary schooling in Catholic schools.[144] This commendable record continues to be sustained up to the mid 90s. Between 1982 and 1988, the percentage passing in Catholic schools ranged from 79% to 91% while the national average ranged from 61% to 66%.[145] In 1995, of the 1951 students

---

[141] *Impact* (Dec 1967).

[142] Between 1968 and 1975, of the 7,962 candidates presented by Catholic schools, 769 (9.6%) obtained Div I, 1694 (21.2%) obtained Div II, and 2,881 (36%) obtained Div. III, in the Cambridge Overseas and G.C.E. examinations with 677 failures (8.5%). Source: *Impact* (April 1976).

[143] *Impact* (1972).

[144] *Impact* (April 1976).

[145] "Progressive Grade 12 Results." CSA.

accepted for study at the University of Zambia who had indicated on their entry forms the secondary school from which they had graduated, 32% came from Catholic aided schools. In a context in which Catholic agency schools provide about 16% of the Grade XII candidates, this is significant.

As we have indicated, the post-Independence government placed high priority on the provision of secondary schooling. In 1969, as part of this policy, the Ministry of Education decided that some secondary schools would henceforth cater for the whole nation as opposed to regions. In this way, pupils were selected to Form I solely on merit and to mitigate the regional inequalities in educational opportunity as well as to enhance national unity. The national headquarters in Lusaka selected.[146] The effect of this policy decision on a number of Catholic schools who had good academic records was that they received a large percentage of the most academically able students in the country. From the perspective of the Church, the less satisfactory side of this was that a large number were non-Catholic. This was rarely, if ever, seen as an opportunity to convert other Christian denominations to Catholicism. The overall result was that the Catholic student populations in such schools declined dramatically in the years following. For instance, at the oldest Catholic secondary school in the country, the intake of 80% Catholics in 1969 dropped to 53% Catholic intake in 1973. While the policy may have been helpful in creating "one Zambia one nation," as the President expressed it, it had serious consequences for Catholic schools.[147] At the time, it is far from clear that it caused any special anxiety among Catholic proprietors. It took some years before any open criticism became evident. Looking back years later one critic wrote: "We seemed to pay undue attention to neutralism as the Education Authorities officially sponsored."[148]

Partly as a result of this policy, the notion of Catholic school became blurred. Not only had the numbers of Catholics in the Catholic-run schools dwindled, but, as in the primary schools, the Religious Education syllabus from 1971 onwards was interdenominational.[149] Moreover, as in the Teacher Colleges, the proportion of LMATs and G.

---

[146] *Ministry of Education, Annual Report 1969* (Lusaka: Government Printer, 1970), p. 5.

[147] Carmody, "Denominational Secondary Schooling in Post-Independence Zambia," p. 250; On the "one Zambia-one nation," idea, see: E. Colson, "The Bantu Botatwe," p. 70.

[148] Bro C. Murray S.J., Teacher at Canisius secondary school, 1971-79. As quoted in Carmody, *Conversion and Jesuit Schooling*, p. 101.

[149] John Mujdrica, "An Evaluation of the Zambian Secondary School R.E. Syllabuses" (M.Ed. thesis, University of Birmingham, 1995), p. 26.

A.E.s declined while it became increasingly difficult to maintain a preponderance of Catholic staff. At the time of the handover of the primary schools, the Education Secretary General of the Catholic Secretariat had predicted:

> It is to be foreseen that in the secondary sector as in the primary sector the present practically total autonomy which the Catholic agencies have in regard to the running of schools will be eroded and eventually eliminated. First of all it is to be expected that the number of Religious teachers will decrease and secondly that the number of Zambian staff will naturally be members of the Zambian Teaching Service Commission, so that autonomy with regard to posting which is presently employed by the Catholic agencies, will be gravely affected by these developments.[150]

As in the Teachers' Colleges, the allocation of teachers to Catholic secondary schools became a major problem in the 1980s. This exacerbated the problem of dwindling numbers of Catholic students. Among other factors, it led to some questioning of the apostolic value of the twenty-two secondary schools the agency then had. However, after some discussion, the Bishops were determined to keep these schools because:

> Our schools have been to a large extent responsible for the general goodwill towards the Church in our Zambian society.... In practice it means that our schools are one of the important ways to build up the Church and especially to build up future lay Catholic leaders.[151]

On the whole, it is far from evident that much attention was paid to the Catholic dimension of the schools until the early 1980s even though, as we have seen, the problem dated back to 1969. When the Catholic school proprietors and administrators began to take some steps to redress the situation, they established some Catholic clubs or groupings with the sole purpose of catering to Catholic needs. Subsequently, Catholic proprietors revised constitutions, drafted mission statements, and set up Boards of Management to monitor the situation. Constitutions usually required that heads and deputies should be Catholics, but at almost no time is there evidence of any attempt to restrict freedom of worship within the institutions. Some non-Catholic staff became concerned that they might not be welcome any longer and so there was a period of some unease in this matter. One positive outcome in the mid-1980s was that the Catholic schools had developed a new sense of identity and purpose.

---

[150] *Impact* (February 1973)
[151] Reflections on our Schools, p. 4. (C.S.A.)

During the first twenty-five years of Zambia's Independence, the Catholic Church continued its long-standing commitment to the education of Zambia's youth. The eventual break with government in the administration of primary schools, though somewhat inevitable in the context, today appears to have been rather unfortunate in the eyes of both Zambians and missionaries. On the secondary and teacher training levels, the Church institutions are widely acclaimed by Zambians. From the proprietors' viewpoints, however, much of the autonomy that was lost in the post-Independence years needs to be reclaimed. As we end the 1990s, with the appearance of a new political system, it appears that the stage may be set for a new era of fruitful partnership.

CHAPTER FOUR

CONVERSION AND SCHOOLS TODAY[1]

Since we have traced the development of Catholic schools over almost a century, it is time to situate the Church in the contemporary social setting. In doing so, we will give particular attention to the current nature of Catholic conversion in Zambia.

In November 1991, after twenty-seven years of Independence, the Zambian people chose a new President, Mr. Frederick Chiluba, replacing Dr. Kenneth Kaunda while Chiluba's party, Movement for Multiparty Democracy (M.M.D.) took the majority of seats in Parliament thereby replacing the United National Independence Party (U.N.I.P.). This heralded a new era in the life of the nation with M.M.D.'s promise of greater democracy and prosperity through a more capitalist route to development. Together with other Churches, the Catholics had contributed to this new dawn. Most of the main political leaders acknowledged that the Churches played a major role in the re-introduction of multiparty politics in Zambia.[2] One M.M.D. politician, when asked if the Catholic Church had supported the shift to multipartyism in Zambia replied:

> Yes, I think the Catholic Church did support it through and through in terms of its philosophy which Catholic goers believed in, mainly the ideas of justice and freedom. All our Catholic populace supported the change. They did not necessarily support M.M.D., but the philosophy of freedom and independence.[3]

Over the years, with much caution, the Christian Churches criticised the working of the Kaunda government under a one party state.[4] One of the first voices of more daring criticism appeared from the

---

[1] Much of the present chapter has appeared in "Catholic Schools in Zambia-whither?" *African Christian Studies* 13, 3 (1997), pp. 49-76.

[2] See: Sr. Casmir Chanda, Paper written for RS 312, October 1996; See also: Paul Gifford, "Some Recent Developments in African Christianity," *African Affairs*, 93, (1994), p. 513; See also: Gifford, ed. *The Christian Churches and the Democratisation of Africa*, pp. 1-13.

[3] Elias Chipimo, Interview, Lusaka, 9 March 1997.

[4] G. Lungu, "Church and state in Zambia: The role of critical observers in a one party state," *African Affairs*, vol. 83, 340 (July 1986), pp. 385-410; after the period analysed by Lungu, in 1987 another significant inter-church criticism appeared, *Christian Liberation, Justice and Development: The Churches concern for human development in Zambia* (Ndola:

Catholic Bishops after the 1990 food riots. Subsequently, the Church became less and less supportive of Kaunda's way of running the state and some of the most overt criticism came from magazines like *Icengelo* on the Copperbelt, which caused Kaunda to become progressively more antagonistic toward the Church[5].

NEW CONTEXT FOR CHURCH STATE CO-OPERATION: THE PRIMARY SCHOOLS

Perhaps because of the positive role played by the Churches in bringing about the new political climate, one of the first initiatives of the new M.M.D. Government included an offer to hand back some of the primary schools that had been taken over in the 1970s, as well as a promise to facilitate greater autonomy in the grant-aided secondary schools and Colleges.[6] The Churches, especially the Catholic Church, responded with interest to the prospect of repossessing some primary schools and receiving greater autonomy in the other institutions. While there was hesitation on the part of the Church authorities about getting involved again in the administration of primary schools, some felt that:

> ...we see the offer as a unique opportunity for the Church to exert influence on the youth of our country. If we opt out now we leave the young generation without the Church.[7]

There followed much re-evaluation of the Catholic educational endeavour in an attempt to respond creatively to the new opportunity. Concrete outcomes have remained slow, but in 1996 the dioceses of

---

Mission Press, 1986): Hinfelaar, *Bemba-Speaking Women*, pp. 154-178. On the wider context, see: Haynes, *Religion and Politics in Africa*, p. 117.

[5] Perhaps one of the best Episcopal statements was "Economics, Politics and Justice." (Catholic Secretariat, Lusaka, 23 July 1990). On Kaunda's reaction, see: "Church Leaders accused of smear campaign," *Times of Zambia* (14 August 1990); "State didn't kill Mutale say bishops," *Times of Zambia* (21 August 1990); Bishop de Jong "Pastoral Statement of the Bishops," *Impact* No. 125 (Nov, 1990), pp. 7-8; M.E. Kashimani, "A Fragile Stability: The rise and demise of Zambia's Second Republic 1972-1991." (Ph.D. dissertation, University of York, 1994), pp. 312 ff.

[6] For details, see: Government of Zambia, *Statutory Instrument No. 43 of 1993* (Lusaka: Government Printer); on the declaration of Zambia as a Christian nation, see: Gifford, "Christian Fundamentalism," in Westerlund, ed. *Questioning the Secular State*, p. 211; "Catholic Church's Stand on the Declaration of Zambia as a Christian Nation," *Daily Mail* (20 February 1995); Gifford, *The Christian Churches and the Democratisation of Africa*, p. 26.

[7] Minutes of Meeting of Heads, Principals, and Representatives of Managing agencies of Catholic Schools, Lusaka, 31 January 1992. C.S.A; Bishop Paul Lungu stressed the notion of "unique opportunity." Interview, 21 July 1997.

Kasama and Mansa had taken definite steps to repossess certain schools on mission property.[8] What appears clear is that the Church had no intention of a major repossession of the primary schools, largely because it did not have the resources to do so. Any resumption of the administration of primary schools would be selective, and worked out at the parish rather than the diocesan level.[9]

Undoubtedly, the handover of the primary schools in 1973-4 represented a loss for the Church. As the former Bishop of Monze explained: "For a while afterwards we had practically no influence on most schools at all. Suddenly we had lost about 100 centres."[10] It was a painful time for the Church. After so many years of close alliance with the schools, suddenly they were separate. Although Catholic authorities in many cases had seen this as an inevitable outcome, the Church on the whole seemed unprepared.

As we have noted earlier, the teacher-catechists formed the backbone of Catholic evangelisation in the 1920s and 30s. From the 1950s, however, much of the Catholic Church's outreach was achieved through the dedicated services of many teachers. With the handover, again the catechist as distinct from the teacher became the key figure. The time had come when Church priorities needed to be placed again in the Churches themselves which in 1928 Monsignor Hinsley had counselled to neglect, if necessary.[11] In the mid 1970s, the Church adopted a new pastoral approach—Small Christian Communities—that greatly helped its development.[12] Perhaps with this development and even before it, the local church began to assume greater responsibility for its direction. In the words of a long-serving Jesuit missionary:

> My experience is that what did bring a definite improvement in Sunday attendance whether in a school or a Church building was the starting of "Sunday service", led by the people themselves and held every Sunday... Being asked to do their own thing had a vivifying effect on the Congregation.[13]

---

[8] *Impact* (October, 1996), p. 1.
[9] John Counihan, "The Management of Primary Schools in the light of Focus on Learning." p. 3. (Counihan personal files, Monze.)
[10] Bishop James Corboy, Bishop of Monze 1962-1992. Interview, 1 March 1984.
[11] Hastings, *Church and Mission in Modern Africa*, p. 59.
[12] See: James O'Halloran, *Small Christian Communities: a pastoral companion* (New York: Orbis Books, 1996); James Healey, "Basic Christian Communities in Africa and Latin America," *Afer* 26, 4 (August, 1984), pp. 222-32; G.L.K. Afagbegee, "Inculturation and Small Christian Communities," *Afer* 27, 5 (October, 1985), pp. 279-85; Haynes, *Religion and Politics in Africa*, pp. 149-52.
[13] Letter from Fr. Bernard Collins to the author, dated 1 March 1987. J.A.C.

The responsibility for forming young Catholics fell again to the local parish community. As Oger commented: "One could then witness a slow divorce between priests and schools, priests and teachers."[14] However this so-called slow divorce between priests and teachers perhaps also included teachers and pastoral workers between whom a rift had long existed in that "there was a tendency for pastoral workers to stay clear of teachers."[15] According to one parish priest, the handover of the primary schools made the need to form Small Christian Communities more urgent. After Independence, it was possible for the priest or catechist to teach the Catholic children in non-Catholic schools. This however changed with the handover of the schools and the introduction of the common syllabus. From 1974, only the class teachers could teach religion. Catechists then had to provide instruction on Saturdays or Sundays. Until then the Church used the schools, normally with due permission, for its instructions and services. Not surprisingly, this too became less and less feasible:

> In many schools there used to be a folding door with the purpose of having two rooms for the Sunday Mass. In one case, I remember the folding door was closed and then there was no hope of having people for Mass so we decided to build prayer houses.[16]

It is possible that the separation between the primary school and the Church eventually helped the Church to stand on its own feet. In certain areas, this seemed true especially when, as we noted, the Small Christian Community ideal began to be implemented in Zambia after 1976.[17] As the Bishop of Ndola recalled:

> The handover helped the Church as we had relied too exclusively on the school. In a sense, the parish base was strengthened and then we made every effort to have catechists and especially the B.C.C.s (Small Christian Communities), men and women.[18]

In a survey conducted in 1988, out of 219 parish priests who were asked to comment on whether they considered that the handover of the primary schools helped the Church to become more self-sufficient, 119

---

[14] Oger, *Where a Scattered Flock*, p. 189.

[15] Fr. Desmond O'Brien S.J. Interview, Chikuni, 1983. Fr. O'Brien worked for many years in the 1970s as parish priest and as Chaplain to the Laity in the Monze diocese.

[16] Fr. Frank O'Neill, parish priest in Monze diocese from the late 1960s. Interview, 31 December 1983.

[17] Brendan Carmody, "Mission Primary Schools and Conversion: Help or Hindrance to Church Growth?" *Missiology: An International Review* XVII, 2 (April 1989), p. 188.

[18] Denis de Jong, Interview, Ndola, 29 July 1996; This was also very much emphasised by Bishop Corboy. Interview, Monze, March, 1984.

(54%) responded positively. Fifty-two percent agreed that the handover had helped the Church to become more self-ministering. More specifically, in a further survey inquiring about what instruction was being given to Catholic children, it was found that 50% received some instruction on weekends. Such instruction concentrates on the basics needed for the sacraments of Baptism and Confirmation and was given mainly by non-teachers. In a 1995 survey of 72 parishes, it was found that of those who responded to the question: Who are the main catechumenate class teachers, 48% claim that it was Small Christian Communities, 31% mentioned teachers and 21% mentioned parents.[19] One parish priest from a long-established mission station in the 1980s noted: "Usually the local leaders are not teachers. Some Catholic teachers are helpful and co-operative but they are not many."[20] It would appear that non-teachers continue to form the core of the instructors, which in the eyes of a long-serving parish priest in the Lusaka archdiocese may need attention because: "as dedicated as the majority of these are, they are not always themselves well instructed in the basics of the faith."[21] In the 1990s, it would seem that new approaches may be more effectively addressing the issue of non-teacher instructors. The Rite of Christian Initiation of Adults (R.C.I.A.) is proving to be both popular and effective.[22]

Although, as we have observed, some benefits resulted from the handover of the primary schools, the overall picture in the 1990s hardly inspires great confidence that young Catholics are receiving a good foundation in their faith. One retired Catholic teacher noted:

> Pupils need to be taught the Catholic faith progressively from childhood. At the moment, most Catholics who learn Catechism at the Church know very little about the faith.[23]

This view was very much confirmed by the Archbishop of Kasama who remarked:

> The handover was a retrogressive step for the Church...Today youth get very little from the point of view of the Church. The common syllabus, from our perspective, is minimalist...There has been no real replacement

---

[19] Survey (1995).

[20] Fr. Colm Brophy S.J., Parish Priest at Chikuni parish, Interview, 9 April 1984.

[21] Fr. L. Tomazin S.J. in J.C.T.R. review No. 15 (January 1993).

[22] Sr. Alexandrina Mwansa, S.S.F., co-ordinator for catechetics in the Livingstone diocese feels that the R.C.I.A. approach is very effective, but in her area, teachers using it have a year's training. (Interview, Livingstone, 10 January 1997). For more detail, see: *Catholic Update* (St. Anthony's Press, 1615 Republic St., Cincinnati, OH.45210).

[23] A.Y. Nyoni, Lecturer, Mongu Teachers' College. Interview, Mongu, 1995.

for the schools...There is lack of depth in the faith of the young. As a result, our youth are a prey to other sects.[24]

Whether this situation would have been greatly different if the schools had not been handed over is difficult to say. Since the common syllabus had become the norm for all schools, Catholic instruction would largely have been limited to out of class time, even if the schools were retained. What might have been significantly different is that the links between the Church and the children, their parents, and their teachers would probably have been closer. Such contact with the teachers clearly would have had important consequences. However, what appears to be true also is the fact that:

> The Church had not done anything comparable to what was done in the schools in terms of providing books, teaching aids, etc. Fr. Lane's catechism was an attempt, but some kind of response to the catechism would be useful.[25]

Perhaps this lack of provision can be explained by the fact that there continues to be in some instances a lingering expectation in Catholic circles that the schools' religious education programmes should be catechetical. A long-serving inspector of Religious Education reflected:

> Many church leaders continue to look back to the good old days of the 1950s and 1960s when each mission taught its own particular brand of doctrine and prepared the pupils for Christian initiation. That mission schools were used as direct instruments of evangelisation is part of Zambia's educational history, but surely that cannot be church policy for the twenty-first century.[26]

Whatever the reason, the Catholic Church's preparation of catechesis appears to leave a good deal to be desired.

Severing the link between church and school probably had positive effects on the conversion process. Many of the social imperatives that facilitated conversion in earlier days disappeared. The association of the Church with school children in the minds of many, which O'Sullivan

---

[24] V. Revd. James Spaita, Archbishop of Kasama. Interview, Kasama, 17 July 1996.

[25] Fr. John Henze, M. Afr. Regional Inspector for Religious Education, Curriculum Development Centre, Ndola. Interview, Ndola. 28 July 1996. The book to which Henze refers is: *A Light for Our Path* (Ndola: Mission Press, 1992). There are others also: *A Lamp for Our Steps* (Lusaka: Catholic Secretariat, 1995); Kieren Shorten, *The Way, the Truth, the Life* (Ndola: Mission Press, 1988)

[26] Fr. B. Henze, *Resources* no. 22, p. 1; D.M. Nguluwe, "The History of Religious Education in Zambia." (Diploma dissertation: University of Birmingham, 1995), p. 20; *Resources* is a regular newsletter for Religious Education teachers in Zambia, produced by the Religious Education Inspectorate at Ndola.

noted in the Western Province, but which was fairly widespread became less clear.[27] Becoming a Catholic and attending school have become quite distinct issues. Thus today the decision to become a Catholic is more likely to be free of the kinds of social imperatives connected with attending a denominational school. This was confirmed by the 1988 survey where it was found that 55% of the children in the catechumenate were considered to have been there because they so wanted and not because of parental or peer influence or because of some form of enhanced social status.[28] Teachers, of course, also are freer in that their choice of being catechists is voluntary and is not dictated by the fact that they are teachers in a Catholic school.[29] Thus, both from the point of view of the teachers and the students, the days of "school Catholics" are now over. Maybe, in these circumstances, conversion results preponderantly from a sense of the superior explanatory power of the new religion as proposed by Horton.[30] In any event, whatever the dominant motivation, conversion to Catholicism should be a more free decision, now made outside the walls of the school.

While the handover of the primary schools had some positive effects on the Church, the current separation between Church and primary schools remains undesirable, from the overall perspective of the Catholic instruction of children. Oftentimes, though located on mission property, the priest has little or no contact with what goes on in the school. The bishops and the Episcopal Education Commission, set up in 1994, have focused particularly on such schools with a view to possible repossession.[31] When the Bishop of Livingstone was asked why he would have interest in repossessing some schools, he replied:

> It would mean better contact with the pupils and better education even though of course much would depend on the parish priests.[32]

Despite the problems involved, he and other bishops felt ready to

---

[27] O'Sullivan, *A History of the Capuchins in Zambia 1931-81*, p. 62; See also: Hastings, *African Catholicism*, p. 10; B. Collins, Letter on this topic to B. Carmody, where he stressed this aspect of early conversions. JAC.

[28] "Catholic Religious Instruction in Zambia." JAC.

[29] For this reason repossession of primary schools seemed undesirable to Fr. John Counihan, Education Advisor to the Bishop of Monze. He felt that the Church should not get back into controlling laity. For him, this is a kickback to the vision of the 1960s. Counihan, Interview, Lusaka, 9 May 1997.

[30] Carmody, *Conversion and Jesuit Schooling*, p. 141.

[31] See: Minutes of the Meeting of the Education Commission, 14 December 1994 (C.S.A.).

[32] Rt. Revd. Raymond Mpezele, Bishop of Livingstone, Interview, Livingstone, 10 January 1997.

resume responsibility for a number of primary schools.

CATHOLIC TEACHERS' COLLEGES

At the Teachers' College level, the handover of the primary schools had important consequences. Henceforth, students were posted to any school, irrespective of the Church's wishes or the student's preference. As the Principal of Charles Lwanga wrote:

> Of late the government seems to have taken large-scale control in staffing these institutions. As a result, many teachers irrespective of their religious and moral background, have been posted at these schools.[33]

As a result, Catholic students found themselves in predominantly non-Catholic areas, while at the same time schools that had been Catholic and were in a densely Catholic area received non-Catholic teachers. Thus, in some cases, it was difficult for the Church to count on the support of the local teachers. As Oger says, rifts grew. Some attempts to regain contact with the teachers or to retain contact with newly trained teachers from the Colleges followed. In Mbala diocese, for instance, a priest and sister assisted in the training of resource teachers, eventually leading to the formation of the Institute for Christian Leadership at Mpika.[34] In Livingstone, as we noted earlier, Fr. Herlihy formed a group to cater for the Catholic education of children. From 1986, in the Monze area, the Bishop appointed a chaplain. His idea was to form and support a group of dedicated Catholic teachers who would actively promote Catholic programmes. Even then, the initiative was welcomed by both Catholics and non-Catholics as well as by the local education officers.[35] In the mid-1990s, perhaps in response to the new interest in repossessing some primary schools, similar initiatives have been taken in Chipata, Kasama, and Mansa, to form a group of dedicated Catholic teachers.

As we have mentioned already, the Colleges themselves had come to cater for large non-Catholic populations. In 1994, for instance, only 61% of Charles Lwanga's students and 27% of Mongu Teachers' College students were Catholic. Moreover, from the point of view of students, roughly 16% chose Mongu because of its Catholic character and 23%

---

[33] B. Haambote, Principal C.L.T.C., letter to Fr. O'Leary, Jesuit Provincial, dated 10 July 1981. JAC.

[34] Oger, *Where a Scattered Flock*, p. 220.

[35] Fr. Klaus Cieszynski S.J., Interview, Lusaka, 26 December 1996. Fr. Cieszynski was the chaplain in the Monze diocese for three years.

chose Lwanga for this reason. In both cases, the dominant reason for the choice of institution was convenience to their homes.[36] For many years, Catholic students in the Colleges have received minimal Catholic doctrine and almost no practical experience in teaching the elements of the Catholic faith. As already mentioned, the initiative of Sr. Aileen Waldron at Charles Lwanga in the late 1970s of assisting the local parish on Sunday mornings with Catholic trainee teachers was eventually discontinued as was that of Sr. Dympna O'Leary at Mongu. There were various reasons for this lack of continuity including diverging perspectives on whether the teachers should be integral to the teaching of Catholic children in the Church when this should be the responsibility of the parish, not the school. In any event, Catholic trained teachers for the most part receive little to prepare them to teach specifically Catholic material even though they are best equipped pedagogically to do this.

The Colleges respond primarily to the teacher needs of the nation not of the Catholic Church.[37] It is true that Catholic students receive special pastoral care. At Mongu and Lwanga, there has been a catechumenate over the years, whereby people can receive Baptism in the Catholic Church. The average number in both colleges is roughly 12 yearly. In a survey carried out by the Lwanga College chaplain, Fr. James McGloin, on why people chose to become Catholics in the College, he found that 38% spoke in terms of personal conviction which, combined with a Catholic background, indicated that the College gave a number of men the opportunity to make a formal commitment. Fewer women were in a similar position.[38] A possible reason advanced was that many such students had been to non-Catholic secondary schools.[39]

It is possible moreover that there can still be some pretence on the part of students whereby if they show some level of Catholic commitment, they may receive some favours. This was mentioned in an earlier set of interviews with lecturers who wondered why so few of the students remain good Christians when they go into the field. In a study

---

[36] Survey conducted in both Colleges in June 1994 involving roughly 100 students in both Colleges.

[37] This was very much how Bishop Corboy saw things in the 1980s and so he and others would have been very careful to avoid any impression that Catholics were using the College for narrowly denominational interests. Interview, Monze, March, 1984.

[38] James McGloin, "Why students wanted to be baptised," JCTR *Bulletin* No. 28 (October 1995), pp. 17-18.

[39] This trend is likely to continue in the light of the fact that so many Catholics will now be attending basic schools as well as more non-Catholic secondary schools with the overall increase in secondary school populations.

done by Nyambe at Mongu, he noted that this element of pretence applied not only to students but to lecturers as well. At Mongu, some students feared that they might be penalised if they were not found to be practising Christians, since on their entry form they had declared themselves committed Christians. Lecturers seemed conscious of the fact that their promotion or prospect of further study rested with the proprietors who take commitment to Church practices into consideration.[40]

As well as their commitment to Catholic students, the Colleges prepare many non-Catholic teachers professionally. One of the areas of this professional training of course is that of Religious Education. This means that their graduates can be posted anywhere throughout the country. From the religious perspective, much is thus being achieved in the promotion of Christian unity. In a nation attempting to create a sense of identity from divergent tribes and religious creeds, this appears to be a significant contribution. Even from the more limited point of view of the Catholic Church, the fact that so many Protestant students, some of whom originate from rather anti-Catholic denominations, leave Catholic institutions with a positive attitude towards Catholicism is surely significant. In a survey of about 100 Protestant students in both Colleges, almost none of the students felt unwelcome in the College or under any undue pressure to conform to Catholic norms. Nonetheless at Charles Lwanga, such tolerance was not seen to be sufficient by itself. The principal noted:

> There is a Catholic atmosphere but there is need for greater ecumenism. Fr. Hidaka (former chaplain) spoke of the need for an ecumenical service on Sunday evenings...Here (at the College) there is need not so much for vision. That is there but many non-Catholics do not feel part of it.[41]

Indeed, there may be some need to make non-Catholics feel part of the institutions as Mr. Chasha implied, especially since in 1995 Mongu had 55% non-Catholic lecturers while Charles Lwanga had 34%. Certainly when the College constitution at Charles Lwanga was revised in the early 1980s, there was apprehension among the non-Catholic lecturers. One long serving member said:

> Members of staff especially non-Catholics feel that they are unwelcome...

---

[40] L. Nyambe, "School as a means of Conversion at Mongu Teacher Training College, Western Province" (Project course at University of Zambia, Lusaka, 1995), pp. 7, 10.

[41] Charles Chasha, Principal. Interview, 12 June 1995. The need to do more was identified by many administrators at their Monze diocesan meeting in Monze Homecraft Centre on 17 May 1997, at which the author was present.

> At one meeting it was said openly that they would like to have more Catholic staff and one gets the impression that it is only a question of time when we will be asked to leave in favour of Catholic staff.[42]

Though clearly non-Catholic staff at times felt some apprehension, it does not appear to have been a major long-standing issue. On the whole, non-Catholics have been welcomed and Catholic authorities have occasionally regretted that they could not promote such people to the level of principal or deputy. In order to maintain a Catholic identity, the proprietors of both Colleges feel that such restrictions are necessary. Such regulations appear to have been widely accepted and have been incorporated into the 1993 Education Act.[43]

At the Teachers' Colleges' level, a repossession of some primary schools would have advantages. When questioned about this, the Principal of Charles Lwanga stated:

> They (repossessed schools) would be more effective in that it would be a local body that would be in charge. Students would get more Catholic background. At present, we have lost touch so it would help to gain some feedback and we would have better demonstration schools.[44]

More close co-operation between the College and primary schools should help create an atmosphere for the children, where Religious Education would not only feature as a subject in the curriculum but where it would become a more lived community experience, in terms of prayers, liturgy, and festivities. From the point of view of the colleges, greater integration would also be possible whereby these primary schools could serve more effectively as models and where, as Mr. Chasha noted, more immediate and effective feedback would be available.

CATHOLIC SECONDARY SCHOOLS

As we have noted earlier, in the post Independence period, the Catholic Church greatly extended its commitment to secondary schooling. The Catholic schools gained and sustained a reputation for excellence, especially for good examination results. Many non-Catholics chose and continue to choose Catholic schools because of such reputations. In a 1996 survey conducted among 684 Catholic and

---

[42] B. Sidono, Non-Catholic Lecturer at Charles Lwanga, 1979-92. Interview, Chikuni, March 1984.
[43] Government of Zambia, *Statutory Instrument No. 43 (1993)*, para. 12.2 and para. 13, 1, 2, and 3.
[44] Charles Chasha, Interview, Chikuni, 28 January 1997.

Protestant graduates from Catholic schools, it was found that 73% of them said that they had attended Catholic secondary schools because they were the "best from the viewpoint of standards".[45] In that same survey, 17% Catholics chose Catholic schools because they were specifically Catholic.

Historically, the concentration on academic achievement was enhanced by the national school concept which government adopted in 1969. There are a variety of further reasons why mission schools perform better academically than government schools. These include the fact that they often have higher entry points, more strict discipline, better teacher and student morale, more qualified and experienced staff, more adequate equipment and organisation, and frequently they are single sex institutions.[46] Allowing for the special advantages that the Catholic schools often had, nonetheless the record of academic success remains admirable. From the point of view of the Catholic Church's religious mission, however, the "success" record needs qualifications. In many cases, with declining numbers of Catholic staff and students, the Catholic, even religious, dimension of the institutions have been overshadowed.[47]

In the late 1970s, as we noted earlier, when the Catholic authorities became more aware of the quickly evaporating identity of Catholic secondary schools, they made efforts to rectify that trend. From the specifically Catholic perspective, the schools had moved from a period

---

[45] The survey in question included 55% current students and 11% teachers/lecturers at University of Zambia, Lusaka, 49% men and 51% women. Schools most highly represented were Fatima, Dominican Convent, Ndola, Canisius, Ibenga, St. Clement's, St. Raphael's, St. Joseph's, and Charles Lwanga College. Representatives from Lwitikila, Chilubula, and St. Mary's, Kawambwa were few, while there were none from Chikuni Girls and Lukulu.

[46] See: Kelly, *Education in a Declining Economy*, p. 83; For more empirical data on the issue, see: M. Banda, "Why Mission schools perform better academically?" (U.N.Z.A: Religious Studies Library, Project 1995); M. Chisulo, "Why Mission schools perform better academically?" (U.N.Z.A: Religious Studies Library, Project 1995); O.M.J. Hambwalula, "Why Mission schools perform better academically?" (U.N.Z.A: Religious Studies Library, Project 1995); E. Nkhoma, "Why Mission Schools perform better academically?" (U.N.Z.A: Religious Studies Library, Project 1995). John O'Leary, "A Study of School Effectiveness in the Southern Province of Zambia." (Ph.D. thesis: Cork University, 1997). While the schools in question are grant-aided, not strictly private, they do share some elements of private schools such as some autonomy in choice of staff, establishment of disciplinary code, homework policies, more recently rate and use of school fees and some flexibility in adapting the curriculum. Thus like private schools elsewhere, they appear to be more effective at boosting school achievement. See: Jimenez & Lockheed, *Public and Private Schooling in Developing Countries*, p. 20.

[47] Bishop Paul Lungu, S.J. Interview, Monze, 21 July 1997.

when they had an almost entire Catholic student body and staff in the 1960s to a time when only a fraction of the students and staff were Catholic. As we already saw, some Catholic schools reacted by creating special Catholic groups where Catholic teaching was given usually outside of class time. Moreover, Catholic authorities attempted to reclaim certain autonomies from government, especially in the area of selection of teaching staff.

Nevertheless, even though many Catholic schools had become more conscious of their Catholic identity by the early 1980s, 66% of the schools surveyed in 1995 claimed that they have ecumenical services at least a few times yearly. In 1995, of 26 Catholic schools that responded to a questionnaire, only 37% of their student body of 14,039 were Catholic. Furthermore, Catholic schools continue to have a large percentage of non-Catholic teaching staff, which includes many different denominations.[48] Overall, approximately 45% of the teaching staff of the 26 schools were non-Catholic, while 48% of the general staff were non-Catholic. Despite the high numbers of non-Catholics in these institutions, their potential for promoting Church unity is weakly recognised. When asked about this issue, administrators tended to say that non-Catholics experience freedom of worship or are under the care of some pastor or patron. However, there seemed little awareness of the opportunities for the creation of more ecumenical and pluralistic communities which such situations presented. At the same time, development of the whole person is presented as a core ideal in Catholic institutions. Catholics and Protestants alike attest to the reality of this ideal when they speak of the dedication and personal interest shown by the staff for their welfare. Such a personalised approach is sometimes further articulated in terms of the institution as a community though in most cases this remains vague.[49]

The Catholic schools seem to have decided to pay special pastoral attention to their Catholic minorities, not neglecting the non-Catholics

---

[48] Of 18 schools surveyed in 1994-5, there were approximately 42% Catholic students and staff, while the remaining 58% came from 24 different denominations. Source: *Impact* No. 142 (1995), p. 10. This estimate is conservative for at St. Raphael's, Livingstone, 28 denominations were recorded. Paper presented at Meeting of Heads and Principals (Lusaka, August 1997).

[49] See: A.S. Bryk et al. *Catholic Schools and the Common Good* (Cambridge: Cambridge University Press, 1993), pp. 275, 289-90, 298-9; On the ambiguity connected with community development in a pluralistic setting see, N. Noddings, "On Community," *Educational Theory* 46, 3 (1996), pp. 245-67; This dimension has been stressed in recent Catholic thinking, see: "The Catholic School on the Threshold of the Third Millennium," *L'Osservatore Romano* (16-22 April 1998), pp. 8, 9.

but taking few initiatives on their behalf. The impression created is that when and if ever government permits, they will probably make the Catholics less and less a minority in these schools, though there seems little evidence that there is a desire to create Catholic schools where students or staff would be totally Catholic. Even in 1995, when the schools' populations were dominantly non-Catholic, those in charge of all the schools surveyed claimed that they were "Catholic" schools. They had various ways in which they felt this claim could be substantiated. Many alleged that the school was Catholic because it made provision for the celebration of Mass perhaps on Sundays or, in the case of day schools, on occasions through the year. Frequently the existence of specifically Catholic groups like the Pioneers or the Catholic Identity groups were noted and occasionally prayers before class, celebration of Catholic feasts, Crucifixes on the wall, and compulsory Religious Education were mentioned. However, as the diversity of replies indicates, there is no univocal concept of what constitutes or might constitute a "Catholic" school. Some spoke more of a Catholic ethos in a predominantly Christian school, but in general it seems that the issue remains somewhat ambiguous. If it is true, as we have mentioned earlier, that there can appear to be rather inward looking attitudes focusing on narrowly defined Catholic schools and teacher associations, it does not represent the mainstream mood of the Catholic Church at this time.[50]

Most administrators continued to regret having so little say on admissions of students, which for many constituted the main problem in maintaining a Catholic school. Seventy-five percent of the administrators surveyed in 1995 considered that for the majority of students, academic takes precedence over religious motives when choosing the school. As we have noted in the context of our 1996 survey, this perception appears accurate. The headmistress of one prestigious school stated:

> Many use the place...Some of our graduates are certainly good but some behave while here. Some are told (by parents) "Behave while there until you get out."[51]

Other important factors in preventing the emergence of "Catholic" schools included the difficulty of procuring and retaining good quality Catholic teachers, government control of curriculum, and lack of clear

---

[50] Letter from B. Henze in *Impact* No. 128 (1991), p. 23.
[51] Sr. Christine Mwale O.P. Headmistress, Fatima. Interview, 27 July 1996; This viewpoint was generally perceived to be exaggerated when reported to Catholic administrators at Monze on 17 May 1997.

vision.⁵² In a number of cases, it was regretted that there are so few meetings at a national level for Catholic administrators. When asked how they see the school contributing to the growth of the Catholic Church, practically all emphasised that these schools produce vocations to the priesthood and religious life.⁵³ Moreover, all stressed the schools' role in the formation of Catholic lay leaders as well as their contribution to communicating both Catholic and Christian values. Nonetheless, in the 1996 survey, only 22% of past graduates from Catholic schools mentioned that they had received special leadership training while at a Catholic institution, while 31% of them felt that the laity in the Catholic Church are poorly prepared for leadership roles.

When asked how the Catholic ideals were realised, administrators stressed the need for staff formation.⁵⁴ In some instances, much emphasis was placed on the role of the chaplain or pastoral director in an institution. Often this person is a priest. Theoretically, he/she is regarded as a king-pin for the religious and moral atmosphere of the setting. However, individual chaplains claim to be rather peripheral to the operation of the school or college. In addition, quite a number feel unprepared for the task in terms not only of skills but also in terms of job description. It is often vague and ill-defined. In a number of instances, the chaplain does not even have an office set aside for his/her work. In general, among chaplains themselves there appears to be an awareness of the need for a team approach to pastoral care in these

---

⁵² Retention of staff is a major problem given the inadequate salaries and poor conditions of service. This is further compounded at Catholic schools as they resisted allowing their teachers to do out of school tuition called A.P.U. (Academic Production Unit). See: "Educating Our Future. Some Reactions from the Zambia Episcopal Conference to the Ministry of Education's Policy Statement." July, 1997, pp. 3-4. (C.S.A.)

⁵³ Certainly, many priests, sisters and brothers have emerged from these schools. Possibly the girls' schools promote more vocations to sisterhood than brothers' or priests' schools to brotherhood or priesthood. In 1996, from the available data, it would appear that 16% of the diocesan clergy had been to Catholic secondary schools, while 10% of the students at Emmaus (pre-seminary training) between 1989-96 had come from such schools and about 45% of the sisters had come through such Catholic schools. The majority of the students entering Emmaus appear to come from the minor seminaries.

⁵⁴ Initiatives have been taken, especially in the Monze area, since 1985. Seminars have been held for both personal development using such things as Myers-Briggs, Training for Transformation, Enneagram, sexuality workshops and for creating and communicating vision in various institutions. Rarely are staff sponsored by the agency for special training, though some thought is being given to this. John Counihan, Monze Diocesan Committee Chair 1985-1990, Interview, Lusaka, 7 May 1997; On parallel developments in the United States, see: *The Principal as Educational Leader* (U.S. Catholic Conference, 1993); *The Principal as Spiritual Leader* (U.S. Catholic Conference, 1993); *Expectations for the Catholic School Principal* (U.S. Catholic Conference, 1996)

institutions. Realising this is seen to be difficult, particularly since there is almost no provision made for on-going formation of staff in Catholic institutions.[55]

There is little follow-up of former students at any institution. When asked if many past pupils live as practising Catholics in later life, administrators generally responded positively, but since there is generally no systematic follow-up at any institution, they could not be too specific. One administrator, however, from a very prominent secondary school stated: "I do not have the impression that most Catholic pupils live as practising Catholics and actively support the Church."[56] However, when later interviewed, she observed that while many appear to leave the Church for some time, a good number later returns to live as good Catholics. In a 1996 survey of past students of Catholic secondary schools and training colleges, it was found that 64% claim that they attend Sunday Mass regularly while 60% are active members of their Small Christian Communities, both of which activities are taken to be key indicators of Catholic involvement. Of the 244 Catholics who indicated that they were married, 26% replied that they had been married in Church.

What thus emerges is that even if the Catholic schools assist only a small percentage of the Catholic students in their Catholic development, they help to create a positive rapport with non-Catholic students, many of whom could be from their own tribe or local community. The freedom which non-Catholic staff and students experience in Catholic institutions, together with cordial school community relationships and occasional ecumenical gatherings have undoubtedly helped to create a more open community. In the 1996 survey, over 90% of all past students noted that they enjoy meeting former teachers and administrators, generally indicating happy memories of their days in these institutions. Overall, Catholic institutions seem to have responded well to the religiously pluralistic nature of their post Independence educational setting. This pluralistic atmosphere in large part has resulted because of government's preoccupation with the academic and professional needs of the new nation. Surely, such a positive ecumenical ambience should be welcome in a country where so much denominational rivalry existed from the earliest days of the missionary enterprise. What perhaps remains is to

---

[55] On the chaplain role, see: Bryk et al. *Catholic Schools and the Common Good*, pp. 140-1; See also B. Carmody, "Religious Education and Human Development" *JCTR* 39 (January, 1999), pp. 20-21.
[56] A Dominican sister from Ndola.

explore ways to enhance such inter-church and inter-religious dialogue.

Moreover, Catholic secondary schools and teachers' colleges have contributed significantly to governments' concern for meeting the labour needs of the country, through, among other things, producing good teachers in the Colleges and good academic results in the schools that enable their students enter various careers and fields of service. Repeatedly, government officials praise the Catholic authorities for the contribution that they have made on this level. From the perspectives of some Catholic authorities, however, there are regrets and misgivings about being so tied to the current academic system, when the country appears to have more and more educated unemployed who have little or no practical skills that would enable them to make a living.[57] Of the past students surveyed in 1996, 73% considered that the Catholic Church should open institutes for drop-outs.[58]

While it is true that the Catholic institutions have produced large numbers of professionals at all levels, is there evidence that these men and women have carried the Word of God with them into the larger world? To paraphrase Muwele, one might ask: Do the graduates from Catholic schools have any better answers about the issues of life and death and truth than others? Is justice and respect for human rights more part of their lives? Is corruption less common among them?[59] When asked if Catholic past students live up to the ideals of their Church, one prominent politician and former student replied:

---

[57] B. Carmody, "Catholic Beliefs, Attitudes and Practice in Zambia," *African Christian Studies* Vol. 12, No. 1 (1996), p. 37; In 1996-7, 34% of the 117, 283 candidates got places in Grade VIII, (*Times of Zambia*, 4 Jan 1997) 20% of the 95, 833 received places in Grade X (*Times of Zambia*, 31 Jan 1997) and of the 26, 922 students who sat for Grade XII examinations, (*Times of Zambia*, 27 March 1997) about 30% of the latter would be absorbed in the world of work or get places at higher institutions. From this statistic alone we realise that there is a large annual increase in the unemployment figure which in 1990 revealed that only about 40% of the 7.8 million in the population had formal employment (*Census of Population* 1990 vol. 10, p. 183.) This does not take account of the many redundancies that have taken place since 1991 under the new restructuring programme, (S.A.P.). See: "Social Dimensions of the 1997 Budget of the Government of the Republic of Zambia: Statement of the Catholic Commission on Justice and Peace." 14 February 1997. J.A.C. In dealing with the unemployment figures, it has to be noted that many find employment in the informal sectors but again it does not seem that school graduates are well prepared for this.

[58] It needs to be pointed out here that many programmes already exist in terms of homecraft centres, agricultural centres, the Education Development Programme in Monze and the Village Oriented Programme in Chipata, and primary schools in Lusaka. For details see: *Catholic Directory 1996* (Ndola: Mission Press, 1996).

[59] The questions are adapted from those posed in C. Muwele, "Features," *Sunday Times of Zambia* (23 July 1995), p. 7.

I don't know. But I think the Catholic upbringing is so principled in that we have little to be ashamed of. They (past pupils) have come up to various high positions and fewer of them than others have caused the Catholic Church any disgrace.[60]

From our 1996 survey, it would appear that 64% of these graduates felt that they had become either better Catholics or Christians while at Catholic schools, and only 8% felt that they had become less interested in either Christianity or Catholicism during their stay in these schools. Of the overall population surveyed, 52% percent agreed that they were prepared to act maturely rather than to obey authority blindly, while 79% felt that hard work had been a cardinal value combined with a sense of competition. Other values that ranked highly included honesty and personal responsibility. Moreover, 54% stressed that they had been encouraged to assist the underprivileged.

On the less positive side, 30% noted that little had been done to make them proud of their Zambian heritage and 46% regretted receiving so little preparation for married life, including 67% who felt that there had been too little contact between the sexes during their school years. It is possible that Catholic schools are no poorer than others in terms of promoting Zambian traditions and cultural identity. Catholic schools, however, have attempted to inculturate the liturgical life of the students and occasionally attention has been given to using Zambian art to decorate. The issue of not sufficiently promoting awareness of local traditions and culture appears wider than Catholic settings for, despite much stress on Zambianization by post-Independence governments, the schools' curricula have generally neglected indigenous languages and heritage. Rather ironically, as Professor Kashoki noted:

> ...the colonial government in the British Empire, together with missionaries did more for indigenous African languages than anything nationalist governments have done since the attainment of Independence.[61]

Again, it is difficult to know how Catholic schools compare with others on matters of sex education. In any event, it is an area that needs much attention at a time when the AIDS pandemic is causing so much havoc.

What the Catholic schools do for Catholic Church growth is difficult to pinpoint. In a 1995 survey of 326 adult Catholics, 158 of

---

[60] Elias Chipimo, Interview, Lusaka, 9 March 1997.
[61] Mubanga Kashoki, "A Battle lost on the frontline," *Africa Insight* vol. 24, 4 (1994), p. 290; This point was also emphasised by Frank Wafer who spoke in terms of people leaving the rural areas as well as their traditions through schooling. (F. Wafer, Interview, Chikuni, 19 July 1997); See also: *Focus on Learning*, p. 9.

whom had been to Catholic secondary schools, it was found that in general those who had attended Catholic schools rated considerably higher on willingness to encourage a child to be a priest/brother/sister (84%-60%), to welcome a visit from a priest/sister/catechist (96%-61%), and to concur with the Church's total prohibition of artificial birth control (45%-32%).[62] Catholic graduate students from Catholic institutes tended to be more traditional in such things as approval of local food and drink for Mass (28%-57%), and fewer would consider that use of drums at liturgy is good (38%-55%). However, as in the 1996 survey mentioned already, being at a Catholic school appeared to help participation in Church life. Those who had been to Catholic schools were more active in Small Christian Communities (55%-44%). In a further mini-survey of 230 men and women who were serving on Church councils or had Church leadership positions in 1995, 38% had been to a Catholic seminary, secondary school, or College. Of the 41 teachers who were serving in leadership capacities, 71% had been to either Charles Lwanga or Mongu Colleges.

Of the past Catholic students surveyed in 1996, 65% felt that they had learned most about their Catholic faith during Church services and 44% through observing the behaviour of priests, brothers, or sisters at an institution. On the other hand, only 23% mentioned the classroom instruction in this regard. It is true that only 49% felt that they were better Catholics because of being at a Catholic institution. Approximately, six percent said that they had become less interested in Catholicism during their time at the institution, which means that a large section of the Catholic population felt that they changed very much during their stay at the Catholic institution.

From the 1996 research, it would appear that Catholic graduates from Catholic institutions have a high level of commitment to the Catholic Church as evidenced in such things as attendance at Sunday Mass and membership of Small Christian Communities. They also seem to retain positive attitudes towards the priesthood where 64% would encourage a son to be a priest and 58% would encourage a daughter to be a sister. Moreover, in a situation where many clergy are still expatriate, 72% favour continuing to receive missionaries from abroad and only 3% favour a moratorium on receiving expatriate missionaries. However, 18% of the expatriate priests were perceived not to listen sufficiently to the laity as opposed to 15% of the Zambian priests. Of the values that the Catholic school graduates highlighted are that marriages

---

[62] Survey prepared by B. Carmody and distributed mainly in the Lusaka region in 1995, by Kennedy Mwamba and Daniel Kangwa.

should be blessed in Church, a Catholic should go for Sunday Mass, and the Church should be involved in issues of justice.

While in general it appears clear that Catholic institutions and their graduates have become more sensitive to issues of justice, Catholic educational institutions have progressively become so integrated into the national system of education that it is difficult for their proprietors to offer an alternative social vision even if they might have so wanted. As the Principal of Charles Lwanga commented: "Our secondary schools have become places for the rich—the poor are left out"[63] Catholic school authorities' desire to serve disadvantaged sections of the population in the light of the Catholic Church's post-Vatican II justice agenda has become increasingly difficult to translate into practice. When the Ministry of Education suggested the phasing out of boarding schools in 1984, some Catholic school authorities saw this as an opportunity to cater for less advantaged groups, since a disproportionately large number of children in secondary boarding schools came from middle and upper income urbanised sections of society.[64] Some attempted to use the additional space in as far as possible for children in the school's vicinity though of course the schools' autonomy in this regard remained limited. Roma girls' school in Lusaka was one such school. It had been founded to provide schooling for rural girls, but had become one of the key schools of the Zambian elite. When the proprietors decided to phase out its boarding section, many parents who were part of a powerful elite resisted. In their determination to retain the school's boarding section, they appealed to the State President. In a letter to one of the government ministers of the day, the Archbishop of Lusaka noted:

> Some of the parents, influential as they are, totally refuse to understand the reasons (for becoming a day school) and wish the continuation of the boarding school...In order to create a more comfortable learning situation for their children, the influential parents cannot understand the plight of those who could be admitted to Grade VIII, if the boarding were not phased out. In this case, the professed Christianity and humanism gives way to unreasonableness and this, what is more difficult to accept, by using their power and influence.[65]

---

[63] Charles Chasha, Interview, Chikuni, 28 January 1997.
[64] E.R.I.P., p. 426.
[65] Adrian Mungandu, Archbishop of Lusaka, to Hon. C. Mwananshiku, 13 July 1988. A. A.L.; A somewhat similar earlier protest was made when the Dominican Convent in Lusaka decided to become a grant-aided school. See: "Roman Catholics and African Politics," p. 37; The trend towards serving the poor and less advantaged sectors of the population has been helped through the shift from boarding to day schools even though

Roma Convent was far from alone in meeting such resistance in becoming more open to day students.

Similarly, conscious of the adverse effects which the re-introduction of fee-paying would have on the poorer sectors of the school population, a group of Catholic university students, in an open letter, pleaded with their leaders, the Zambia Episcopal Conference, to urge government to reconsider its decision to re-introduce boarding fees. In the students' view, such action would unduly hurt peasant families and favour those who could pay. They wrote:

> The decision to re-introduce fees is but another case of the manner in which the gap between the world of the poor and that of the rich is created and maintained.[66]

Subsequently, the Bishops made a representation to government in February 1986. As they realised that the re-introduction of fees was inevitable in the economic climate of the day, they pleaded that the fees should be affordable to the majority of the students. They appealed thus:

> We realise that the Ministry of General Education and Culture...is not in a position to provide all boarding expenses...In our estimation not even half of the parents, especially in the rural areas will be able to pay...we appeal to you to influence those responsible for the introduction of boarding fees to lower them to a reasonable amount, which even the poorer population could afford.[67]

Most Catholic authorities were unhappy with the prospect of the adverse effects on the poorer sectors of society which the fees would bring. The Regional Superior of a group of brothers complained:

> The brothers are very worried about the possibility of one third of the present pupils being forced out of the school due to these fees...and so as a consequence of the expected rush from urban well-off families to place their children in the school.[68]

When many Catholic schools subsequently began to charge fees, they created some form of bursaries to assist needy students. About the

---

there is still a loud cry for boarding schools from both poor and rich. (Sr. Madeline Kelly, R.S.C., Interview, Chikuni, 20 July 1997); Bishop Paul Lungu of Monze also welcomed this direction. (Interview, Monze, 21 July 1997).

[66] Open letter to the Catholic Bishops of Zambia from The Catholic Community, University of Zambia, Lusaka, 6 December 1985. C.S.A.

[67] Bishop J. Spaita, Chairman Zambia Episcopal Conference, to Hon. K. Musokotwane, 2 February 1986. CSA.

[68] Regional Superior Marist Brothers, to Proprietor, St. Paul's Secondary School, Kabwe. 15 April 1986. C.S.A.

same time, government also set up a bursary system that seemed somewhat ineffective initially. After the re-introduction of boarding fees in 1985, 4,000 pupils had to withdraw as they could not pay. Nonetheless, it was reported that same year that the government bursary scheme had been under-utilised. This was later confirmed by Himpyali's study, where he found that grant-aided schools did a better job at administering the bursaries.[69] It is difficult to estimate how many children have been denied schooling in Catholic secondary schools because of the fees. Himpyali found that the numbers were low, but with increasing inflation and unemployment, this is likely to become a bigger problem. In most instances, the Catholic authorities have tried to work out some strategies to protect the most vulnerable but, as of 1999, the preferential option for the poor was becoming increasingly difficult to maintain as government subsidies becomes less and less adequate.[70] At the same time, however, staff in Catholic schools appear to view their institutions as having special concern for the poor and less advantaged in society.[71]

Conclusion

This period in Zambian Catholic Church history was not one of primary evangelisation. By the mid 1970s, 24% of the population were estimated to be Catholic. Between 1970 and 1980, the Church grew at about 4.2% annually. In 1996, it was considered that about 28% of the population was Catholic. Since 1974, the primary schools have not been direct instruments of conversion, for Catholic instruction at the primary school level has progressively been done more independently from the school. In this period too, the secondary schools have become less and less Catholic in the sense of having a preponderantly Catholic student and staff population, and they have become less autonomous in their co-operation with government. The situation in the two Catholic Colleges was not significantly different. What role then did these Catholic institutions have in the remarkable growth of the Church in the period

---

[69] Editorial, *Times of Zambia*, 21 May 1987; Barnabas Himpyali, "The relationship between educational fees and the dropout rate in selected boarding schools in Southern Province." (M.Ed. thesis, University of Zambia, Lusaka, 1993), pp. 17, 50, 53.

[70] Among others, Bishop Lungu of Monze acknowledges this with regret (Interview, Monze, 21 July 1997). See also: "Educating Our Future: Some Reactions from the Zambia Episcopal Conference Policy Statement," p. 4. (J.A.C.).

[71] Out of 164 teachers/lecturers from 11 Catholic institutions in 1997, 79% agreed that their respective institution has a special concern for the poor and less advantaged in society. See: "The Catholic School on the Threshold," pp. 8, 9.

we are discussing?

What appears true is that in a rather general way the Catholic institutions have supported what has been taking place in the parishes. However, the connections with the parishes in many instances are far from clear. Frequently, there is little direct contact between a Catholic secondary school and a local parish, while the contact with the primary schools is often minimal. As secondary schools become progressively more full of day pupils, this will change since these students will be clearly part of the parish. Co-operation between the teachers' colleges and the local parishes also appears weak even though this may change with the appearance of a special chaplain to the primary teachers as has happened in the Monze diocese. As we saw, some direct participation by Charles Lwanga students in the Chikuni parish catechumenate under Sr. Aileen Waldron blossomed only briefly. Similarly, the initiatives of Sr. Dympna O'Leary at Mongu have not continued. Follow-up of former student-teachers through the chaplaincy programme of the Monze diocese, which we mentioned, may bring some positive results, as the foundation of the Institute of Christian Leadership at Mpika did. It is moreover clear that more systematic and close co-operation between parishes and Catholic institutions would be of much benefit to the interests of the Catholic Church.

One of the major achievements of this era, from a religious perspective, would appear to be the largely unintended ecumenical atmosphere that has been created. For instance, among past students from Catholic higher institutions, we find that only 7% would agree that the Catholic Church is the one true Church while 46% would like the Catholic Church to unite with other Christian Churches. About 64% felt that they had become either better Christians, or where appropriate, better Catholics while they were in these institutions. A factor that may need some attention in this context is the fact that 15% of all past students from Catholic institutions felt that attendance at Sunday Mass was unfairly imposed and, hardly surprisingly, 17% of non-Catholic students had this reaction. Otherwise, both non-Catholic staff and students at Catholic schools appear satisfied with the respect that they received. This is indeed a commendable achievement, facilitating, among other things, the formation of a Religious Studies unit at the University of Zambia that caters for students of numerous denominations.

On the specifically Catholic level, certain positive elements seem clear. In practically all the Catholic schools and Colleges, a definite

Catholic character has been identified. It is a Catholic identity that respects and welcomes other Christian traditions but yet wishes to remain distinctive. Since the Religious Education syllabus is interdenominational, specifically Catholic doctrines and practices are not dealt with in the classroom. Much is being done out of class to create Catholics who are loyal and dedicated. It appears, nevertheless, that more precision is needed when specifying what constitutes a Catholic school and how such an institution can remain Catholic yet creatively ecumenical.

What perhaps remains a more difficult challenge for the Catholic institutions is to maintain and enhance not only an ecumenical dimension but especially to continue their commitment to the liberation of the poor. For various reasons as should now be clear, the Catholic institutions have become an integral part of the present socio-political system. By doing this, they have shown their willingness to identify with and promote national policies. Many such policies have greatly contributed to the creation of a Zambia that can today take its place among the nations. Howsoever, in becoming so closely allied to the system, the Catholic schools' specifically Catholic and Christian messages have become difficult to proclaim effectively.[72] Perhaps what a Church historian foresaw has come to pass when he questioned:

> If the missions co-operate with governments, are they likely to lose their Christian character in serving a scheme over the details of which they have no control, and the aim of which is different from their own?[73]

Although current Catholic thinking strongly advocates a commitment to justice and liberation of the underprivileged, Catholic schools in the present Zambian social system have come to favour those who already have means. The Catholic Church apparently has become less able to cater for the schooling needs of those who have to drop out of the system because they do not have the resources needed to continue. Catholic schools and their proprietors have been part of a system that has historically helped the poorest of the poor to stand on their feet. Over the past two decades, however, that system has progressively assumed the role of class reproduction rather that of social mobility, thereby becoming more and more inimical to the interests of the poor. Surely, this is a great reversal of a mission that started in the 1890s,

---

[72] The over-identification of the Catholic Church with the existing system has been documented clearly especially as it effects the liberation of women by Hinfelaar, *Bemba-Speaking Women*, pp. 154 ff.

[73] S. Neil, *Colonialism and Christian Missions* (London: Lutterworth Press, 1966), p. 331.

where the missionaries were welcomed as liberators of the poor.⁷⁴ Though the overall trend of the school system favours those who have, it is true that Catholic schools, in accord with government policy, assist poorer sectors of society by, among other ways, replacing boarding with day schools and providing bursaries for the needy.⁷⁵

Moreover, as Zambia and other African nations struggle to sustain democratic institutions in the aftermath of rather dictatorial regimes, Catholic schools may need to highlight leadership for democracy even though, as Hastings and others have noted, the Catholic Church itself is far from democratic in operation.⁷⁶ While it has been found that schooling generally supports the maintenance of formally democratic political institutions, the effects are not invariant.⁷⁷ While Catholic schools in Zambia appear to be sensitive to individual rights, they vary considerably on how they promote democracy among both their staffs and students. Of the 164 teachers and lecturers surveyed from eleven Catholic institutions in 1997, 62% felt that the administration of their

---

⁷⁴ On the changing role of the school in Zambian society, see: Carmody, "Denominational Secondary Schooling in Post-Independence Zambia: A Case study," *African Affairs*, Vol. 89 (355), p. 260; on how the early Catholic missionaries were perceived, see: Hinfelaar, *Bemba-Speaking Women*, p. x. This was explicitly acknowledged at the vote of thanks during the meeting of Heads and Principals of Catholic Schools and Colleges, 19-22 August 1997. C.S.A.

⁷⁵ Becoming day schools in some cases means becoming co-educational which may have adverse effects on girls. See: Bryk et al. *Catholic Schools and the Common Good*, pp. 225-41; V.E. Lee & M.E. Lockheed, "The effects of single sex schooling on achievement and attitudes in Nigeria," *Comparative Education Review* 34, 2 (1990), pp. 209-31; E. Jimenez & M.E. Lockheed, "Enhancing girls' learning through single sex education: evidence and a policy conundrum," *Education and Policy Analysis* 11, 2 (1989), pp. 117-42; V. Lee and A.S. Bryk "Effects of single sex schools on student achievement and attitudes." *Journal of Educational Psychology* 78 (1986), pp. 381-95; H.W. Marsh, "Effects of attending single-sex and co-educational high schools on achievement, attitudes, behaviours and sex differences," *Journal of Educational Psychology* 81, 1 (1989), pp. 70-85.

⁷⁶ Hastings, "The Churches and Democracy," in Gifford, ed. p. 40; De Cruchy, *Christianity and Democracy*, p. 255; For more detail on the relationship between democracy and religion, see: B. Badie, "Democracy and Religion: logics of culture and logics of action," *International Social Science Journal* XLII, 3 (1991), pp. 511-21; W.V. D'Antonio, "Autonomy and democracy in an autocratic organisation: the case of the Roman Catholic Church," *Sociology of Religion* 55 (1994), pp. 379-96.

⁷⁷ See: Kamens, "Education and Democracy: A comparative institutional analysis," *Sociology of Education* Vol 61, 2 (1988), pp. 114-27; For further data on the relationship between education and democracy, see: A. Benavot, "Education and Political Democratisation: Cross National and Longitudinal Findings," *Comparative Educational Review* 40, 4 (1996), pp. 377-403; N.F. McGinn, "Education, Democratisation, and Globalisation: A Challenge for Comparative Education," *Comparative Education Review* 40, 4 (1996), pp. 341-57.

respective institution was democratic, 60% felt that staff criticisms were well received, while 53% agreed that students are frequently consulted in the running of the school or college. Though the picture appears positive, direct involvement of students in democratic life of institutions may need further emphasis since it has been found that direct participation in political affairs seems to be the best school for democracy.[78]

From the perspective of Catholic conversion, we have found that greater emphasis has been placed on people's religious experience after Vatican II, especially through the schools' religious education programmes, though of course these only partly reflect Catholic input.[79] The old catechism approach has been largely replaced, giving way to some shades of inculturation. Certainly, many Catholics and Christians are becoming more critical of the Catholicism which they had received. Attempts have been made to listen more attentively to the religious experiences of Zambians and to find ways of integrating them in to the teaching and liturgy. The task remains difficult particularly where roughly 60% of the religious men and 40% of the religious women are expatriates, who often unwittingly may support as traditional what is not so. The point may be illustrated by a comment from Professor Kashoki:

> Have dancing, ululating, cavorting and throwing of arms *akimbo* anything to do with African custom and tradition in so far as prayer is concerned? The answer is a categorical no. In African traditional forms of worship, we did not, in this part of the world, I submit, dance and ululate when in communion with God and the ancestral spirits. The moment called for solemnity and drum-free reverence. Thus, what we are doing today does not seem to be based on or derived from custom and tradition...what we are doing is in fact utterly alien to the manner we worshipped in the past.[80]

On the other hand, it appears true that many Western ways including forms of worship continue to be rather alien to Zambians' experiences. To some, even the Eucharist as it is celebrated today may not greatly appeal. As one person expressed it:

> The Mass—that's not the way Africans carry on. They would be really

---

[78] McGinn, "Education, Democratisation and Globalisation," p. 356; This point has also been emphasised by Bryk et al., p. 289; Paulo Freire, *Pedagogy of Hope* (New York: Continuum, 1993), p. 113.

[79] Mujdrica, "An Evaluation of the Zambian Secondary School R.E. syllabuses," pp. 31, 34, 37; While serious efforts have been made towards inculturation of the syllabi, much more needs to be done in terms of using traditional resources such as proverbs etc. (F. Wafter, Interview, 19 July 1997).

[80] Mubanga Kashoki, *Impact* No. 138 (Feb, 1994), pp. 12-13.

happy to have something in the open air with plenty of dancing. Now it's so formal and rigid. Africans like spontaneity...even God is a bit abstract... you have the feeling that Jesus was white...we would love to feel that Jesus was black.[81]

Evidently, the issue is complex and described by the recent African Synod as "a difficult and delicate task, since it raises the question of the Church's fidelity to the Gospel and the Apostolic Tradition amidst the constant evolution of cultures."[82] In the words of a middle aged Zambian Catholic:

> Fundamentally, Christianity is true and the source of salvation, but I agonise that I have to become an expert in an alien culture (like Judaism) or else take it all blindly like I learned Latin. The urge to indigenize is right but it has to be taken carefully.[83]

The persistence of what Mwamba terms "pagan" beliefs and practices indicates however that there is still a long way ahead before some satisfactory integration between tradition and Catholicism is achieved.[84] When Bishop Lungu of Monze was asked if the faith of Zambians was still very foreign, he replied: "Yes, it is still very foreign."[85] Thus, while the intellectual dimensions of conversion remain paramount in Catholic schools, much greater attention is now being given than formerly to Zambians' experience on the religious, emotional and moral levels. In this way, perhaps conversion in a deeper sense is being effected even if to quote Kent, at the end of Shakespeare's *King Lear*: "(We) have a journey shortly to go. Our master calls, (we) must not say no"[86]

---

[81] Chewa, Catholic, Interview, Lusaka, November, 1990.

[82] *Ecclesia in Africa*, p. 63; For details on the evolution of "inculturation," see: R.R. McAuliff, "Inculturation and Western Education: a challenge to the Church in Micronesia." M.Th. thesis, Jesuit School of Theology at Berkeley, 1992.

[83] Dominic Mulaisho, Interview, Lusaka, 11 April 1997.

[84] Benedict Mwamba, "Vernacular Christianity and African Theology in the context of an African philosophical debate." (M.A. School of Oriental and African Studies, London: 1996); See also Gifford, "Some recent developments in African Christianity," pp. 521-2; Hastings, *African Catholicism*, pp. 20, 136, 138-55; Carmody, "Conversion to Roman Catholicism," pp. 5-24; T. Rasing, *Passing on the Rites of Passage* (Leiden: African Studies Centre, 1995).

[85] Interview, Monze, 21 July 1997.

[86] King Lear, Act V, Sc. III from *The Complete Works of William Shakespeare* (London: Spring Books, 1970), p. 892.

SELECTED BIBLIOGRAPHY

Abernethy, David B. *The Political Dilemma of Popular Education.* Stanford: Stanford University Press, 1969.

Abbott, Walter M., ed. *The Documents of Vatican II.* New York: Guild Press, 1966.

Afagabegee, G.L.K. "Inculturation and Small Christian Communities." *Afer* 27, 5 (October 1985): 279-85.

Alexander, D.J. "Problems of Educational Reform in Zambia." *International Journal of Educational Development* 3 (1983): 203-222.

Apple, Michael W. "Curriculum as Ideological Selection." *Comparative Educational Review* 48 (November 1978): 495-503.

- *Ideology and Curriculum.* London: Routledge and Kegan Paul, 1979.
- ed. *Education and Power.* Boston: Routledge and Kegan Paul, 1982.
- ed. *Cultural and Economic Reproduction.* London: Routledge and Kegan Paul, 1982.

Badie, B. "Democracy and Religion: logics of culture and logics of action." *International Social Science Journal* XLIII, 3 (1991): 511-21.

Baldwin, R.E. *Economic Development and Export Growth.* Berkeley: University of California Press, 1966.

Baur, John. *2000 Years of Christianity in Africa.* Nairobi: Paulines Publications, 1994.

Bediako, Kwame, *Christianity in Africa.* Edinburgh: Edinburgh University Press, 1995.

Beidelman, T.O. *Colonial Evangelism: A Socio-historical study of an East African Mission at the Grassroots.* Bloomington: Indiana University Press, 1982.

Benedict XV, Pope. "Maximum Illud." In *Modern Missionary Documents and Africa,* pp. 22-47. Edited by Raymond Hickey. Dublin: Dominican Publications, 1982.

Berman, E.H. "American Influence on African Education: The Role of the Phelps-Stokes Fund's Education Commissions." *Comparative Education Review* XV (June 1971): 132-45.

- *African Reactions to Mission Education.* New York: Teachers' College Press, 1975.
- "African Responses to Christian Mission Education." *African Studies Review* XVII (December 1974): 528-31.

Bernstein, Henry. "Notes on Capital and Peasantry." *Review of African Political Economy* 10 (1977): 60-73.

Blakemore, Kenneth, and Cooksey, Brian. *A Sociology of Education for Africa.* London: George Allen and Unwin, 1980.

Bordieu, Pierre, and Passeron, Jean-Claude. *Reproduction in Education, Society and Culture.* Beverly Hills: Sage Publications, 1977.

Bosch, D.J. *Transforming Mission.* New York: Orbis Books, 1994.

Bowles, Samuel, and Gintis, Herbert. *Schooling in Capitalist America.* New York:

Basic Books, 1976.

Bryk, A.S., Lee, V.E., Holland, P.B. *Catholic Schools and the Common Good.* Cambridge, Mass: Harvard University Press, 1993.

Burke, Thomas J. ed. *Catholic Missions: Four Great Missionary Encyclicals.* New York: Fordham University Press, 1957.

Carey, F. *Women and Children first.* Ndola: Mission Press, 1988.

Carmody, Brendan. "Conversion to Roman Catholicism in Zambia: Shifting Pedagogies." *African Christian Studies* IV, 2 (1988): 5-24.

- "Conversion and School at Chikuni: 1905-39." *Africa* 58, 2 (1988): 193-208.
- "Mission Primary Schools and Conversion: Help or Hindrance to Church Growth?" *Missiology* XVII, 2 (April 1989): 177-92.
- "A Post Independence Zambian Secondary School." *African Affairs* 89 (1990): 247-63.
- "Secular and Sacred at Chikuni: 1905-40." *Journal of Religion in Africa* XXX 2 (1991): 130-48.
- "Jesuit Mission School: Ally of Zambian Nationalism?" *Zambia Journal of History* 5 (1992): 37-56.
- *Conversion and Jesuit Schooling in Zambia.* Leiden: E.J. Brill, 1992.
- "Catholic Beliefs, Attitudes, and Practice in Zambia," *African Christian Studies* 12, 1 (1996): 30-45
- "Catholic Schools in Zambia—whither?" *African Christian Studies* 13, 3 (1997): 49-76.
- "Religious Education and Human Development." *JCTR* 39 (1999), PP.19-21.
- "Conversion to Catholicism in Zambia: 1891-1924," *Missiology* xxvii, 2 (1999): 195-205
- "Catholic Schools in Zambia: 1891-1924." *History of Education* 28, 1 (1999): 73-86
- "The Catholic Church and its Primary Schools in Zambia: 1926-1973." *Afer* (in press).
- "Zambia's Catholic Schools and Secularization" *History of Education* 29, 4 (2000)

Carnoy, Martin. *Education as Cultural Imperialism.* New York: David McKay, 1974.

Castle, E.B. *Growing up in East Africa.* London: Oxford University Press, 1966.

Catholic Directory 1996. Ndola: Mission Press, 1996.

Catholic Education in the Service of Africa. Catholic International Education Office Regional Secretariat for Africa and Madagascar, 1965.

Christian Education in Africa. London: Oxford University Press, 1963.

Clarke, P.B. "The Methods and Ideology of the Holy Ghost Fathers in Eastern Nigeria: 1885-1905." *Journal of Religion in Africa* VI (1974): 81-108.

Coleman, James S. *Nigeria: Background to Nationalism.* Berkeley: University of California Press, 1958.

- *Education and Political Development*. Princeton: Princeton University Press, 1965.

Colson, Elizabeth. *Marriage and the Family among the Plateau Tonga*. Manchester: Manchester University Press, 1958.

- *The Plateau Tonga of Northern Rhodesia*. Manchester: Manchester University Press, 1962.
- "Converts and Tradition: The Impact of Christianity on Valley Tonga Religion." *South-western Journal of Anthropology* 26 (1970): 143-56.
- "The Bantu Botatwe: Changing Political Definitions in Southern Zambia." In *The Politics of Cultural Performance*, pp. 61-80. Oxford: Berghadn Books, 1996. Edited by David Parkin, Lionel Caplan, & Humphrey Fisher.

Coombe, Trevor. "The Origins of Secondary Education in Zambia." *African Social Research* 3 (June 1967): 173-205;

- "The Origins of Secondary Education in Zambia." *African Social Research* 4 (December 1967): 283-315.
- "The Origins of Secondary Education in Zambia." *African Social Research* 5 (June 1968): 365-405.

Coombs, Philip. *World Education Crisis*. London: Oxford University Press, 1968.

- *The World Crisis in Education: The view from the Eighties*. New York: Oxford University Press, 1985.

D'Antonio, W.V. "Autonomy and Democracy in an autocratic organisation: the case of the Roman Catholic Church." *Sociology of Religion* 55 (1994): 379-96.

Davidson, Basil. *The Black Man's Burden*. New York: Random House, 1992.

DeCruchy, J.W. *Christianity and Democracy*. Cambridge: Cambridge University Press, 1995.

DeGuibert, Joseph. *The Jesuits: Their Spirituality, Doctrine and Practice*. Chicago: Loyola University Press, 1964.

Developing in Christ: A Post Primary Series in the Christian Faith for Africa Today. London: Geoffrey Chapman, 1970.

Dillon-Malone, C. *Zambian Humanism, Religion and Social Morality*. Ndola: Mission Press, 1989.

Dixon-Fyle, Mc. "Reflections on Economic and Social Change among the Plateau Tonga of Northern Rhodesia: 1890-1935." *International Journal of African Studies* XVI (1983): 423-39.

- "The Seventh Day Adventists (S.D.A.) in the protest politics of the Tonga Plateau, Northern Rhodesia." *African Social Research* 26 (December 1978): 453-67.

Donovan, Vincent J. *Christianity Rediscovered*. New York: Orbis Books, 1978.

Doran, R.M. *Subject and Psyche: Ricoeur, Jung and the Search for Foundations*. Washington D.C.: University of America Press, 1977.

Dore, Ronald. *The Diploma Disease*. Berkeley: University of California Press, 1976.

Draisma. T. *The Struggle against Underdevelopment in Zambia since Independence:*

What role for Education. Amsterdam: The Free Press, 1987.
Dulles, Avery. *Models of the Church.* New York: Image Books, 1978.
Education in East Africa. London: Edinburgh House Press, n.d.
Ekechi, F.K. "Colonialism and Christianity in West Africa: The Igbo Case: 1900-1915." *Journal of African History* XII (1970): 103-15.
Etherington, N. "Mission Station Melting Pots as a Factor in the Rise of Black Nationalism." *International Journal of African Historical Studies* 9 (1976): 592-605.
- "Recent Trends in the Historiography of Christianity in Southern Africa," *Journal of Southern African Studies* 22, 2 (1996): 201-19.
Evangelisation. A Report of the General Missionary Conference of Northern Rhodesia. Broken Hill, July 15-21, 1931. Lovedale Institution Press, n.d.
Expectations for the Catholic School Principal. U.S. Catholic Conference, 1996
Fashole-Luke, E. ed. *Christianity in Independent Africa.* London: Rex Collings, 1978.
Fisher, Humphrey. "Conversion Rediscovered: Some Historical Aspects of Religious Conversion in Black Africa." *Africa* XLIII (January 1973): 27-40.
- "The Juggernaut's Apologia: Conversion to Islam in Black Africa." *Africa* 55, 2 (1985): 153-73.
Flies, J. *The Missionaries of Africa: 100 years in Zambia.* Ndola: Mission Press, 1991.
Franklin, P. "Early Church state relations in African Education in Rhodesia and Zambia." *The World Year Book of Education.* London: Evans, 1966.
Fry, Gerald W. "Schooling, Development and Inequality: old myths and new realities." *Harvard Educational Review* 51, 1 (February 1981): 107-115.
Foster, Philip. *Education and Social Change in Ghana.* Chicago: University of Chicago Press, 1965.
Freund, B. *The Making of Contemporary Africa.* Bloomington: Indiana University Press, 1984.
Gadsden, Fay. "Education and Society in Colonial Zambia." In S.N. Chipungu, ed. *Guardians in their Time*, pp.97-105. London: MacMillan, 1992.
- "Patriarchal Attitudes: Male control over and polocies towards female education in Northern Rhodesia: 1924-63." *Zambia Journal of History* 6/7 (1993/4): 25-45.
Gann, L.H. *Birth of a Plural Society: The Development of Northern Rhodesia under the British South Africa Company 1894-1914.* Manchester University Press, 1958.
- *A History of Northern Rhodesia: Early Days to 1953.* London: Chatto and Windus, 1964.
- *A History of Southern Rhodesia.* London: Chatto and Windus, 1965.
Garvey, Brian. "Bemba Chiefs and Catholic Missions, 1898-1935." *Journal of African History* 18 (1977): 411-426.
- *Bembaland Church: Religious and Social Change in South Central Africa 1891-1964.* Leiden: E.J. Brill, 1994.

- "Colonial schooling and missionary evangelism." *History of Education* 23, 2 (1994): 195-206.

Gifford, Paul. "Some recent developments in African Christianity." *African Affairs* 93 (1994): 513-34.

- ed. *The Christian Churches and the Democratisation of Africa.* Leiden, E.J. Brill, 1995.

Giroux, Henry. *Ideology, Culture and the Process of Schooling.* Philadelphia: Temple University Press, 1981.

Gray, Richard. "Christianity and Religious Change in Africa." *African Affairs* 77, 306 (January 1978): 89-100.

- *Black Christians and White Missionaries.* New Haven: Yale University Press, 1990.

Gelpi, Donald L. "The Converting Jesuit," *Studies in the Spirituality of Jesuits* 18 (1986): 1-38.

Gerovac, Ivan. *The Lay Apostolate in Zambia from 1965 to 1975.* Rome: Pontificia Universita Lateranense, 1984.

Goody, J. *The Logic of Writing and the Organisation of Society.* Cambridge: Cambridge University Press, 1986.

Hall, Richard. *Zambia 1890-1964.* London: Longman, 1976.

Hammond, Phillip E. ed. *The Sacred in a Secular Age.* Berkeley: University of California Press, 1985.

Hannecart, Karl. *Intrepid Sowers: From Nyasa to Fort Jameson.* Rome: Gregorianum Press, 1991.

Hastings, Adrian. "Patterns of African mission work." *Afer* VIII, 4 (October 1966): 291-8.

- *Church and Mission in Modern Africa.* London: Burns and Oates, 1967.
- *A History of African Christianity 1950-1975.* Cambridge: Cambridge University Press, 1979.
- *African Catholicism: Essays in Discovery.* London. S.C.M. Press, 1989.
- *The Church in Africa.* Oxford: Clarendon Press, 1994.

Haynes, Jeff. *Religion and Politics in Africa.* Nairobi: East African Educational Publishers, 1996.

Healey, James. "Basic Christian Communities in Africa and Latin America." *Afer* 26, 4 (August 1984): 222-32.

Hefner, R.W. (ed.) *Conversion to Christianity.* Cambridge: Cambridge University Press, 1993.

Heise, David. "Prefatory Findings in the Sociology of Missions." *Journal for the Scientific Study of Religion* VI, 1 (Spring 1967): 49-58.

Henkel, Reinhard. *Christian Missions in Africa: A Social Geographical Study of the Impact of their activities in Zambia.* Berlin: Reimer Verlag, 1989.

Herskovits, Melville J. *The Human Factor in Changing Africa.* New York: Vintage Books, 1957.

Hinfelaar, Hugo. *Bemba-Speaking Women of Zambia in a century of Religious Change.* Leiden: E.J. Brill, 1994.

Hogan, Edmund. "Conversion to Roman Catholicism." *Afer* 24, 2 (April 1982): 71-80.
Holmes, T. "French Missionaries and British Treaties in Southern Africa 1830-1900." *Zambia Journal of History* 6/7 (1993-4): 1-24.
Horton, Robin. "African Conversion." *Africa* XLI (April 1971): 85-108.
- "On the Rationality of Conversion." Part I. *Africa* 43 (1975): 219-35.
- "On the Rationality of Conversion." Part II. *Africa* 45 (1975): 373-99.
- *Patterns of Thought in Africa and the West: Essays on magic, religion, and science*. Cambridge: Cambridge University Press, 1993.
- and Peel, J.D.Y. "Conversion and Confusion: A Rejoinder on Christianity in Eastern Nigeria." *Canadian Journal of African Studies* X (1976): 481-98.

Ifeka-Muller, Caroline. "White Power: Social Structural Factors in Conversion to Christianity, Eastern Nigeria, 1921-66." *Canadian Journal of African Studies* VIII (1974): 55-72.
Ipenburg, A. *All Good Men: The Development of the Lubwa Mission, Chinsali, Zambia 1905-1967*. Frankfurt-am-Main: Peter Lang, 1992.
Isichei, Elizabeth. *A History of Christianity in Africa*. London: S.P.C.K. 1995.
Jimenez, E. & Lockwood, M.E. "Enhancing girls' learning through single sex education: evidence and a policy conundrum." *Educational Evaluation and Policy Analysis* 11, 2 (1989): 117-42.
- *Public and Private Secondary Education in Developing Countries: A comparative study*. Washington, D.C.: The World Bank, 1995.

John Paul II, Pope. *Post Synodal Apostolic Exhortation Ecclesia in Africa of the Holy Father John Paul II*. Rome: Vatican City, 1995.
Kamens, David. "Education and Democracy: a comparative institutional analysis." *Sociology of Education* 61, 2 (1988): 114-27.
Kaplan, S. (ed.) *Indigenous Responses to Western Christianity*. New York: New York University Press, 1995.
Kashoki, Mubanga. "A Battle Lost on the Frontline." *Africa Insight* 24, 4 (1994):
Kaunda, Kenneth. *Humanism and a guide to its implementation*. Parts I & II. Lusaka: Zambia Information Services, 1974.
Kelly, Michael J. *Education in a Declining Economy. The Case of Zambia, 1975-85*. Washington D.C.: The World Bank, 1991.
Kieren, J.A. "Some Roman Catholic Missionary Attitudes in 19th Century East Africa." *Race* X (January 1969): 341-59.
Lee, V.E. & Lockheed, M.E. "The effects of single sex schooling on achievement and attitudes in Nigeria." *Comparative Education Review* 34, 2 (1990): 209-301.
Lee, V. & Bryk, A.S. "Effects of single sex schools on student achievement and attitudes." *Journal of Educational Psychology* 78 (1986): 381-95.
Lewis, L.J. *Phelps-Stokes Reports on Education in Africa*. London: Oxford University Press, 1962.
Linden, Ian and Jane. *Catholics Peasants and Chewa Resistance in Nyasaland*.

London: Heinemann, 1974.

Lonergan, Bernard. *Method in Theology*. London: Longman and Todd, 1973.

Lulat, Y.G.M. "Political Constraints on Educational Reform for Development: lessons from an African experience." *Comparative Educational Review* 26 (1982): 235-53.

Lungu, Gatian. "The Church, Labour and the Press in Zambia: The role of critical observers in a one party state." *African Affairs* 83, 340 (July 1986): 385-410.

MacKenzie, C. "Demythologising the Missionaries: A reassessment of the functions and relationships of Christian missionary education under colonialism." *Comparative Education* 29, 1 (1993):

Mackie, R. ed. *Literacy and Revolution: The Pedagogy of Paulo Freire*. New York: Continuum Press, 1981.

Marsh, H.W. "Effects of attending single-sex and co-educational high schools on achievement, attitudes, behaviours and sex differences." *Journal of Educational Psychology* 81, 1 (1989): 70-85.

Maxwell, Kevin B. *Bemba Myth and Ritual: The Impact of Literacy on an Oral Culture*. New York: Peter Lang, 1983.

McCracken, John. *Politics and Christianity in Malawi: 1875-1940: The Impact of Livingstonia Mission in Northern Province*. Cambridge: Cambridge University Press, 1967.

- "Underdevelopment in Malawi: The Missionary Contribution." *African Affairs* 76, 303 (April 1977): 195-210.

McGarry, C. "Ecclesia in Africa." *Hekima Review* 14 (January 1996): 57-63.

McGinn, N.F. "Education, Democratisation and Globalisation: a challenge for comparative education." *Comparative Education Review* 40, 4 (1996): 341-57.

McLaren, Peter. *Schooling as a Ritual Performance*. London: Routledge & Kegan Paul, 1986.

Miller, Elmer S. "The Christian Missionary: Agent of Secularisation." *Missiology* 1 (January 1973): 96-106.

Miller, Jon. "Missions, Social Change and Resistance to Authority: Notes towards and understanding of the relative autonomy of religion." *Journal for the Scientific Study of Religion* 32, 1 (1993): 29-50.

Moreau, Joseph. "Bakule Menyo." *Nada* XXVII (1950): 34-38.

Morris, Colin. *The Hour after Midnight*. London: Longmans, 1961.

Mufuka, K.N. *Missions and Politics in Malawi*. Kingston: The Limestone Press, 1977.

Mulaisho, Dominic. *The Tongue of the Dumb*. London: Heinemann, 1971.

Mwanakatwe, John. *The Growth of Education in Zambia Since Independence*. Lusaka: Oxford University Press, 1968.

Neil, S. *Colonialism and Christian Missions*. London: Lutterworth, 1966.

Noddings, N. "On Community." *Educational Theory* 46, 3 (1996): 245-67.

Ogbu. John. *The Next Generation*. New York: Academic Press, 1974.

- *Minority Education and Caste: The American System in Cross Cultural Perspectives.* New York: Academic Press, 1978.
- "Investment in Human Capital: Education and Development in Stockton, California, and Gwembe, Zambia." *Kroeber Anthropological Society Papers* 63 & 64 (1984): 104-14.

Oger, Louis. *Where a scattered flock gathered: Ilondola.* Ndola: Mission Press, 1991
- *Forget Me Not.* Ndola, Mission Press, 1992.
- "La Sorcellerie lieu d'inculturation." *Petit Echo* 860 (1994/5).

Ogez, J.M. *Where it all began.* Lusaka: Missionaries of Africa, 1991.

O'Halloran, James. *Small Christian Communities: A pastoral companion.* New York: Orbis, 1996.

O'Loghlen, Desmond. Book review. *Studies* (Autumn 1992): 344-46.

Omenka, Nicholas I. *The School in the Service of Evangelisation.* Leiden: E.J. Brill, 1989.

O'Shea, Michael. *Missionaries and Miners.* Ndola: Mission Press, 1986.

O'Sullivan, Owen. *A History of the Capuchins in Zambia 1931-81.*

Parkin, David. ed. *Town and Country in Central and Eastern Africa.* London: Oxford University Press, 1975.

Paul VI, Pope. *Populorum Progressio.* New York: Paulist Press, 1967.
- *Evangelii Nuntiandi.* Washington D.C.: Catholic Conference, 1976.

Peters, H.E. *Education and Achievement.* Lusaka: Institute of African Studies, 1976.

Pityana, N. Barney. "The Evolution of Democracy in Africa." *Journal of Theology for Southern Africa* 86 (1994): 4-13.

Proceedings of the General Missionary Conference of Northern Rhodesia 1924. Lovedale: Institution Press, 1929.

Pro Mundi Vita: Dossiers 7/8 (March, 1979)

Ragsdale, J.P. *Protestant Mission Education in Zambia, 1880-1954.* London: Associated Press, 1986.

Rahner, Karl. "Anonymous Christianity and the Missionary task of the Church." *Theological Investigations,* vol. XII, pp. 161-78. Translated by David Bourke. New York: The Seabury Press, 1974.
- "The Experience of God." *Theological Investigations,* vol. XI, London: Longman & Todd, 1974.

Rambo, Lewis R. "Psychological Perspectives on Conversion." *Pacific Theological Review* XIII (Spring 1980)
- *Understanding Religious Conversion.* New Haven & London: Yale University Press, 1993.

Rasing, T. *Passing on the rites of passage.* Leiden: African Studies Centre, 1995.

Roberts, Andrew. *A History of Zambia.* London: Heinemann Educational Books, 1976.

Roof, W.C. (ed.) *World Order and Religion.* Albany: State University of New York, 1991.

Rotberg, Robert I. *Christian Missionaries and the Creation of Northern Rhodesia 1880-1924*. New Jersey: Princeton University Press, 1965.

Salvodi, V. and Sesana, R.K. *Africa The Gospel belongs to us*. Ndola: Mission Press, 1986.

Sanneh, Lamin. "Christian Mission in the Pluralist Milieu: The African Experience." *Missiology* XII, 4 (1984): 421-434.

- *Translating the Message: The Missionary Impact on Culture*. New York: Orbis Books, 1989.
- *Encountering the West: Christianity and Global Cultural Process: The African Dimension*. London: Marshall Pickering, 1993.

Sanyal, B.C. et al. *Higher Education and the Labour Market in Zambia*. Unesco, 1976.

Samoff, Joel. "School Experience in Tanzania: Private Initiatives and Public Policy," *Comparative Education Review* 31, 3, (August, 1987): 333-60.

Scherer, J.A. and Bevans, S.B. eds. *New Dimensions in Mission and Evangelisation* 2. New York: Orbis Books, 1994.

Schmidlin, J. *Catholic Mission History*. Techny, Illinois: Mission Press, 1933.

Schultz, T.W. "Investment in Human Capital." *American Economic Review* LI (March 1961): 1-17.

Scudder, Thayer and Colson, Elizabeth. *Secondary Education and the Formation of an Elite: The Impact of Education on Gwembe District, Zambia*. New York: Academic Press, 1980.

Shorter, A. *African Christian Theology*. New York: Orbis Books, 1977.

Smith, Adrian. *Interdenominational Religious Education in Africa*. Leiden: Interuniversitair Instituut Voor Misslogie en Oecumenica, 1982.

Smith, E.M. *African Ideas of God*. London: Edinburgh House Press, 1966.

Snelson, P.D. *Educational Development in Northern Rhodesia 1883-1945*. Lusaka: Neczam, 1974.

Strayer, R.W. "Mission History in Africa: New Perspectives on an Encounter. *African Studies Review* XIX (1976): 1-15.

Steedly, M.M. "The Importance of proper names: language and "national" identity in colonial Karoland." *American Ethnologist* 23, 3 (1996): 447-75.

The Catholic School on the Threshold of the Third Millennium (L'Osservatore Romano, 16-22 April, 1998)

The General Missionary Conference of Northern Rhodesia. Ndola: June 7-13, 1935.

The Principal as Educational Leader. U.S. Catholic Conference, 1993.

The Principal as Managerial Leader. U.S. Catholic Conference, 1993.

Thompson, A.R. *Education and Development in Africa*. New York: St. Martin's Press, 1981.

Thompson, E.P. "Time, Work-Discipline and Industrial Capitalism." *Past and Present* 38 (December 1967): 56-97.

Tiberondwa, Ado K. *Missionary Teachers as Agents of Colonialism: A study of their activities in Uganda, 1877-1925*. Lusaka: Neczam, 1978.

VanBinsbergan, Wim M.J. *Religious Change in Zambia: Exploratory Studies*.

London: Kegan Paul, 1981.
Vickery, Kenneth. *Black and White in Southern Zambia.* New York: Greenwood Press, 1986.
Wakeford, J. *The Cloistered Elite.* New York: Praeger, 1969.
Weller, J. and Linden, J. *Mainstream Christianity to 1980 in Malawi, Zambia and Zimbabwe.* Gweru: Mambo Press, 1984.
Westerlund, D. ed. *Questioning the Secular State.* London: Hurst, 1996.

UNPUBLISHED WORKS

Banda, M. "Why mission schools perform better academically?" Project for Religious Studies programme. University of Zambia, 1995. Religious Studies Library, University of Zambia.
Calmettes, J-L. "The Lumpa sect, rural reconstruction and conflict." M.Sc. thesis. University of Wales, 1978.
Carey, Francis. "Conscientization and in-service education of primary school teachers." Ph.D. dissertation. University of London, 1986.
Chanda, Casmir. "The Role of the Catholic Church in post-Independence Zambia." Essay for Religious Studies course no. RS 312 : October 1986
Change, E., Luwewe, I. and Mwansa, P. "Some Factors related to high boarding fees in grant-aided secondary schools and the effects of high boarding fees on the pupils' accessibility to these schools." Research Report for Ed 408, October 1995.
Cheyeka, Austin. "The Declaration of Zambia as a Christian Nation by President Chiluba." M.A. thesis. University of Birmingham, 1995.
Chileshe, Winfridah. "The Attitudes of the University Community towards Church Marriage." Project for RS 920 (1995). University of Zambia, Religious Studies Library, 1995.
Chilufya, R. "The Impact of Catholic Secondary Schools on University of Zambia Students' academic and religious life." Project for Religious Studies programme, University of Zambia, 1996. Religious Studies Library, University of Zambia.
Clarke, Roy. "Policy and ideology in Educational Reform in Zambia: 1974-78." M.A. thesis. University of Lancaster, 1978. Special Collections, University of Zambia.
Darragh, M. "The Development of Girls' Education in Barotseland." Essay for the Post Graduate Certificate in Education programme, 1968. Special Collections, University of Zambia.
Hambwalula, O.M.J. "Why mission schools perform better academically?" Project for Religious Studies programme. University of Zambia, 1995. Religious Studies Library, University of Zambia.
Hazemba, W. "The Seventh Day Adventist Church and the State in Zambia: 1905-1990." Project for Religious Studies programme. University of Zambia, 1996. Religious Studies Library, University of Zambia.

Himpyali, Barnabas. "The relationship between educational fees and the dropout rate in selected boarding schools in Southern Province." M.Ed. thesis. University of Zambia, Lusaka, 1993. Special Collections, University of Zambia.

Kagulura, Sylvia. "The Catholic Church's Contribution to the Education of Girls in Zambia 1894-1994." Project for Religious Studies programme. University of Zambia, Religious Studies Library, 1995.

Kalilombe, Patrick. "From Outstation to Small Christian Communities: A Comparison between two pastoral methods in Lilongwe diocese." Ph.D. dissertation. Graduate Theological Union, 1983.

Kashimani, M.E. "A fragile stability: The rise and demise of Zambia's Second Republic 1972-1991." Ph.D. dissertation. University of York, 1994. Special Collections, University of Zambia.

Katulushi, Clement. "Religious Education in a secular institution. A case study of Nkrumah Teachers' College, Kabwe, Zambia." M.A. thesis. University of Leeds, 1996.

Lane, William. "Jesuit Religious Education: Zambezi to Zambia 1875-1975." M. Ed. thesis. University of Dublin, 1976.

Machila, E. "A History of the Malende among the Tonga of Southern Province of Zambia. A case study of Chief Hanjalika's area 1890-1986." M.A. thesis. University of Zambia, 1990. Special Collections, University of Zambia.

McAuliffe, R.R. "Inculturation and Western Education: a challenge to the Church in Micronesia." S.T.M. thesis, Jesuit School of Theology at Berkeley, 1992.

Mhoswa, A.M. "A Study of the Educational Contribution of the Jesuits at Chikuni and the Adventist Mission at Rusangu 1905-64." M.Ed. thesis. University of Zambia, Lusaka, 1980. Special Collections, University of Zambia.

Mujdrica, John. "An evaluation of the Zambian secondary school R.E. syllabuses." M.Ed. thesis. University of Birmingham, 1996.

Murphy, Edward. "Changing Educational Policy of the Catholic Voluntary Organisations with reference to Zambia". Paper presented for the post Graduate Certificate of Education at the University of Zambia, Lusaka, 1972. Special Collections, University of Zambia.

Muyatwa, V. "The Development of Catholic Education in Western Province Zambia 1931-1995." M.A. thesis, Leeds University, 1998.

Mwansa, Benedict. "Vernacular Christianity and African Theology in the context of an African Philosophical debate." M.A. thesis. London: School of Oriental and African Studies, 1996.

Mweemba, Clement. "Bana ba Mutima Church 1954-1985." Essay. University of Zimbabwe, 1986.

Nankwenya, I.A.J. "Christian Influence on Education in Malawi up to Independence with special reference to the role of the Catholic Missionaries." Ed.D. dissertation, University of South Africa, 1977.

Nguluwe, D.M. "The History of Religious Education in Zambia." Diploma essay. University of Birmingham, 1995.

Nkhoma, E. "Why Mission schools perform better academically?" Project for the Religious Studies programme. University of Zambia, 1995. Religious Studies Library, University of Zambia.

Nyambe, L. "School as a means of conversion at Mongu Teachers' College, Western Province." Project for Religious Studies programme. University of Zambia, 1995. Religious Studies Library, University of Zambia.

Nyeko, J. "Development of female education in Northern Rhodesia 1925-63." M.A. thesis. University of Zambia, 1983. Special Collections, University of Zambia.

O'Leary, John. "A Study of School Effectiveness in the Southern Province of Zambia." Ph.D. dissertation, Cork University, 1997.

Robertson, P. "Katondwe Mission School." School of Education final year research project, n.d. Special Collections, University of Zambia.

Saxby, John. "The politics of Education in Zambia." Ph.D. dissertation. University of Toronto, 1980. Special Collections, University of Zambia.

Simpson, A.J. "Religious formations in a post-colony: an ethnographic study of a Zambian mission school." Ph.D. dissertation. University of Manchester, 1996.

Sitondo, M. "Brief history of St. Mary's secondary school, Maramba, Livingstone". History project. University of Zambia, n.d.

Skillman, C.J. "Some aspects of Women's education in Zambia." Research Project, n.d. Special Collections, University of Zambia.

SELECTED INTERVIEWS

Anonymous Woman teacher. Interviewed by Kennedy Mwamba. Kasama, June 1995.

Banda, A. & A. Teachers in 1930s and 1940s. Interview, Minga Mission, June 12, 1996.

Bantungwa, Ives. Priest. Education Secretary for Kasama archdiocese. Interview, Kasama, July 17, 1996.

Beenzu, Wilson. Farmer. Pre-1924 student at Chikuni. Interview, Chikuni, November 1983.

Boron, Joseph. Brother. (S.J.). Missionary in Zambia:1928-1993. Interview, Kasisi, October 20, 1983.

Bowdren, Donald. Priest. (Fidei Donum). Chaplain at St. Mary's Secondary School, Livingstone. Interview, June 16, 1995.

Brophy, Colm. Priest. (S.J.) Missionary. Interview, Chikuni, April 8, 1984.

Chakobe, Henry. Teacher in 1940s and 1950s. Interview, Ilonola, Chinsali, July 12, 1996.

Chasha, Charles. Principal, Charles Lwanga College. Interview, Chikuni, June, 1995.

- Interview, Chikuni, January 28, 1997.

Chibale, R.K. Headmaster, St. Clement's Mansa. Interview, July 23, 1996.

Chikolokoso, Lazarus. Teacher from 1949. Interview, Chilonga, Mpika, July 9, 1996.

Chilala, Sebastian. Former headmaster, St. Mary's, Livingstone. Interview, Livingstone, June 14, 1995.

Chilala, Agnes. Sister. (H.B.V.M.). One of the first Zambian sisters. Interview, Lusaka, December 1983.

Chimuka, Silverio. Civil servant. Canisius: 1950-54. Interview, Lusaka, June 26, 1984.

Chintu, Magdalene. Religious Sister. (Kasisi) Student at Canisius:1952-4. Interview, Kabwe, May 31, 1984.

Chipimo, Elias. Diplomat. Student at Canisius: 1950-2. Interview, Lusaka, December 14, 1983.

- Interview, Lusaka, March 9, 1997.

Chirwa, Victoria. Sister. (M.I.C.) Pastoral team, Chipata diocese. Interview, Chipata, June 14, 1996.

Chisanga, M. Teacher at St. Francis, Malole. Interview, July 17, 1996.

Chisanga, Teddy. Teacher at Lwitikila Girls' School. Interview, July 10, 1996.

Chisenga, George. Member of Chikuni mission's founding party. Interview, Chikuni, December 30,1983.

- Interview, Chikuni, March 3, 1984.
- Interview, Chikuni, April 4, 1984.
- Interview by Kenneth Hamwaka, Chikuni, August, 1986.

Chisha, Aaron. (Bishop of Mansa). Interview, Mansa, July 26, 1996.

Chisopa, Andrew. Teacher. Interviewed by Kennedy Mwamba, Kasama, March 1995.

Chitauka, Augustine. Teacher, manager of schools. Student at Chikuni:1940-48. Interview, Chikuni, December 29, 1983.

Chona, Matthias Mainza. Lawyer. Student at Chikuni in 1940s. Served in many capacities under the U.N.I.P government. Interview, Lusaka, December 17, 1983.

Cieszynski, Klaus. Priest. (S.J.). Diocesan chaplain to primary teachers,1986-9. Interview, Lusaka, December 26, 1996.

Clarke, A. Priest. (S.J.) Missionary educator. Interview, Lusaka, October 28, 1983.

Clarke, Josephine. Religious Sister. (R.S.C.) Former lecturer at Charles Lwanga College and instrumental in promoting the new Religious Education programme in the schools. Interview, Lusaka, December 1983.

Collins, Bernard. Priest. (S.J.) Missionary. Interview, Chikuni, December 20, 1983.

Corboy, James. (Bishop of Monze: 1962-91). Interview, Monze, March 1, 1984.

Cousineau, Denise. (M.I.C.). Teacher at St. Moncia's Chipata. Interview, St. Monica's, June 13, 1996.

Counihan, John. Priest. (S.J.) Interview, Chikuni, January 2, 1984.
- Interview, Lusaka, May 9, 1997.
Cunningham, Joseph Helen. Sister. (R.S.C.) Teacher at Chikuni: 1949-63. Interview, Dublin, August 13, 1984.
Cremins, Richard. Priest. (S.J.) Interview, Lusaka, October 1983.
DeJong, Denis. (Bishop of Ndola). Interview, Ndola, July 29, 1996.
Daka, E. Student at Chassa Secondary School at time of interview. Interview, Chassa, June 12, 1996.
Flannery, Denis. Priest. (S.J.). Chaplain to primary teachers, Monze diocese. Interview, Lusaka, January 3, 1997.
Flynn, Edwin. Priest. (O.F.M.Cap.) Involved in promoting the new Religious Education programme. Founder lecturer in Religious Studies at the University of Zambia, Lusaka. Interview, Lusaka, December 1983.
Forcier, Jeannine. Sister. (M.I.C.) Teacher at St. Monica's Secondary School, Chipata. Interview, St. Monica's, June 13, 1996.
Folta, Marion. Priest. (S.J.). Missionary 1942-89. Interview, Lusaka, October 27, 1983.
Froch, A. Priest. (S.J.) Missionary 1928-1998. Interview, Lusaka, October 22, 1983.
Funga, P. Priest. (Mansa diocese). Chaplain at St. Clement's Mansa, and Education Secretary General in 1970s. Interview, Mansa, July 24, 1996.
Gaydos, Joseph. Brother. (S.J.). Missionary 1928-88. Interview, Lusaka. June 21, 1984.
Geoghegan, Anthony. Priest (S.J.) College lecturer and chaplain. Interview, Kitwe, December 1983.
Haambote, Bruno. Teacher. First Zambian principal of Charles Lwanga College: 1972-81. Interview, Livingstone, March 21, 1984.
Haamonga. Chikuni Convert of pre-1920 vintage. Interviewed by M. Phiri. at Chikuni. August 5, 1986.
Haamujompa, Patrick. Teacher in late 1960s. Lecturer at Charles Lwanga and later at the University of Zambia. Interview, Lusaka, December, 1983.
Haangala, Cosmos. Teacher. Student at Chikuni: 1939-43. Interview, Kalomo, March 21, 1984.
Hayes, Joseph. Priest. (S.J.) Missionary educator. Interview, Chikuni, February 4, 1984.
Henze, John. Priest (M.Afr.) Lecturer and inspector of Religious Education. Interview, Lusaka, December 3, 1984.
- Interview, Ndola, July 28, 1997.
Himpyali, Barnabas. Student, teacher and later headmaster at Canisius secondary school. Interview, Chikuni, March 14, 1984.
Igoe, Michael. Priest. (S.M.A.). Chaplain, Fatima Secondary School. Interview, July 27, 1996.
Imeebo, M. Teacher. Interview, Livingstone, June 20, 1995.
Kachesa, Elias. Civil servant. Student at Canisius: 1966-69. Interview, Lusaka,

June 20, 1984.

Kachesa, Peter. Farmer. Student at Chikuni: 1930-4. Interview, Chikuni, December 28, 1983.

Kalale, John. Priest. (Lusaka Archdiocese). Student at Chingombe mission and at Chikuni from 1935-39. Interview, Lusaka, November 21, 1983.

Kalebwe, Felix. Priest. (S.J.). Student at Canisius: 1963-4. Interview, Kitwe, December 11, 1983.

Kapaya, George, Headmaster, Dominican Convent, Ndola. Interview, July 26, 1996.

Kashoki, Mubanga. University Professor and former student at Canisius. Interview, Lusaka, March 13, 1997.

Kasia, Elias. Former teacher from 1940s to 1970s. Student at Katondwe in 1940s and Chikuni 1945-7. Interview, Kasisi, November 5, 1983.
- Interview, Kasisi, June, 1995.

Katapazi, Bernard. Teacher. Interview, Livingstone, June 20, 1995.

Kaunda, Kenneth D. Former Head of State. Interview, Lusaka, February 19, 1999.

Keenan, Francis. Former Director of Catechetics Monze. Interview, Lusaka, December, 1983.

Kelly, Michael. Priest. (S.J.) Missionary educator. Interview, Lusaka, December 1983.

Kosloviecki, Adam. (First Archbishop of Lusaka). Interview, Lusaka, November 28, 1983.
- Interview, Kabwe, June 1996.

Kuchler, DeSales. Sister. (O.P). Assistant chaplain and long-serving teacher, Fatima Girls' School. Interview, Fatima, July 27, 1996.

Lane, William. Priest. (S.J.) Missionary and former education secretary in the diocese of Monze. Interview, Lusaka, December 15, 1983.

Lombe, Charles. (S.H.) Chaplain and teacher at St. Francis, Malole. Interview, Malole, July 17, 1996.

Lubasi, M. Teacher. Interview, Livingstone, June 20, 1995.

Lubinda, V. Teacher in 1960-80 period. Interviewed by Oscar Mate, Mongu, June, 1995.

Lungu, Amos. Teacher. Student at Canisius: 1949-51. Interview, Lusaka, November 24, 1983.

Lungu, Gatian. University lecturer. Student at Canisius: 1960s. Interview, Lusaka, June 5, 1984.

Lungu, M. Headmaster, Chilonga Primary School. Interview, Chilonga, July 8, 1996.

Lyamibaba, John. Priest. (Kasama diocese). First Zambian priest. Interview, Chilubula, July 16, 1996.

Lyiempe, Seraphina. Teacher. Student at Kasisi and Chikuni 1947-50. Interview, Kabwe, May 30, 1984.

Mainza, Gabriel. Farmer. Pre-1924 student at Chikuni. Interview, Chikuni,

March 11, 1984.

MacDonald, Norman. Priest. (S.J.). Missionary. Member of the Tonga Bible translation team. Interview, March, 1997.

Malambo, Luke. Born 1904. Interviewed by D. Muwowo. August, 1986.

Malambo, Stephen. Teacher and education secretary from 1950s in Monze and Lusaka. Interview, Chikuni, June 1995.

Mary Regis. Sister. (S.N.D.). Teacher at Chikuni 1946-8. Interview, Liverpool, England, July 25, 1984.

Matongo, M. Teacher in 1950s and 1960s. Interview, Chikuni, June 1995.

Masase, Genevieve. Sister. (S.C.J.). One of the early Zambian sisters. Interview, Chilubula, July 16, 1996.

Mbewe, Julia. Sister. (M.I.C.) Teacher and assistant chaplain, St. Monica's, Chipata. Interview, St. Monica's, June 13, 1996.

Mbozi, Bart. Catechist. Interview, Mulongalwiili, Chikuni, March 14, 1984.

McKenna, Bernadette. Sister. (R.S.C.). Community development in Chikuni area in the 1970s. Interview, Chikuni, March 1984.

McKenna, Donald. Priest. (S.J.) Missionary educator. Former headmaster of St. Canisius. Interview, November, 1983.

McGloin, James. Priest. (S.J.) Missionary educator. Interview, February 16, 1984.

McGivern, Thomas. Priest. (S.J.). Missionary. Education Secretary General 1990s. Interview, Lusaka. June, 1984.

Milimo, John. University lecturer. Student at Chikuni: 1953-55. Interview, Lusaka, December 8, 1983.

Miyanda, Charles. Catechist. Interview, Chivuna, January 29, 1984.

Miyanda, Elias. Farmer and former teacher. Student at Chikuni 1940s. Interview, Choma, March 21, 1984.

Monze, Antonio. Teacher and Jeanes Supervisor. Student at Chikuni: 1927-9. Interview, December 30, 1983.

Moore, Bernadette. Sister. (R.S.C.). Lecturer at Charles Lwanga in the 1970s. Interview, March 4, 1984.

Mooya, Cynthia. Pre-1924 student at Chikuni. Interview, Singonia, Chikuni, February 1984.

Mooya, Dominic. Teacher of 1960s. Interview, Chikuni, June 12, 1995.

Mooya, Fidelina. Sister. (H.B.V.M.). One of the early Zambian sisters. Interview, Lusaka, December, 1983.

Moriarty, Fred. Priest. (S.J.) Promoter for development in diocese of Monze for many years. Interview, Monze, February, 1984.

Moya, Peter. Teacher and farmer. Student at Chikuni: 1932-4. Interview, Chivuna, January 30, 1984.

Mpezele, Raymond. (Bishop of Livingstone). Student at Canisius 1955-7, 1961-2. Interview, Lusaka, December 7, 1983 and January 10, 1997.

Muhau, F.L. Teacher at Holy Cross Secondary School. Interview by Oscar Mate, Mongu, June, 1995

Muhau, Rose. Teacher at Holy Cross Secondary School. Interview by Oscar Mate, Mongu, June, 1995.

Mufuzi, George. University lecturer. Student at Canisius: 1956-60. Interview, Lusaka, June 1984.

Mukalamba, Simon. Teacher 1947-81. Interview by K. Mwamba. Kasama, July 19, 1995.

Mulaisho, Dominic. Teacher, diplomat, businessman. Student at Chikuni: 1946-8. Interview, State House, Lusaka, December 1983.

- Interview, Lusaka, April 11, 1997.

Mulenga, Anastasia. Sister. (H.B.V.M.) Student at Chikuni: 1940s. Interview, Lusaka, February 4, 1984.

Mulenga, K. Teacher, Dominican Convent, Ndola. Interview, Ndola, July 26, 1996.

Mulenga, Faustina. Sister. (L.S.M.I.), One of the first girls to attend secondary school at Canisius: 1952-4. Interview, Lusaka, December 15, 1983.

Mulenga, Mary Rose. Sister. (L.S.M.I.) Teacher and administrator at Lwitikila Girls' School. Interview, Lwitikila, July 10, 1996.

Mulongoti, A.G. Teacher at St. Monica's Chipata. Interview, St. Monica's, June 13, 1996.

Mulumbe, M. Teacher at St. Francis, Malole. Interview, Malole, July 17, 1996.

Mumpangwe, P. Teacher. Interview, Mansa, July 23, 1996.

Mungandu, Adrian. (Archbishop of Lusaka: 1984-97). Student at Chikuni 1937-9. Interview, Lusaka, November 26, 1983.

Mungwa, Benedict. Former teacher and farmer. Student at Kasisi and Chikuni: 1934. Interview, Lusaka, November 5, 1983.

Munjebe, M. Teacher at St. Monica's Chipata. Interview, St. Monica's, June 13, 1996.

Musonda, Annie. Teacher after 1968. Interview by K. Mwamba. Kasama, July 21, 1995.

Musonda, M. Teacher at Dominican Convent, Ndola. Interview, Ndola, July 29, 1996.

Musonda, Simon. Teacher after 1964. Interview by K. Mwamba, Kasama, July 21, 1995.

Mutale, Abel. Teacher of 1950-60 period. Interview, Chilubula, July 16, 1996.

Mutale, Elias. (Former Archbishop of Kasama) Student at Chikuni: 1947-9. Interview, Lusaka, December 12, 1983.

Mutamba, Felicity. Teacher after 1956. Interview by K. Mwamba, Kasama. July 20, 1995.

Mutembo, M. Teacher at St. Clement's Mansa. Interview, July 24, 1996.

Muuma, Claver. Teacher and headmaster at Canisius and St. Edmund's. Interview, Chikuni, February 5, 1984.

- Interview, Mazabuka, June 1995.

Muwowo, H. Teacher at St. Francis Malole. Interview, Malole, July 17, 1996.

Muyovwe, Nicholas. Teacher. Student at Canisius 1933. Interview, Pemba,

March 23, 1984.

Muzeta, Paul. Teacher and lecturer. Interview, Lusaka, June 5, 1984.

Mwale, Christine. Sister. (O.P.). Headmistress, Fatima Secondary School. Interview, Ndola, July 27, 1996.

Mwalye, Helen. Sister. (S.S.F.). One of the first students at St. Mary's, Livingstone. Interview, Livingstone, June 1995.

Mwansa, Alexandrina. Sister. (S.S.F.) Co-ordinator for catechetics in Livingstone diocese. Interview, Livingstone, January 10, 1997.

Mwananshiku, Luke. Diplomat. Student at Canisius 1957-9. Interview, Lusaka, July 14, 1984.

Mweemba, Patrick. Chikuni convert of the 1910-20 period. Interview, Chikuni, August, 1986.

Mweempa, Jacob. Catechist. Interview, St Mary's Monze, January 15, 1984.

Mweene, Vincent. University lecturer. Student at Canisius: 1974-8. Interview, Lusaka, July 1984.

Mweene, Yolanta. Sister. (R.S.C.) Student at Canisius: 1961-3. Interview, Chikuni, March 1983.

Mwiinga, Bruno. Teacher and former Principal of Charles Lwanga College. Interview, Chikuni, March 1984.

Mwiinga, L. Old convert at Chikuni. Interviewed in his 80s by N. Mwiinga, Chikuni, August 6, 1986.

Ncete, Dominic. Priest (Monze diocese). Teacher, manager of schools. Interview, Chikuni, April 7, 1984.

Nduna, Nicholas. Student at Chikuni, 1938. Interview, Njola, January 28,1984.

Nkandu, Stephen. Student at Chikuni, 1930s. Interview, Chikuni, March 8, 1984.

Nkhoma, Francis. Businessman. Student at Canisius, 1955-8. Interview, Lusaka, June 22, 1984.

Nkomo, E. Former lecturer at Charles Lwanga, Interview, Chikuni, February 23, 1984.

Nkwemu, Simon. Student at Chikuni in late 1920s. Catechist. Interview, Chikuni, March 1984.

Nyanga, Cosmos Moya. Former headmaster of Canisius. Interview, Chikuni, February 6, 1984.

Nyoni, A.Y. Teacher and later lecturer at Mongu Teachers' College. Interview, Lusaka, May 1996.

O'Brien, Desmond. Priest. (S.J.). Missionary. Interview, Chikuni, February, 1984.

O'Brien, Thomas. Priest. (S.J.). Missionary educator. Interview, Lusaka, December 4, 1983.

O'Holohan, John. Priest. (S.J.). Missionary educator. Interview, Lusaka, December 1983.

O'Leary, Dympna. Sister. (H.C.). Missionary teacher. Interview, Lusaka, May, 1996.

O'Loghlen, Desmond. Priest. (S.J.) Missionary teacher. Interview, Lusaka, May 15, 1884.
O'Neill, Francis. Priest. (S.J.). Missionary. Interview, Lusaka, December 31, 1983.
O'Riordan, Colm. Priest. (S.J.). Education Secretary General in 1970s. Interview, Monze, January 15, 1984.
O'Reilly, J. Brother. (C.F.C.). Headmaster, St. Raphael's, Livingstone. Interview, Livingstone, June 1995.
Phiri, Yambani. Teacher and later manager of schools in Chipata. Interview, Chipata, June 15, 1996.
Prokoph, Max. Priest. (S.J.) Missionary. Founder of Canisius Secondary School, education secretary. Interview, Lusaka, October 1983.
- Interview, Lusaka, June, 1984.
Sakala, M. Teacher at St. Francis, Malole, Kasama. Interview, Molole, July 17, 1996.
Sakala, R.M. Teacher at Lwitikila Girls' School. Interview, Lwitikila, July 10, 1996.
Sidono, Bruno. Former lecturer at Charles Lwanga. Interview, Chikuni, February 22, 1984.
Sokoni, Jonas. Teacher in 1940s and 1950s. Interview, Ilondola, Chinsali, July 12, 1996.
Spaita, James. (Archbishop of Kasama). Interview, Kasama, July 17, 1996.
Tembo, S.G. Teacher and chaplain. Chassa Secondary School, Nyimba. Interview, Chassa, June 12, 1996.
Tilomboyi, M. Farmer and mission cook in 1920s. Interview, Chikuni, February 15, 1984.
- Interviewed by R.L. Sishawa. Chikuni, August 8, 1986.
Thayden, Roy. Priest. (S.J.). Missionary. University chaplain 1970s. Interview, Lusaka, May 1984.
Thompson, Robert. Priest. (S.J.) Missionary. Editor of *The Leader* in the 1960s. Interview, Kildare, Ireland, August 1983.
- Interview, Kildare, Ireland. August 1984.
Titland, Peter. (S.J.) Missionary. Parish priest. University Chaplain, 1980s. Interview, Lusaka, June 15, 1984.
Tremblay, Martha. Sister. (S.O.L.A.). Teacher. Interview, Kasama, July 17, 1996.
Tyaila, Killian. Priest (Monze diocese). Student at Canisius 1960s. Interview, Choma, March 19, 1984.
Vielfavre, Louis. Priest. (M.Afr.). Chaplain, St. Mary's, Lwitikila, Mpika. Interview, Lwitikila, July 11, 1996.
Waldron, Aileen. Sister. (R.S.C.) Catechetical co-ordinator for the diocese of Monze 1970s. Interview, Chikuni, March, 1984.
Walusiku, Francis. Politician. Student at Canisius 1964-6. Interview, Lusaka, June 20, 1984.

Wegner, Ingeberg. Sister. (S.O.L.A.). Teacher. Interview, Kasama, July 17, 1996.
Wilms, Gabrielle. Sister. (O.P.). Administrator, Dominican Convent, Ndola. Interview, Ndola, July 27, 1996.
Ziwa, M. Teacher at St. Monica's, Chipata. Interview, St. Monica's, June 13, 1996.
Zulu, M. Teacher. Chassa Secondary School, Nyimba. Interview, Chassa, June 12, 1996.
Zysk, Stanislaw. Priest. (S.V.D.). Interview, Livingstone, January 3, 1997.

OFFICIAL REPORTS AND PUBLIC STATEMENTS

NORTHERN RHODESIA

Department of Native Education/Department of African Education. *Annual Reports*, 1927-63.
African Education Advisory Board Minutes, 1926-63.
Department of Native Education. *Report of sub-Committee on Female Education 1937* Lusaka: Government Printer, 1938.
The African Education Ordinance 1939. No. 12 of 1939.
African Education Department Plans: 1945-55. Lusaka: Government Printer, 1945.
Northern Rhodesia Ordinance no. 38 of 1951.
Legislative Council Debates. November 10-December 21, 1951.
Ten Year Development Plan for Northern Rhodesia as approved by Legislative Council on February 11, 1947. Lusaka: Government Printer, 1960.
Report of the Commission of Inquiry into disturbances in certain African schools. Lusaka: Government Printer, 1960.

REPUBLIC OF ZAMBIA

Ministry of Education, *Annual Reports* 1964-79.
Education Act (1966)
"Republic of Zambia: Educational Policy" in *World Survey of Education*. Vol. V. Unesco, 1966.
Manpower Report 1965-66. Lusaka: Government Printer, 1966.
"Permanent Secretary's Address to Secondary School Committee." December 17, 1968.
Education in Transition. Rogers' Report. Lusaka: Government Printer, 1969.
"Minutes of Secondary Education Committee." November 24, 1969.
Report on the National Education Conference held at Evelyn Hone College. Lusaka: Sept.30-October 2, 1969.
Zambian Manpower. Lusaka: Government Printer, 1970.
Education for Development: Draft Statement on Educational Reform. Lusaka:

Ministry of Education, 1976.
Educational Reform: Proposals and Recommendations. Lusaka: Ministry of Education, 1977.
Educational Statistics 1980 (August, 1982).
Focus on Learning. Lusaka: Ministry of Education, 1992.
Government of Zambia: *Statutory Instrument no. 43 of 1993*. Lusaka: Government Printer.
Census of Population 1990 Vol. 10. Lusaka: Government Printer, n.d.
Educating Our Future. National Policy on Education (February 1996).
Towards the implementation of Zambia's Education Reform under demographic and economic constraints. Lusaka: University of Zambia, 1986.

UNITED NATIONS AND GREAT BRITAIN

Education Policy in British Tropical Africa. Cmd. 2374. H.M.S.O. (1925).
Memorandum on Education of African Communities. Col. No.103. H.M.S.O. (1940).
Education for Citizenship in Africa. Colonial Office, 1948.
African Education: A Study of educational policy and practice in British Tropical Africa. Oxford: Colonial Office, 1953.
U.N. *Economic Commission for Africa and Unesco Conference of African States on the Development of Education in Africa*. Addis Ababa, 1961.

NATIONAL ARCHIVES OF ZAMBIA

Sec 1/459	Village school
	African Membership on Central Advisory Board.
Sec 1/443	African Female Education 1935-48.
Sec 1/444	Report of the Proceedings of the Meeting of the Central Advisory Board, 1935.
	Acting Director of African Education to Secretary for Native Affairs. September 5, 1947.
	Minutes of a conference of Education Officers, June 23, 1948.
Sec 1/455	Minutes of the Advisory Board on Native Education. July 12-13, 1933.
Sec 1/457	More assistance to Mission education.
Sec 1/458	Junior sec school at Munali.
	Minutes of Standing Committee 1940
Sec 1/460	Advisory Board—composition of.
Sec 1/462	The African Education Advisory Board.
	Governor to Sec. State for the Colonies. September 21, 1948.
Sec 1/509	Letter from Gov. Maybin to Sec. State.
Sec 1/511	Despatch from Hon. Chief Secretary commenting on Education.

	Director of African Education to Chief Secretary. January 1, 1946.
Sec 1/524	African Education on the Copperbelt.
Sec 1/525-	African Education provincial reports.
Sec 1/548	Acting Chief Secretary to Msgr. Wolnik S.J.
Sec 1/550	Annual Reports on Mission Education
	Minutes of a meeting of the Standing Committee of the Advisory Board on African Education, Lusaka, April 26, 1948.
Sec 1/556	Letter of Director of Native Education to Chief Secretary, June 28, 1940.
	Letter from Governor to Secretary of State for the Colonies, Nov 25, 1941.
	Letter of Apostolic Delegate to Director of Native Education.
Sec 1/557	Letter from acting director of African Education to Secretary for Native Affairs. September 17, 1947.
	Letter from George Hewitt, Secretary to the Christian Council of Northern Rhodesia to Director of African Education.
	Letter from J.A. Cottrell to Sec Nat Affairs. July 1947.
	Letter from Governor to Sec for Native Affairs September 25, 1947.
	Memorandum from Commission for Native Development to Hon. Sec Native Affairs.
	Minutes of a meeting in the Chief Secretary's room, Lusaka: October 30,1947.
	Note for Executive Council African Secondary Education
	Proposed new secondary school in Northern Rhodesia: Archbishop Mathew's Personal approach.
Sec 1/463	African Education tour reports, 1928-35.
KDC 2/16/1	Mission and Native Education
KDB 6/6/1	Report on Chikuni: 1916.
	Moreau to Administrator. November 10, 1923.
	Moreau on Initiation of Girls.
ZA/7/1/1/3	Sec for Native Affairs, reports for 1915
ZA/7/1/2/3	Sec for Native Affairs. Reports for 1915
ZA/71/3/3	Sec for Native Affairs. Reports for 1916.
C/18/7/2	Foreword to Reports on village schools under the Jesuits, Chikuni.
RC/711	Spheres of Influence.
	Proceedings of the General Missionary Conference 1924.
RC/1690	Jesuits.
RC/1691	Moreau to D.C. Mazabuka. December 11, 1935.
RC/1721	Northern Rhodesia policy on education.
RC 365	Resolutions adopted at the General Missionary Conference of Northern Rhodesia.

A3/10/9	Les Peres Blancs. Report by Fr. Guilleme (1902).
HM 42	Snelson Papers.
KDH 1/1	Kasama Notebook.
BS 3/197	vol. 1 Proclamation of 1916.
NR2/287	vol. 1. Effects of Education on Village Life. Local Education Authorities.
NR2/287	vol. VI. Mission independence in education.
Ed 1/5/1	Cottrell to Dir. Native Education.
Ed 1/5/2	Report on Rosa training school. June 5, 1932.
Ed 1/5/3	Van Sambeck to Keith re denominational schools. May 5, 1931.
Ed 1/5/8	Spheres of Influence cannot be imposed. Director Native Education to Sec. Dept. Lands. January 2, 1931.
Ed 1/5/16	Ulendo 1932 Cisungu ceremonies.
Ed 1/5/29	Chilubula Teachers' College. White Fathers—Eastern Province. Tour Report 1951.
Ed 1/5/36	Superintendent Native Education to Director, Native Education. Feb 8, 1934. Malole.
Ed 1/5/47	Headmaster to African Eagle March 15, 1953.
Ed 1/5/103	Malole
Ed 1/5/169	St. Paul's Mulungushi.

JESUIT ARCHIVES CHELSTON, LUSAKA.

Moreau, Joseph, The Chikuni Mission: How it came to be started. Box Moreau.
Coyne, John. History of the Jesuits in Zambia. Lusaka, n.d.
Letter from A. Casset to Superior, December 22, 1919. Box Casset.
"Minutes of Missionary Conference" held at St. George's, Bulawayo, June 22-27, 1920. Box Education.
"Memoriale of Jesuit Visitor to the Province 1924-5."Box Moreau.
Letter from J. Moreau to Superior, August 27, 1932. Box Moreau.
Report of Education work at Chikuni, 1933. Box Education.
Minutes of Ordinaries' Meeting of 1942. Box Bishops' Conferences.
Letter from A.B. Mathew to Msgr. Wolnik. September 5, 1947. Box Education.
Statement to the Christian Council Executive by Director of African Education. April 2, 1948. Box Education.
Letter from Richard Cremins to Irish Provincial. April 10, 1960.
Draft Minutes of Educational items of Bishops' Conference Lusaka June 1951. Box Bishops' Conference.
Minutes of the Northern Rhodesian Ordinaries Conference January 9-15, 1951. Box Bishops' Conference.
Bishops' Memorandum to Government, January 15, 1951. Box Bishops'

Conference.

Matters dealt with by the Binns study group session, September 1951. Box Education.

Letter from the Catholic Education Secretary General to Chairman, Bishops' Conference. January 14, 1952. Box Bishops' Conference.

Catholic Education Secretary General, letter to Ordinaries, January 3, 1952. Box. Education.

Minutes of Education Advisory Board, June 23-6, 1953. Box Education.

Letter from Irish Jesuit Provincial to Msgr. Pailloux W.F. September 23, 1954. Box Charles Lwanga.

Letter from Patrick Walsh to Irish Provincial, March 3, 1957. Carmody papers.

Letter from Bernard Collins to Irish Provincial, July 19, 1961. Carmody papers.

Minutes of Lusaka Vicariate Superiors' Meeting. July 26-7, 1956. Box. Missionary Conference.

Report on schools, 1963. Box Education.

Record of Archbishop's address to the Education Secretaries of East and Central Africa, July 31, 1963. Box. Education.

Minutes of the Administrative Board Meeting held at Northern Rhodesia Catholic Secretariat, September 3, 1964. Box Bishops' Conference.

Minutes of Education Secretaries Meeting held on August 29, 1966. Box Education.

Radio Broadcasting Interview. September 1966. Box Communications.

Primary school statistics, 1972. Box Education.

Max Prokoph, "Our Mission and Education." Box Prokoph.

President Kaunda, Talk to the Synod of the United Church of Zambia, April 4, 1967. Box Communications.

Education Secretary, Monze, letter to Education Secretary General. January 31, 1972. Box Education.

Max Prokoph, "The Involvement of the Churches in Education in Lusaka." October 18, 1974. Box Education.

Bruno Haambote, "Education for Development." November 25, 1976. Box Education.

Chisengalumbwe, Edward. "The Repercussions of Colonial Religions in Independent Africa." Address to the Historical Association of Zambia, Lusaka, November 12, 1976. Carmody papers.

Memorandum of Education Secretaries Lusaka and Kabwe, n.d .Box Education.

"Towards Teachers' deeper involvement." Reflection paper, n.d. Box Education.

Letter from B. Haambote to Fr. J. O'Leary, Jesuit Provincial. July 10, 1981. Box Charles Lwanga.

"Humanism and Development." Presidential Address to Church leaders at the Humanism and Development Seminar. Lusaka, March 18-19, 1982.

Speech by His Excellency the President, Comrade Dr. Kaunda, at the Golden Jubilee Celebrations of Regiment Church, November 1989. Box Parishes.

Letter from Bernard Collins to B. Carmody. March 1987. Carmody papers.
Letter from Elizabeth Colson to B. Carmody. July 2, 1987. Box Carmody papers.
Letter from Louis Oger to B. Carmody. November 24, 1995. Carmody papers.
Letter from Vincent Chichecki to B. Carmody. March 9, 1997. Carmody papers.
A set of the *Zambezi Mission Record* is held here.
Impact (Newsletter of the Catholic Secretariat) is held here.
JCTR bulletins are held here.
Northern Star held here.
The Leader held here.
The Catholic Teacher held here.
Northern Rhodesia African Education, some numbers held here.
Christian Liberation Justice and Development. Ndola, Mission Press, n.d.
"Marxism Humanism and Christianity." (August, 1979).
Charles Lwanga Teachers' College 25th Anniversary.
"Economics Politics and Justice." Catholic Secretariat, July, 1990.
"The Future is Ours." (February 1992).
"Education and the Status of Women." Paper by S. Mwananshiku. Carmody papers.
St. Ignatius Parish 50 years, 1937-1987.
A Church on the move 50 years on the Copperbelt 1930-1980. (W. Lane).
"Thirty Years of Canisius 1949-79." *The Canisian* vol. 3 no. 1.

JESUIT ARCHIVES, ROME.

Remarks regarding the Conference held at St. George's, Bulawayo, 1920.

CATHOLIC EDUCATION SECRETARIAT ARCHIVES

Catholic Ordinaries Meeting Minutes, February 4, 1947.
Minutes of Ordinaries' Conference, July 30, 1954.
The Joint Pastoral Letter of the Catholic Bishops of Northern Rhodesia, 1958.
Record of XVII Meeting of the Northern Rhodesian Bishops' Conference, Lusaka, May 7-9, 1958.
Minutes of Northern Rhodesia Bishops' Conference, October 13-14, 1959.
Minutes of Meeting of Education Secretaries held on January 11-12, 1961.
Minutes of the Plenary Meeting of Northern Rhodesian Episcopal Conference, Lusaka, July 9-10, 1963.
Minister's Speech at the Advisory Board Meeting. October 13, 1964.
Some Proposals for consideration by the College authorities at Charles Lwanga Teachers' Training College, n.d. (1960s).
Handover of Primary Schools 1966-7.
Political Education File.
Zambia Episcopal Conference Administrative Board Meeting, Catholic Secretariat, Lusaka: February 11-12, 1970.

Letter from Catholic Education Secretary General to Permanent Secretary, Ministry of Education and Culture, July 31, 1973.
Zambia Episcopal Conference Meeting of Principals and Heads of Colleges and Secondary schools, November 5, 1976.
Mongu Teachers' Training College Staff Meeting, June 18, 1976.
Letter of Acting Principal Mongu Teachers' College to Mother Provincial, Holy Cross Sisters, July 24, 1980.
B.M. Haambote, Letter to Proprietor, Charles Lwanga, July 10, 1981.
Notes on the Seminar held at Evelyn Hone College, March 13, 1982.
Letter from Fr. Vincent Cichecki to Permanent Secretary, Ministry of Education and Culture, November 19, 1984.
Open Letter to the Catholic Bishops of Zambia from the Catholic Community, University of Zambia, Lusaka, December 6, 1985.
Letter from Bishop James Spaita, Chairman, Zambia Episcopal Conference to Hon. K. Musokotwane, February 2, 1986.
Letter from Regional Superior, Marist Brothers, to the Proprietor, St. Paul's Secondary School, Kabwe, April 15, 1986.
"Reflections on our school situation." Position paper, n.d.
Minutes of Meetings of Heads Principals and Representatives of Managing agencies of Catholic Schools, Lusaka, January 31, 1992.
Address of Kenneth Kaunda, President of the Republic of Zambia on the occasion of the Centenary Celebration, August 1991.
Minutes of the Meeting of the Education Commission, December 14, 1994.

ARCHDIOCESAN ARCHIVES LUSAKA

Minutes of the Meeting of Ordinaries of Northern Rhodesia, April 10-13, 1945.
Minutes of the Ordinaries' Conference Jan 30 to Feb 1, 1947.
Minutes of a Conference on Catholic Secondary Education for Northern Rhodesia, July 1-4, 1948.
Education Secretary General circular to all Ordinaries. Ref. no. CAO/7/55.
Minutes of the 17th Meeting of the Northern Rhodesian Bishops' Conference, May 7-9, 1958.
Letter from Adrian Mungandu, Archbishop, to Hon. Clement Mwananshiku, July 13, 1988.

ARCHIVES OF LIVINGSTONE DIOCESE

"Notes on the Director of Education's tour in Barotese Protectorate." December 4-8, 1955.
Letter from Fr. Edwin Flynn to Education Secretary General. March 22, 1960.
Letter from Bishop of Livingstone to Permanent Secretary, Ministry of General Education and Culture, April, 1982.

ARCHIVES OF MANSA DIOCESE

Letter from the Chairman of the Bishops' Conference to the Anglican Bishop of Northern Rhodesia in reply to a special day of prayer. October 8, 1953.
Letter from the Chief Education Officer, Ministry of Education, to Vicar General, Diocese of Mansa, December 1991.

ARCHDIOCESAN ARCHIVES KASAMA

Letter from Bishop Courtemanche to Chairman, Zambia Episcopal Conference. November 17, 1966.
Letter from Vicar Apostolic to the P.E.O. Kasama. March 15, 1953.
Memorandum on the education of women and girls. April 22, 1960.
Bishop of Kasama, Memo, December 7, 1966.
Bishop of Mbala to Education Secretary General. November 24, 1966.
Chilubula Memo. September 23, 1969.
School Leavers. Ministry of Education Cir. ME 53/2/57.
The Link, diocesan newsletter.

ARCHIVES OF MBALA-MPIKA DIOCESE

Letter from Apostolic Delegate to a Bishop. June 23, 1948.
Letter from Apostolic Delegate, Mombasa, to Sir Thomas Lloyd, Colonial Office, London. July 28, 1952.
Letter from Bishop to Archbishop Mathew. November 8, 1952.
Letter from P.E.O. to Dir. African Education. August 18, 1953.
Letter from Education Secretary General to Ordinaries. March 20, 1953.
Letter from Vicar Apostolic, Abercorn, to Education Secretary General. June 17, 1955.
Letter from Education secretary, Mbala, with report on Management of schools. Jan 12, 1972.
Minutes of meeting in Bishop's office, Mbala. March 29, 1973.

ARCHIVES OF THE DIOCESE OF MONZE

Letter Education Secretary General to Permanent Secretary August 30, 1963.
Diocese of Monze, Consultation November 11, 1967.
Allocation of time for Religious Instruction, circular ME.S/3/10, 1967
Chief Education Officers' Conference, January 7-8, 1969.
Diocese of Monze, Consultation August 29, 1969.
Letter from T.P. O'Shea, Bishop of Livingstone, to Bishop James Corboy, March 3, 1973.

MISSIONARIES OF AFRICA ARCHIVES ROME

Dupont, J. Letter a Son Excellence, Monsieur Le Gouverneur de la British Central Africa a Blantyre. Doss 106.2
Etat de la Mission (Bangwelo) Doss 213 no. 1.
Perraudin, J. "Mons Dupont, l'apotre des Babemba." Notice Biographique B2 Divers 5.
Lettre de Mgr. Guilleme, 12-3-1919. Cote Q 41.
Circulaires 1911-1935 Cote Q41.
Lettre de Mgr. Hinsley a Mgr. Guilleme. Q 41.
Lettre a Confreres Chilubula, November 1, 1928.
A set of *Rapports Annuels* is held here.
Dupont, J. Premier voyage des missionaires chez Mwamba, 1897.
- La Mission de L'Ubemba et le gouvernement anglais, 1920.
Pailloux, P.R. La Place de la femme chez les Babemba, 1953.

MISSIONARIES OF AFRICA ARCHIVES LUSAKA

The Mponde Mambwe Diary 1891-1895.
Oger, L. Our Missionary Shadow.
Corbeil, La Femme Bemba. MC 98.
Elements of Pedagogy for Std III and IV. ME 5
Method of Teaching Religious Instruction. ME.6
Calmettes, J-L. "Politique et Ideologie." Manuscript. MG 6.
History of the Congregation of the Sisters of the Child Jesus. MH37.
Nyassa, 1928. MH 69.
Arab and European Contact with Zambia before the arrival of White Fathers. MH 74.
Diary Reflections MI 10
Dupont, "Chilubula." Des 34.
Statutes of Lwangwa Vicariate 1934. Des 3.
Ilondola Superiors Meeting Aug 26-30, 1960. Des 33
Decisions du Conseil Vicarial a propos des ecoles Protestantes, Aug. 1926. Des 26.
Circulaire sur notre catechumenate, 1938. Des 40.
Sunday Mass-Chilubula Juillet 25, 1920. Des 39.
Letter from Fr. Oger to A. Roberts, 22-2-1967. Box MH 28.
A set of *Petites Nouvelles* is held here.
A set of *Rapports Annuels* is held here.

PUBLIC RECORDS OFFICE, KEW, LONDON

Report on Native Affairs, dated 31-3-1925.

Annual Colonial Reports for Northern Rhodesia no. 1410 for 1927 CO 799-2

ARCHIVES OF THE ARCHDIOCESE OF WESTMINSTER

Fides Service (October 1929) Aaw Hi/139/36.

NEWSPAPERS

African Eagle
African Mail
Livingstone Mail
Mirror -
Northern News
Sunday Times of Zambia
Times of Zambia

INDEX

Abbott, Walter, 95n
Abernethy, David, 67n, 88n, 101n
Addis Ababa Conference, 100
Advisory Committee on Native Education in Tropical Africa, 7, 40
Afagbegee, G.K.L., 133n
Africa, Church in, 21n, 22n, 25n, 30n, 45n, 85n, 90n; democratisation of, 88n, 97n, 131n, 132n; independent, 78n, 89n, 91n; Missionaries of, see White Fathers; modern, 4n, 27n, 133n; and new world order, 30n; politics in, xviii; second liberation of, 97; West, 5
African(s), Basic communities, 133n; Bishops, 94; Christian theology, 98n; cosmology, xiv; custom, 30; dialogue with Europeans, 85; education, xxiin, 6n, 41n, 43, 46n, 49, 50, 54, 55, 56n, 59, 60n, 64n, 65, 68; frustration, 76; girls, 69, 75, 100; heritage, 28; ideas of God, 21n; interests, 82; local authority, 53; local government, 52; manager, 57; opposition, 83; politician, 87; priest, 57, 78; religion, 30; religious experience, 35; secondary schools for, see schools; Sisters, 75; teaching service, 54, 56; wage earner, 36
African Eagle, 86n
African Education Advisory Board, 41, 44, 52, 60, 64, 65, 66, 68n, 74n, 84, 91, 107
African Education Ordinance, 56n
African National Congress, 76, 84
African Synod, 157
Alexander, D.J., 104n
AMECEA, 94
Apostolic Delegate, 53, 55n, 65, 66, 83, 84n
Apple, Michael W., xxin
Badie, B., 155n
Banda, M., 142n
Bangweulu, 2, 10, 20
Baptism, admission to, 23; adult, 26; of children, 77; consultation on, 14; desire for, 16; at Charles Lwanga and Mongu Colleges, 139; preparation for, 22; requirements for, 23; sacrament of, 135; essential for salvation, 5, 25; school as path to, xv, 77; and Torrend, 22; and White Fathers, 22
Barotse National School, 6, 50
Barotseland, 48, 49
Baur, John, 4n, 5n

Bediako, Kwame, xxiin
Beenzu, Wilson, 19n, 20n, 44n
Beidelman, T.O., 4n, 34n
Bemba, 1, 2, 20, 21, 25, 26, 31, 32, 36, 86, 88, 89, 91
Bembaland, 1, 2, 10, 30n, 32
Benavot, A., 155n
Benedict XV (Pope), 5, 39
Beresford Stooke, G., 42n
Berman, Edward, xiin, 5n, 18n, 34n, 35n, 41n, 43n, 88n
Binns Commission, 43, 54, 55, 60
Binns Study Party, 55
Bishop(s), of Ft. Rosebery, 38n; Kasama, 109n, 136n, 166n, 167n; Livingstone, 110n, 114n, 119n, 122n, 137n, 166n; Lusaka, 150n, 165n; Mansa, 164n, Mbala, 109; Monze, 38n, 114n, 123n, 133n, 137n, 152n, 165n; Ndola, 165n
Bishops' Conference, 56n, 57n, 58n, 79n, 83n, 84n, 89n
Blakemore, Kenneth, 104n
Blantyre, 2
Bosch, David, 95n
Bourke, David, 95n
boys: academic education for, 74; Catholic secondary schools for, see schools; first students at Kayambi, 15; higher education for, 68; interest in school, 34; numbers of in school, 58, 69, 73, 77, 82n, 94, 101, 103, 126; search for work, 18
British South Africa Company (B.S.A.C.), xv, 6, 7, 8, 40, 100
Broken Hill, 38n, 50, 69
Brophy, Colm, 135n
Brothers, 62, 69n, 80, 93, 149n, 151
Brown, B., 49n
Bryk, A.S., 143n, 146n, 155n, 156n
Burke, T.J.M., 4n, 5n
Caldwell, Mr., 51n
Calmettes, J.L., 80n
Cambridge Conference, 43, 55, 56, 60
Canisius, v, 53, 54, 58, 59, 66, 67, 69n, 81, 96, 98, 108
Capuchins, 38n, 39n, 48, 49, 58n, 69
Carey, Frank, 91n
Carmody, Brendan, xvn, xvin, xxn, xxin, xxiin, 3n, 7n, 9n, 14n, 17n, 18n, 22n, 25n, 31n, 32n, 33n, 34n, 35n, 39n, 41n, 42n, 48n, 64n, 71n, 77n, 81n, 84n, 87n, 90n, 91n, 97n, 102n, 103n, 104n, 128n, 134n, 137n, 147n, 155n, 157n
Carnoy, Martin, xxin

187

Cartmel-Robinson, 52
Casset, A., 23n
catechist, aid for, 6; and BCCs, 134; conditions for becoming, 12n; as well established men, 12; itinerant, 9, 16; with Jesuits, 13, 15; literacy levels of, 12, 24; and native teacher, 6; role of, 34, 134; as teacher, 12, 13, 133; training of, 2, 3; voluntary, 137; and White Fathers, 2
Catholic Association for Religious Education (C.A.R.E.), 124
Catholic Association, 53
Catholic Education Secretary General, 54
Catholic Teacher, The, 56n
Catholicism, xiii, xv, xvii, xx, 17, 21, 22, 30, 31, 35, 39, 65, 79, 90, 91n, 93n, 95n, 97, 128, 137n, 140, 148, 149, 157
Chabukasanshi, Clement, 38n, 93
Chakobe, Henry, 76n, 86n
Chanda, Casmir, 115n, 131n
chaplain, 115, 123, 127, 138, 139, 140, 145, 146, 153
Charles Lwanga, 63, 88, 110, 114, 117, 120, 121, 122, 123, 124, 125, 138, 140, 141, 142, 149, 150, 153
Chasha, Charles, 140n, 141n, 150n
Chibote, 2
Chikolokoso, Lazarus, 74n, 86n
Chikuni, xv, 3, 13, 14, 17, 18, 19, 20, 22, 26, 28, 32, 33, 34, 35, 36, 37, 43, 44, 48, 53, 58, 61, 62, 63, 64, 68, 69, 71, 74, 75, 79, 81, 82, 88, 89, 90, 106, 112, 114, 120, 124, 134, 135, 141, 142, 148, 150, 153
Chilala, Agnes, 74, 79n
Chilembwe, 6, 40
Chilonga, 2, 74, 86
Chiluba, Frederick, xi, 131, 132
Chilubi, 2
Chilubula, 2, 120
Chilufya, Rosemary, xixn
Chimuka, Silverio, 90n
China, xvi, 85
Chingombe, 3
Chinsali, 157
Chipembi, 64, 68
Chipimo, Elias, 88n, 89n, 104n, 131n, 148n
Chisenga, George, 35n, 78n, 89n
Chisengalumbwe, Edward, 78n, 89n
Chishimba, C.P., 125n
Chisopa, Andrew, 111n
Chisulo, Mark, vi, 142n
Chitimukulu, (Chief), 1
Chobana, L., 37n
Choma Trades Training Institute, 77

Christian Council, 52, 59, 60, 65, 66, 68, 107, 118n
Christian village, 4, 6, 8, 9, 9n, 19n, 26, 37
Church, Anglican, 83; Bana ba Mutima, 78n; Catholic, ix, xi, xiin, xxn, xv, xvi, xvii, xviii, xix, 1, 5, 7, 15, 16, 24, 25, 28, 32, 34, 39, 40, 45, 49, 51, 56, 57, 58, 59, 63, 65, 68, 77, 78, 80, 81, 83, 84, 87, 88, 89, 94, 95, 97, 98, 99, 106, 109, 113, 115, 126, 127, 130, 131, 132, 133, 136, 139, 141, 142, 144, 145; of Christ, 95; Dutch Reformed, 3, 59; leader(s), 118, 119, 120, 136, 149; Lumpa, 80; of Scotland, 83; Seventh Day Adventist, 84n, 114; United, 106, 107
Cichecki, Vincent, vi, 78n, 82n, 112n, 115n, 119n
Cieszynski, Klaus, 138n
Clarke, J., 124
Clarke, P.B., 5n
Clarke, R., 101n
clergy, 5, 27, 39, 45, 63, 79, 122, 124, 145, 149
Clignet, R., 76n
Codrington, R, 2
co-education, 63, 120, 155n
Coleman, J.S., 88n
Collins, Bernard, 133n,137n
Colonial Office, 43n, 83n
Colonial, administration, 20, 45, 47, 83, 86; government, xv, xvi, 43, 86, 97, 148; interests, 37; Karoland, 19n; legacy, 100; neglect, 100; policy, 43n, 69; reports, 44n; schooling, 11n, 14n, 44n; state, xxi, 43, 84;
Colson, Elizabeth, xviiin, 20, 21n, 26n, 28, 75, 88n, 100n, 128n
Commission, Binns, 43, 54, 55, 60; Cartmel-Robinson, 52; De La Warr, 41n, 42; Education, 137; of Inquiry into Disturbances in certain African Schools, 87n; Justice and Peace, 147n; Phelps-Stokes, 7, 40, 41; Zambian Teaching Service, 129
Conference, Addis Ababa, 100; AMECEA, 94; Bishops' 56n, 57n, 58n, 79n, 83n, 84n, 89n; Bulawayo, 9n, 13n. 28n; Cambridge, 43, 55, 56, 60; Episcopal, 109n, 113n, 116n, 145n, 151n, 152n; National Education, 103; Jesuit, 7; Ordinaries, 50n, 53, 54n, 59n, 65, 78, 89n;
Confraternity of Christian Doctrine (C.C.D.), 124
Consterdine, Harold, 63
Conversion, as adhesion, xiv, 35; as

alien, xvii, 89; to Catholicism, xv, xvn, xvn, xxn, 17n, 22, 30n, 35n, 91n, 95, 97n, 157n criteria for, 26; different meanings, xiii; early, 20, 26, 35, 137n; emotional, xiii, xiiin, 157; explanatory power of, 137; first step to, 22; and traditional concept of God, 21; intellectual, xiii, xv, 30, 89, 157; Lumpa, 80; moral, xiii, xv, 30, 157; motivation for, xv, 21, 137; need for, xxii, 39; religious, xiii, xv, xxn, 30, 156, 157; and school, xi, xiii, xvn, 1, 3n, 4, 7n, 9n, 14n, 18n, 22n, 25n, 31n, 32n, 33n, 38, 39n, 41n, 42n, 48n, 57, 64n, 77, 93, 106, 131, 136, 152; social, xviii; stages of, xiv; standards to judge, 23;

convert(s), xi, 8, 20, 21, 24, 34, 35n, 36n, 38, 43, 93, 124

Cooksey, Brian, 104n
Cookson, P.C., 2n
Coombe, Trevor, 42, 43n
Coombs, Phillip H., 102n, 104n, 105
Copperbelt, 32, 50, 58, 70, 75, 81, 87, 101, 132
Corboy, James, 38n, 114n, 123n, 133n, 134n, 139n
Cottrell, J.C., 54, 55n, 67n, 68n
Counihan, John, 62, 82n, 110n, 133n, 137n, 145n
Coyne, John, 6n, 7n, 13n, 14n, 23n, 26n, 27n
Cremins, Richard, 91n
D'Antonio, W.V., 155n
Daily Mail, 132n
Daly, E., 49n
Dar-es-Salaam, 39, 44
De Cruchy, J.W., 88n, 155n
de Guibert, Joseph, 3n
De La Warr Commission, 42
DeJong, Dennis, 118n, 134n
Democracy, xi, xxii, 88n, 131, 155
Dillon-Malone, C., xviiin, 118n
Dominican Sisters, 14, 69, 81n
Donovan, Vincent, 5
Doran, R., xiiin
Dore, R., 103n, 104n
Doyle, J., vi
Draisma, T., 104n, 105n, 118n
Dulles, A., 34n
Dupont, Joseph, 1, 2, 12, 15, 17, 24, 26, 38, 90
E.R.I.P., The Provision of Education for all: towards the implementation of Zambia's educational reform under demographic and economic restraints, xiin, xxiin, 105n, 150n
Eclesia in Africa, 97n
ecumenism, 7, 21n, 95, 98, 121, 122, 140, 143, 146, 153, 154

education, academic, xii, 105; African, xxii, 41n, 43, 46n, 49, 55, 56n, 58n, 60n, 65, 68; agnostic approach to, 82; basic 13, 105; BSAC, 50; Catholic, 53, 54, 55n, 57, 58n, 81, 82, 84n, 87n, 99, 108n, 109, 110, 111, 113, 115n, 119, 129; for citizenship, 60; co-education, 63, 120, 155n; colonial legacy in, 100; control of, 6, 56, 107ff; and democracy, 88n, 155n, 156n; desire for, 45; for development, 103, 104, 116, 117; female, 13n, 14, 24, 74n, 76n; higher, xvi, 40, 43, 69, 74, 77, 81, 86, 101n, 105; human capital approach to, 102; as imperialism, xxi; missionary, 5n, 6n, 7, 8n, 40n, 42n, 51n, 52n, 53n, 56n, 57n, 60, 65n, 71, 76, 81, 91n; and Moreau, 19, 44; political, xviii, 99n, 100n, 102n, 103n, 104n, 117, 118, 120, for priesthood, 55; primary, 52, 53, 56, 101, 102; quality of, 7, 43, 105, 127; religious, xviii, xix, 7n, 8n, 11n, 14n, 23n, 25n, 51n, 89, 91, 108, 109, 116, 117, 118, 120, 122, 123, 124, 128, 136, 140, 141, 144, 154, 156; responsibility for, 47, 109; secondary, xxiin, 42n, 43n, 64, 65, 68n, 75n, 77, 105; and secularisation, 51, 56; as selective, 103; sex, 148; in transition, 109n, and UNIP., 100; value of, 40, 72; values in, 98; vocational, 68;

Education Act, 106, 107n, 108, 141
Education for Development, 103, 104, 116, 117
Education Ordinance of 1927, 71
Education Ordinance of 1951, 53, 54, 56
Education Policy in British Tropical Africa, 41
Education Proclamation of 1918, 6, 7, 12
Education Secretary, 54, 55n, 57, 58n, 81, 82, 84n, 87n, 108n, 109, 110, 111, 113, 115n, 119, 129;
Education, Department of, 46, 47, 48, 50, 52, 56, 59, 60, 61, 64, 66, 70, 74, 91
Education, Director of, 43, 44, 46, 47, 51, 59, 68, 108,
Education, Minster of, 106, 107, 108, 109;
Education, Ministry of, 70n, 99, 103, 106, 111, 113, 116, 119, 121, 122, 128, 150;
Educational Reform, xiin, xviii, 103n,

104, 105, 117
Ekechi, E.K., 5n
English (language), desire for, 17, 18, 19; as part of curriculum, 42, 72, 125; gateway to employment, 18, 71; Moreau and, 33, 44; speaking missionaries, 61, 68, 83
Episcopal Education Commission of 1994, 137
Etherington, N., xivn
Eucharist, 26, 123, 156
Evangelii Praecones, 39, 40
Evangelization in the Modern World, 96
Fashole-Luke, E., 89n, 91n
Federation, xvi, 83ff
Fisher, Humphrey, xiii, xiv, xv, xviiin, 35, 91
Flies, J., 2n, 11n, 17n
Flynn, Killian, 38n, 52, 55, 60, 66, 82
Foster, Philip, 76n
France, 4, 19
Franciscan Missionary Sisters for Africa, 69
Franciscans, 58n, 59, 70
Freeburn, Alan, 124
freedom, 29, 87, 96, 111, 112, 121, 129, 131, 143, 146
Freire, Paulo, xx, xxi, 156n
Freund, B., 83
Ft Rosebery, 61
Fustenburg, Adolf, 38n
Gadsden, Fay, vi, 12, 13n, 14n, 73n, 74n
Gann, L.H., 19, 24, 25, 30n, 83n
Garvey, Brian, 1n, 7n, 9n, 11n, 12n, 14n, 15n, 16n, 17n, 22n, 23n, 24n, 26n, 27n, 29n, 30n, 31n, 32n, 37n, 44n, 47n, 79n, 80n, 83n, 84n
Gaudium et Spes, 96
Gelpi, Donald, xiiin
Geoghegan, Anthony, 124
Gifford, Paul, xxn, 88n, 97n, 118n, 131n, 132n, 155n, 157n
girls, attitudes to school, 15, 33, 73, 74, 75, 76; co-education, 63, 120, 155n; desire for schooling, 13; Dominican Sisters and, 69; drop out of school, xix; education to puberty, 13; higher education for, 64, 68, 69, 73, 74, 75, 79n, 126; initiation of, 28, 75; marriage of, 27, 29; need of schools for, 12; numbers in school, 14, 18, 58, 69, 73, 77, 82n, 101, 103, 126, 127; Sisterhood, 75, 76, 79, 145n; teaching as career, 75;
God, abstract, 157; Christian, 20, 21n; communion with, 156; distant, 90; grace of, 116; idea of, 21n; Leza, 20, 21; new concept, 21; saving plan, 116; Son of, 25; Tonga concept of, 20, 21n; traditional, 20; Word of, xii, 29, 147
Grace, Canon, 66
Grace, John, 63, 120
Grant Aided Educationist (G.A.E), 121, 122, 129
grant-aided schools, xii, xviii, 41, 43, 69, 94, 121, 126, 132, 142n, 150n, 152
grants-in-aid, 41
Gray, Richard, 4n, 21
Gremillion, Joseph, 96n
Haambote, Bruno, 114, 117n, 124, 138n
Haamujompa, Patrick, 121n
Hall, R., 118, 133n
Hambwalula, Obote, 142n
Handmaid, (Sisters), 75, 79
Hastings, Adrian, 4n, 5n, 21n, 22n, 25n, 27n, 30n, 34n, 45n, 85n, 88n, 90n, 97n, 107n, 133n, 137n, 155n, 157n
Haynes, J., xvin, 84n, 97n, 107n, 133n, 137n, 155n, 157n
Hazemba, W., 84n
Healey, James, 133n
Hefner, R.W., xivn
Heise, David, 24n
Hell, 3, 16, 21
Henkel, R., 9n, 10n, 15n, 17n, 49n, 70n, 81n
Henze, John, 136n, 144n
Herlihy, A., 49n, 124n, 138n
Herskovits, Melville, 91n
Hillerich, Rupert, 38n
Himpyali, Barnabas, 152n
Hinfelaar, Hugo, 2n, 10n, 16n, 17n, 47n, 78n, 87n, 112n, 131n, 154n, 155n
Hinsley, Arthur, xvi, 39, 44, 45, 49, 71, 81
Hirmer, Oscar, 94
Hogan, Edmund, 30
Holmes, Timothy, 1n, 10n
Holy Cross Sisters, 63, 69, 120, 122
Hopgood, Cecil, 21n
Horton, Robin, xiii, xiv, xv, 21, 22, 35, 137
Icengelo, 132n
Igbo, 5, 34n
Ilondola, 7n, 38n, 47n, 76n, 80, 86
inculturation, 24n, 89n, 156n, 157
indirect rule, 48
interdenominationalism, xviii, 50, 51, 60, 65, 122, 123, 128, 154
Ipenburg, At., 2n, 17n, 25n, 34n, 84n
Ireland, 62, 66
Irish Jesuits, 61, 62, 68, 84n, 85, 87

Isichei, Elizabeth, 4n, 5n, 7n, 21n, 34, 79
Jaricot, Pauline, 4
Jeanes, 70
Jeanes School, 42, 48, 50
Jeanes Supervisors, 72
Jesuit, xv, xvi, xvii, xxi, 3, 4, 6, 7, 8, 9, 10, 11, 13, 14, 15, 17, 18, 19, 20, 21, 22, 23, 24, 25, 26, 27, 28, 29, 30, 31, 32, 33, 34, 36, 37, 38, 39, 41, 42, 43, 44, 48, 53, 57, 58, 61, 62, 63, 64, 68, 69, 70, 71, 76, 77, 81, 84, 85, 87, 91, 103, 104, 106, 128, 133, 137, 138, 157
Jimenez, Emmanuel, xxiin, 142n, 155n
John Paul II, (Pope), 97
John XXIII, (Pope), 94, 96
justice, xix, xxi, 36, 86, 97, 98, 116, 131, 147, 150, 154
Kabwata, 82
Kachebere, 3, 38n, 39, 93
Kafue, 7, 40
Kalilombe, Patrick, 32n
Kamens, David, 88n, 155n
Kangwa, Daniel, vi, 149n
kapitau, 48
Kaplan, S., 30n
Kapoche, 3, 48
Kasama, xii, 2, 12, 20, 21, 25, 38, 43, 62, 72, 79, 86, 93, 101, 109, 111, 112, 115, 120, 133, 135, 136, 138
Kashimani, M.E., 132n
Kashoki, Mubanga, 21, 24n, 28, 31n, 148, 156
Kasia, Elias, 73n, 90n
Kasisi, 3, 13, 14, 27, 36, 48, 69, 73, 90
Katondwe, 3, 6, 14, 25, 30, 48, 126
Katulushi, C., 123n
Kaunda, Kenneth, xi, xii, xviin, 76n, 85, 86, 103, 106, 115, 118, 131, 132
Kayambi, 1, 2, 11, 15, 87
Keenan, Frank, 123n
Kelly, Madeline, 151n
Kelly, Michael, 101n, 105n, 118n, 119n, 125n, 142n
Kenya, 50
Kieren, J.A., 28n, 136n
Kosloviecki, Adam, 38n, 61n, 66n, 93, 114n, 157n
Lane, William, 7n, 9n, 11n, 14n, 23n, 24n, 25n, 136n
Larue, Etienne, 2, 10, 17, 38
Latham, G., 41, 42, 43
Lavigerie, Cardinal, 1, 22
Lay Missionary Associate Teacher (L.M.A.T.), 121, 122
Leader, The, 85
leadership, in Bishops' hands, 78; Catholic, xvi, 55, 58, 64, 86, 129; Christian, 138, 153; church, 51, 88, 118, 119, 120, 132n, 136, 149; for democracy, 155; handbook for, 49n; lay, 94, 145; local, 135; nationalist, xvi, xvi, xvii, xxii, 76; prayer, 16; religious, 81; training for, xvi, 125, 145
Lee, V.E., 123n, 155n, 156n
Lejeune, Fr., 4
Lenshina, Alice, xvii, 79, 80
liberation, xix, xx, 97, 154
Limpopo, 3
Linden, Ian, 5n
Linden, Jane, 1n, 5n, 27n, 37n, 50n, 79n
literacy, xiv, xx, 21
Livingstone, (town of), xii, 3, 38, 42, 49, 69, 75, 79, 87, 109, 110, 111, 114, 116, 119, 122, 124, 135, 137, 138, 143
Livingstonia, 47, 50n
Lloyd, T., 83n
Local Education Authority, 54, 57, 128
local government, 51, 52, 53, 54
Lochner Concession, 6
Lockheed, xxiin, 142n, 155n
Lonergan, Bernard, xiii, xv, 30
Lukulu, 49, 58, 62, 69, 120, 142
Lulat, Y.G.M., 104n
Lumen Gentium, 95
Lungu, Gatian, 97, 98n, 118n, 131n
Lungu, Paul, 132n, 142n, 151n, 152n, 157
Lungwangwa, G., ix
Lyamibaba, John, 11, 12n, 80
MacKenzie,C., 91n
Mackie, R., xxn
MacKinnon, Mr., 2
MacMahon, B., 62n
Mainza, Gabriel, 33n, 36n
Malambo, Stephen, 112n
Malole, 58, 62, 69, 83, 86, 126
Mansa, xii, xviii, 38, 69, 83, 86, 93, 111, 133, 138
Marist Brothers, 69, 151
Marsh, 31n, 155n
Martin, F., 38n
Marx, K., 119
Marxism, 118
Masase, Genevieve, 75n, 79n
Mason, M., 65, 68
Mass, 16, 24, 26, 89, 90, 120, 134, 141, 144, 146, 149, 153; and Zambian culture, 80, 89, 90, 149
Mathew, Archbishop, 53, 65, 66
Maximum Illud, 5, 39
Maxwell, Kevin, 21n, 24, 25n
Mazabuka, 18, 42, 47, 48, 50, 65, 69
Mazombwe, Medardo, 93

Mazzieri, Fraqncis, 38n
McAuliff, R.R., 157n
McCracken, John, 32n
McDonald, Norman, 21n
McGarry, Cecil, 97n
McGinn, N.F., 155n, 156n
McGivern, Thomas, 121n
McGloin, James, 139
McLaren, Peter, xxi, xxin, 90, 91n
Medellin, 96
Milingo, Emmanuel, 93
Miller, Elmer, 37n
Miller, Jon, 14n, 19n,
Minga, 3
Missio, vi
Mission, xii, xv, xvi, xviii, xxi, 1, 2, 3, 4, 5, 6, 7, 8, 9, 10, 11, 13, 14, 15, 17, 19, 21, 23, 24, 25, 27, 28, 30, 31, 32, 34, 36, 37, 40, 41, 42, 44, 46, 47, 48, 49, 50, 51, 52, 53, 55, 56, 57, 60, 62, 64, 65, 66, 67, 68, 69, 70, 75, 77, 81, 84, 87, 88, 90, 91, 95, 97, 118, 121, 131, 133, 134, 136, 142, 147, 154
missionaries, access to local population, 9; aid to, 41; conditions of service, 112; Conference of, 7, 67; conflict with students, 71; decline in numbers of, 122; education by, 6, 39, 51, 52, 57, 67, 72, 81, 106, 108, 112, 130; English-speaking, 61, 68, 83; French, 22, 30; and Hinsley, 44; as liberators, 16, 155; and local languages and culture, 28, 29, 49, 148; moratorium on, 149; Muslim, xiv; non-British, 83; range of influence, 3, 4, 10, 38; and social development, 33, 34, 36; and women/girls education, see girls; (see also Baptism, Mass, primary schools, secondary schools, teachers colleges, girls.)
modernization, xvi
Mokalapa, 50
Mongu, 49, 63, 69, 86, 109, 111, 117, 119, 120, 122, 123, 124, 125, 135, 138, 139, 140, 149, 153
Monze, Antonio, 48, 72
Monze, xii, 20, 29, 32, 37, 38, 43, 48, 72, 82, 109, 110, 111, 114, 115, 123, 133, 134, 137, 138, 139, 140, 142, 144, 145, 147, 150, 152, 153, 157
Mooya, Cynthia, 33n
Mooya, Fidelina, 79n
Moreau, Joseph, 3, 7, 13, 17, 18, 20, 22, 23n, 28, 29, 32, 33, 36, 37, 43, 44, 63, 67, 74, 81, 90
Morris, Colin, 84n
Moto-Moto, 1
Movement for Multiparty Democracy (M.M.D.), xi, xviii, 131, 132
Mozambique, 3
Mpezele, Raymond, 137n
Mpile, Jerome, 33n, 36n
Mujdrica, John, 128n, 156n
Mulaisho, Dominic, 30, 82n, 88n, 157n
Mulenga, R., 76n
Mulenga, T., 79n
Mulungushi, 69, 86, 118
Mumpangwe, P., 86n
Munali, 64, 65
Mungandu, Adrian, 150n
Murphy, Edward, 99n, 100n, 108n, 110n
Murray, C., 128n
Musokotwane, K., 151n
Mutale, Abel, 86n
Mutale, Elias, 93, 132n
Muwele, C., 147n
Muyowe, Nicholas, 112n
Mwale, Christine, 144n
Mwamba, (Chief), 1, 2
Mwamba, Benedict, 157n
Mwamba, Kennedy, vi, 112n, 149n
Mwanakatwe, John, 77n, 99n, 100n, 101n
Mwananshiku, C., 150n
Mwansa, Alexandrina, 135n
Mweemba, Clement, 78n
Mweemba, Patrick, 35n
Mwiinga, Bruno, 124n
Mwila, C., 19n
Myers-Briggs, 145n
National Education Conference, 103
nationalism, xvin, xxin, 77n, 86, 87, 88
Native Authority School (N.A.S.), 51, 54
native clergy, 39, 79
Native Education Code, 44
Naviruli, 48, 58
Neil, S., 154n
Nguluwe, D.M., 51n, 136n
Ngumbo, 2
Nigeria, 4, 5, 44, 88n, 155n
Nightingale, E., 55, 65
Nkhoma, E., 142n
Nkomo, Mr., 125n
Nkrumah Teachers' College, 101, 117, 123n
Nkumbula, Harry, xvii, 76, 85
Noddings, Nell, 143n
normal school, 42, 43, 44, 49, 53, 58ff; see also, teachers college
Northern Rhodesia, xii, xv, xvi, 1, 3, 4, 6, 7, 8, 9, 13, 15, 18, 20, 21, 26, 31, 32, 33, 34, 36, 37, 38, 39, 40, 41, 42, 43, 44, 49, 50, 51, 54, 55, 56, 57, 58, 61, 63, 64, 65, 66, 67, 68, 69, 70, 74,

192

76, 77, 79, 83, 84, 87, 89, 107
Northern Star, xviin, 85n
Nyamayaro Mufuka, K., 88
Nyambe, L., 140n
Nyasa, 2
Nyasaland, xvi, 5, 6, 32, 39, 40,76
Nyeko, Janet, 76n
Nyoni, A.Y., 135n
O'Brien, Desmond, 134n
O'Brien, Thomas, 122, 123n
O'Grady, L., 62
O'Halloran, James, 133n
O'Leary, Dympna, 124n, 139, 153
O'Leary, J., 138n
O'Leary, John, 142n
O'Loghlen, Desmond, 89n
O'Neill, Frank, 134n
O'Riordan, Colm, 82n, 113, 115n
O'Shea, Michael, 1n, 2n, 9n, 14n, 27n
O'Shea, T.P., 38n, 69, 114n
O'Sullivan, Owen, 49n, 70n, 137n
Ogbu, John, 76n
Oger, Louis, 7n, 10n, 11n, 12n, 15n, 16n, 17n, 22, 24, 31n, 44n, 46n, 67, 80n, 86, 90n, 91, 134, 138n
Ogez, J.M., 1n, 15n, 79n
Omenka, Nicholas, 4n, 5, 18n, 39n, 40n
Ordinaries, 50, 53, 54, 55, 57n, 58, 59, 64, 65, 66, 67, 78, 89n; see also, Conference
Pailloux, Rene, 38n, 61n, 93
Parker, Franklin, 6
Parkin, David, xviiin, 21n
Paul VI, (Pope), 93, 96
Perraudin, J., 2
Peters, Harold, 7n, 11n, 81n
Phelps-Stokes Commission, 7, 40, 41
Phiri, Yambani, 74n, 76n
Pius VII, (Pope), 4
Pius XII, (Pope), 39
Poland, 48
Polish, 3, 48
Populorum Progressio, 96
Portugal, 3
Presbyterian Church, 4
Priest(s), African, 57, 58; attitudes towards, 149; authority of, 78; behaviour of, 149; Dutch, 43; education for priesthood, 5; encourage to be, 149; expatriate, 149; Irish, 85; lifestyle of, 79; parish, 78n, 134, 135, 137; profile of, xvii; and pupils, xix; shortage of, 5, 13; vocations to, 145n; work of, 32; Zambian, 93, 149; see also, Jesuits, White Fathers
Prokoph, Max, 53, 56n, 63, 64, 72, 75, 81, 82, 108n, 115n
Propaganda Fidei, vi, 4, 5
Protestants, xvi, xvii, 4, 6, 7, 8, 10, 17, 25, 26, 30, 32, 40, 41, 42, 43, 45, 46, 47, 48, 49, 50, 51, 52, 53, 56, 57, 59, 60, 64, 65, 66, 67, 73, 82, 84, 140, 142, 143
Ragsdale, J.P., 6, 7, 8, 40, 42, 51, 52, 53, 56, 57, 60, 65
Rahner, Karl, 95n
Rambo, Lewis, xiiin, xxn
Ranger, T., 25n, 34n
Rasing, T., 157n
Religious Sisters of Charity, 69n
Rite of Christian Initiation for Adults (R.C.I.A.), 135
Roberts, A., 78n
Robertson, P., 14n
Rogers Report, 109, 113
Roma Convent, 150
Roof, W.C., 29n
Rosa, xv, 43, 72
Rosary, xv
Rotberg, R.I., 15n, 19
Rusbridger, Mr., 48
Samoff, Joel, xxiin, 105n
Sanneh, Lammen, 30n, 31n
Santa Maria, 49, 58
Sanyal, B., 101n
Saxby, John, 99n, 100, 101n, 102n, 103n, 104n
Scherer, J.A., 95n
Schmidlin, J., 4n
school(s), grant aided, xiin, 48, 49, 58n, 69, 70, 72, 81, 94, 126, 128, 150n, 152; autonomy of, 150; basic, 105, 127, 139n; calendar, 106; Catholic dimension of, 129; Catholic, ix, xix, xx, xxii, 47, 51, 53, 54, 56, 57, 58, 62, 66, 69, 70, 71, 77n, 78, 86, 87, 88, 90, 98, 99, 108, 109, 111, 112n, 113, 114, 116n, 120, 122, 126, 127, 128, 129, 131, 134, 137, 141, 142, 143, 144, 145n, 146, 148, 149, 150, 151, 153, 154, 155, 157; chapel school, 16; co-educational, 155n; control of, 54, 55, 56, 57, 114; government takeover of, ix, 52, 53, 108, 109, 111, 112, 113, 115, 120, 134; Jeanes, 48, 50; leavers, 103; manager of, 56, 74n, 76n, 109, 110, 112n multi-racial, 69; national, 142; neutral, 51; non-racial, 69; primary, xvi, xvii, xviii, 2, 14, 40, 42, 43, 49, 50, 53, 58, 64, 69, 70, 71, 75, 77, 78, 81, 82, 87, 94, 99, 101, 102, 103, 105, 107, 108, 109, 110, 111, 112, 114, 115, 118, 122, 128, 129, 130, 132, 133, 134, 135, 137, 138, 147n; private, 105, 142n;

secondary, xvi, xviii, xix, xixn, xxi, 40, 43, 61, 63, 64, 65, 66, 67, 68, 69, 71, 75n, 76, 77, 81, 86, 87, 88, 94, 100, 101, 102, 103, 105, 106, 107, 116, 119, 120, 125, 126, 128n, 139n, 146, 147, 149, 150, 151n, 152, 153, 156n; see also, Local Education Authority; Native Association Schools; normal schools

Schreiter, R.J., 95n

Scudder, Thayer, 75

Second Vatican Council, xvii, 10, 95, 97,

seminary, xii, 11, 27, 63, 93, 145, 149

Seventh Day Adventist Church, 84n, 114

Shakespeare, 157

Shanahan, Joseph, 4, 5

Shorten, Kieren, 49n, 136n

Shorter, A., 89n

Sidono, Bruno, 141n

Simpson, A.J., 91n

Sisters of Charity of Ottawa, 69n

Sisters of Notre de Dame de Namur, 33

Sitondo, Magdalena, 69n

Small Christian Communities, (S.C.C.), 94, 133, 134, 135, 146, 149

Smith, A.B., 123n

Smith, E.W., 21n

Snelson, P.D., xiin, 6n, 7n, 9n, 15n, 41n, 42n, 44n, 49n, 50n, 51n, 70n, 73n

socialism, 97, 117, 118, 119

Society for the Propagation of the Faith, 4

Sokoni, Jonas, 76n, 86n

South Africa, xv, 6, 8, 50, 94, 97, 116

Spaita, James, 93, 136n, 151n

St. Clement's, 69n

St. John's, 69n, 86, 87

St. Mary's, 69n, 75n, 142n

St. Monica's, 69n, 82n

St. Paul's, 69n, 151n

Stanley, Sir Herbert, 41

Star, The, 85

Sunday Times, The, xviiin, 147n

Sykes, R., 36n

Tanganyika, 51

Tanguy, Fr., 46, 47

Tanzania, 51, 105

teacher(s), A.P.U., 145n; appointment of, 54; association for, 53; as catechist, 6, 9, 11, 12, 13, 15n, 133; Catholic, 50, 53, 56, 58, 86, 108, 111, 113, 120, 124, 135, 138, 139, 144; College, xvii, xviii, 65, 94, 101, 117, 119, 120, 122, 123n, 125, 128, 129, 130, 135n, 138, 140n, 141, 147, 153; control of, 53, 54, 56; as expatriate, 101; Lay Missionary Associate, 121; and nationalism, 86; as overlord, xxi; primary, 12, 91n, 101, 115, 120, 125, 153; R.E., 136n; and takeover of schools by government, 112; training, xii, 14, 41, 42, 43, 48, 54, 58, 59, 60, 61, 62, 63, 64, 71, 72, 78, 94, 101, 107; U.A.T.S., 57; women, 74, 76, 112n, 120;

Teachers' College, 101, 119, 120, 122

Ten Year Development Plan of 1946, 64

Termination of Pregnancy Act of 1972, 97

Thompson, A.R., 77n, 100n, 102n, 104n

Thompson, Robert, 62

Tilimboyi, Mr., 20n

Tomazin, L., 135n

Tonga, 7, 11, 17, 18, 19, 20, 21, 26, 29, 32, 84, 88, 90, 121

Torrend, Jules, 3n, 21n

Tutu, Desmond, 89n, 91n

Tyndale Biscoe, Julian, 51

United African Teaching Service (U.A.T.S), 56, 57

United Missions in the Copperbelt (U.M.C.B.), 50

United National Independence Party (U.N.I.P.), 76, 100, 115, 119, 131

United States, 41, 118, 145

University of Zambia, vi, xi, xiin, xixn, 69n, 81n, 99n, 101, 115n, 121n, 125, 127, 128, 140n, 142n, 151n, 152n, 153

Van Binsbergen, Wim., 80n

Van den Biesen, J., 38n

Van Sambeek, J., 31n, 38n, 43, 46, 47

Vatican II, 94ff, 106, 121, 122, 150, 156

Vickery, Kenneth, 18n, 20n, 32n

village committees, 48

Wafer, Frank, 90n, 148n

Wakeford, J., 88n

Waldron, Aileen, 124, 139, 153

Walsh, Patrick, xvii, 85

Weller, John, 1n, 5n, 6n, 27n, 37n, 50n, 79n

Westerlund, David, 97n, 118n, 132n

White Fathers (Missionaries of Africa), xii, xv, 1, 2, 3, 8, 9n, 10, 11, 13, 14, 15, 16, 17, 19, 20, 21, 22, 23n, 24, 25, 26, 27, 28, 29, 31, 32, 33, 34, 36, 37, 38, 43, 44, 45, 46, 47, 48, 58n, 59, 61, 63, 69n, 70, 71, 72, 73

White Sisters, 2, 12, 14, 69, 75

Winterbottom, J.M., 42n

194

Wolnik, Bruno, 38n, 66n
women, anxious for schooling, 13; as evangelists, 14; Bemba speaking, 2n, 10n, 16, 17n, 47n, 78n, 87n, 97n, 112n, 154, 155n; Catholic, 118, 120; Christian community, 134; on Church Councils, 149; College for, 120, 127; and conversion, 139; education of, 14; emancipation of, 112n, 131n, 154n; and handover of schools to government, 112; importance of, 14; and initiation, 28; Legion of Mary, 79; LMATs, 121n; potential of, 75; professional role of, xiii, 75, 147; religious, 93, 156; as teachers, 74, 76, 120; traditional role of, 16; at University of Zambia, 142n; as wives, 11

Zabdyr, Ladislaus, 48, 71
Zambezi Mission, 3n, 9n, 49n, 70n
Zambia Journal of History, xvin, 1n, 10n, 13n, 74n, 77n, 87n
Zambia, xi, xii, xiii, xv, xvi, xvii, xviii, xix, xx, xxi, xxii, 1, 2, 3, 6, 7, 8, 9, 10, 13, 14, 16, 17, 18, 21, 23, 24, 28, 31, 32, 35, 36, 38, 42, 43, 47, 49, 51, 57, 58, 69, 73, 74, 75, 76, 77, 78, 79, 80, 81, 82, 84, 85, 87, 88, 89, 90, 91, 93, 94, 97, 98, 99, 100, 101, 102, 103, 104, 106, 107, 108, 109, 112, 113, 114, 115, 116, 117, 118, 119, 121, 122, 123, 125, 126, 127, 128, 129, 130, 131, 132, 134, 136, 137, 140, 141, 142, 145, 147, 148, 149, 150, 151, 152, 153, 154, 155, 156, 157
Zambianization, 93, 121, 148
Zimba, R., 91n
Zimbabwe, 1, 9, 78, 118

www.ingramcontent.com/pod-product-compliance
Lightning Source LLC
Chambersburg PA
CBHW070604300426
44113CB00010B/1402